BOOK 1

HOW TO
REALLY
LOVE
YOUR CHILD

BOOK 2

HOW TO
REALLY
KNOW
YOUR CHILD

UNDERSTANDING
AND
NURTURING
YOUR CHILD

Authentic

This omnibus edition first published 2012 by Authentic Media Limited
PO Box 6326, Bletchley, Milton Keynes, MK1 9GG.
www.authenticmedia.co.uk

British Library Cataloguing in Publication Data
A catalogue record for this book is available from the
British Library.
ISBN: 978-1-78078-014-6

Cover design by David Smart.
Printed and bound in the UK by CPI Group (UK Ltd.), Croydon, CR0 4YY.

How To Really Love Your Child

Ross Campbell

Contents

In this book . . .

. . . identify your child's unique character

. . . common misconceptions

. . . developing a healthy bond

. . . understanding how a child feels

. . . conveying love

. . . giving and receiving attention

. . . rewards and punishment

. . . sharing your spiritual life

. . . and more

Foreword

This is a penetrating book, but bringing up children the right way in today's world is no light matter. This book gets down to the real issues of being a parent.

Parents haven't been trained to be parents, and so bringing up children tends to be something done rather haphazardly. Even 'successes' seem to happen accidentally. This book will guide parents in the right directions for today's lifestyles.

The author, Dr Ross Campbell, points to different areas where children will know real love; especially through eye contact, physical touch, and 'focused attention'. He reminds us of the question 'Do you love me?' that children seem to be constantly asking in their different behaviour patterns. He writes sensitively of what discipline is and its place in the home. And all of his writing is set within a Christian framework – not one that just gives pat answers but one that is determined to find a realistic way of enjoying a deeper relationship with our children.

What appealed to us especially was the author's honesty in sharing not only sound principles but also his honesty in relating how these have worked in his own family life. He doesn't shirk the problems but offers some ways out, at the same time giving us instances of both his failures and successes. The thrust of the book is not to condemn us where we have failed, but to point the better ways. What comes through strongly is the joy as well as the responsibilities of being a parent.

Dr Campbell writes as a psychiatrist but his style avoids jargon and is down to earth. We would recommend that you read this book before your children are teenagers. It's a practical book which you will want to read and re-read as you go through the teenage years with your children.

Roy and Fiona Castle

Preface

This book is for parents of children younger than adolescents. Its intention is to give mothers and fathers an understandable and practical way of approaching their wonderful, yet awesome, task of raising each child. My concerns are the needs of children and how best to meet them.

This whole area of child rearing is in itself a complex venture with which most parents today are having great difficulty. Unfortunately, the outpouring of books, articles, lectures, and seminars regarding children have largely frustrated and bewildered parents despite the fact much of the information has been excellent.

I believe the problem has been that many books, articles, and lectures have homed in on one, or at most, only a few specific aspects of child rearing without covering the subject fully, or without clearly defining the specific area they are covering. Consequently, many conscientious parents have earnestly attempted to apply what they have read or heard as the fundamental way of relating to a child, and often fail. Their failure is not usually due to error in the information read or heard, nor in the way it is applied.

The problem, as I see it, usually lies in the parents not having a general, balanced perspective on how to relate to a child. Most parents have the essential information *per se*, but there is confusion about *when* to apply *which* principle under *what* circumstance. This confusion is understandable. Parents have been told what to do, but not when to do it, nor, in many cases, how to do it.

The classic example of this is in the area of discipline. Excellent books and seminars on childhood have addressed the issue of discipline but failed to make clear that discipline is only one way of relating to a child. Many parents, consequently, conclude that discipline is the basic and primary way of treating a child. This is an easy mistake to make especially when one hears the statement, 'If you love your child, you must discipline your child.' This statement is, of course, true, but the tragedy is that many parents discipline almost *totally* while showing little love which can be felt or bring comfort to a child. Hence, most children doubt that they are genuinely, unconditionally loved. So again, the problem is not whether to discipline; the problem is how to manifest our love to a child through discipline and when to show it in other, more affectionate, ways.

I address these problems in a plain, understandable way, in order to demonstrate how to *generally* approach child rearing. In addition, I hope to provide information which will help parents determine the correct action for each situation. Of course, handling every circumstance correctly is impossible; however, the closer we come to this, the better parents we become, the more gratified we are, and the happier our child becomes.

Much of the material in this book has come from lecture series that I have given over past years at numerous conferences on parent-child relationships.

1

The problem

'As Tommy was growing up, he was such a good boy, so well behaved,' Esther Smith, her husband, Jim, at her side, began as the grieving parents unfolded their painful story in my counselling room. 'Yes, he seemed content and never gave us much trouble. We made sure he had the right experiences – scouts, baseball, church and all. Now he is fourteen and is forever fighting with his brother and sister – but that's just sibling rivalry, isn't it? Other than that, Tom – he's no longer Tommy – has never been a real problem for us,' Esther Smith concluded. 'He is moody sometimes and goes to his room for long periods. But he has never been disrespectful or disobeyed or back-talked. His father saw to that.

'There's one thing we *know* he has gotten plenty of and that's discipline. In fact, that's the most puzzling thing of all. How can a child so well disciplined all his life suddenly begin running around with undisciplined peers and do the things they do? And show such disrespect for his parents and other adults? These children even lie, steal, and drink alcohol. I can't trust Tom anymore. I can't talk with him. He's so sullen and quiet. He won't even look at me. He doesn't seem to want anything to do with us. And he's doing so poorly in school this year.'

'When did you notice these changes in Tom?' I asked.

Jim Smith looked up at the ceiling. 'Let me think. He's fourteen now, almost fifteen', he said. 'His grades were the first problem we noticed. About two years ago. During the last few months of sixth grade, we noticed he became bored first with school, then with other things. He began to hate going to church. Later Tom even lost interest in his friends and spent more and more time by himself, usually in his room. He talked less and less.

'But things really worsened when he began junior high school. Tom lost interest in his favourite activities – even sports. That's when he completely dropped his old stand-by friends and began running around with boys who were usually in trouble. Tom's attitude changed and conformed to theirs. He placed little value in grades and wouldn't study. These friends of his often got him in trouble.'

'And we've tried everything.' Mrs Smith took up the account. 'First we spanked him. Then we took away privileges like television, movies, and so on. One time we grounded him for a solid month. We've tried to reward him for appropriate behaviour. I really believe we have tried every recommendation we have heard or read. I really wonder if anyone can help us or help Tom.'

'What did we do wrong? Are we bad parents? God knows we've tried hard enough,' Jim Smith added. 'Maybe it's congenital. Maybe it's something Tom inherited. Could it be physical? But our pediatrician examined him a couple of weeks ago. Should we take him to a gland specialist? Should we get an EEG? We need help. Tom needs help. We love our boy, Dr Campbell. What can we do to help him? Something's got to be done.'

Later, after Mr and Mrs Smith departed, Tom entered the counselling room. I was impressed with his naturally likable ways and handsome appearance. However, his gaze was downcast and when he would make eye contact, it was only for a moment. Although obviously a bright child, Tom spoke only in short, gruff phrases and grunts. Finally, when he felt comfortable enough to share his story, he revealed essentially the same factual material as his parents. Going further, he said, 'No one really cares about me except my friends.'

'No one?' I asked.

'No. Maybe my parents. I don't know. I used to think they cared about me when I was little. I guess it doesn't matter much now anyway. All they really care about are their own friends, jobs, activities, and things.

'They don't need to know what I do, anyway. It's none of their business. I just want to be away from them and lead my own life. Why should they be so concerned about me? They never were before.'

As the conversation progressed, it became clear that Tom was quite depressed, never having times when he felt content with himself or his life. He had longed for a close, warm relationship with his parents as long as he could remember, but during the last few months he had slowly given up his dream. He turned to peers who would accept him, but his unhappiness deepened even more.

So here is a common tragic situation today. An early adolescent boy who, by all apparent indications, was doing well during his early years. Until he was around twelve or thirteen years of age, no one guessed that Tom was unhappy. During those years he was a complacent child who made few demands on his parents, teachers, or others. So none suspected he did not feel completely loved and accepted. Despite his having parents who deeply loved him and cared for him, Tom did not *feel* genuinely loved. Yes, he knew of his parents' love and

concern for him and never would have told you otherwise. Nonetheless, the incomparable emotional well-
being of feeling completely and unconditionally loved
and accepted was not his.

This is truly difficult to understand, because Tom's
parents are indeed good parents. They love him, and
take care of his needs to the best of their knowledge. In
raising Tom, Jim and Esther Smith have applied what
they have heard and read and have sought advice from
others. And their marriage is definitely above average.
They do love and respect each other.

A familiar story

Most parents have a difficult time raising their children.
With pressures and strains mounting every day upon
the family, it is easy to become confused and discouraged. Rising divorce rates, economic crises, declining
quality of education, and loss of trust in leadership all
take an emotional toll of everyone. As parents become
more physically, emotionally, and spiritually drained, it
becomes increasingly difficult to nurture a child. I am
convinced that a child takes the greatest brunt of these
difficult times. A child is the most needy person in our
society, and his greatest need is love.

The story of Tom Smith is familiar today. His parents
do love him deeply. They have done their best in rearing
him, but something is missing. Did you notice what it
was? No, not love, the parents *do* love him. The basic
problem is that Tom does not *feel* loved. Should the parents be blamed? Is it their fault? I don't think so. The
truth is that Mr and Mrs Smith have always loved their
son, but never knew how to show it. Like most parents,
they believed they were meeting Tom's needs: food,

shelter, clothes, education, love, guidance, etc. Yes, they met all these needs but were overlooking his need for love, unconditional love. Although love is within the heart of almost all parents, the challenge is to *convey* this love.

I believe that, despite the problems in today's living, any parents who genuinely desire to give a child what he needs, can be taught to do so. In order to give him everything they can in the short time he is with them, all parents need to know how to truly love their children.

Which form of discipline is most appropriate?

'I remember one time when I was six or seven. Even now it makes me unhappy to think about it, and sometimes it makes me mad,' Tom continued in a session with me a few days later. 'I had accidentally broken a window with a ball. I felt terrible about it and hid in the woods until Mum came looking for me. I was so sorry and I remember crying because I felt I had been very bad. When Dad came home, Mum told him about the window and he smacked me.' Tears had welled up in Tom's eyes.

I asked, 'What did you say then?'

'Nothing,' he muttered.

This incident illustrates another area of confusion in handling children, that of discipline. In this example, the way Tom was disciplined caused him to have feelings of pain, anger, and resentment towards his parents which he will never forget or forgive without help.

Now years afterward, Tom still hurt from that happening. Why did that particular incident make such an unpleasant imprint on his memory? There were other times when he accepted spankings with no problems, and on occasion was even thankful. Could it have been because he already felt sorry and repentant over his breaking the window? Had he already suffered enough for his mistake without enduring physical pain? Could the spanking have convinced Tom that his parents did not understand him as a person or were not sensitive to his feelings? Could he have needed his parents' warmth and understanding at that particular time rather than harsh punishment? If so, how could Tom's parents know? And, if so, how could they discern which form of discipline was most appropriate at that particular time?

What do you think, fellow parents? Should we decide in advance what action we will routinely take in raising a child? Do you think we should be consistent? How consistent? Should we use punishment each time our child misbehaves? If so, should it always be the same? If not, what are the alternatives? What is discipline? Are discipline and punishment synonymous? Should we study one school of thought, for example, Parent Effectiveness Training, and stick by it? Or should we use some of our own common sense and intuition? Or some of each? How much? When?

These are questions every conscientious parent is struggling with today. We are bombarded with books, articles, seminars, and institutes about how to rear our children. Approaches vary from pinching a child's trapezius muscle to the use of candy as a reward.

In short, how could the parents have handled this situation in a way that would discipline Tom and yet maintain a loving, warm relationship with him? We'll look into this difficult subject later.

I think all parents agree that rearing a child today is especially difficult. One reason is that so much of a child's time is under the control and influence of others; for instance, school, church, neighbours, and peers. Because of this many parents feel no matter how good a

job they do, their efforts have little overall effect upon
their child.

The opposite is true

Just the opposite is true. Every study I've read indicates
that the home wins hands down in every case. The influence of parents far outweighs everything else. The home
holds the upper hand in determining how happy,
secure, and stable a child is; how a child gets along with
adults, peers, and different children; how confident a
youngster is in himself and his abilities; how affectionate
he is or how aloof; how he responds to unfamiliar situations. Yes, the home, despite many distractions for a
child, has the greatest influence on him.

But the home is not the only thing that determines
what a child becomes. We should not make the mistake
of totally blaming the home for every problem or disappointment. For the sake of fairness and completeness, I
believe we must take a look at the second greatest influence upon a child.

Congenital temperament

Actually there are many congenital temperaments.
Nine have been identified to date. The research which
has given us this knowledge has been done by Dr Stella
Chess and Dr Alexander Thomas. The data have been
reported in their book. *Temperament and Behavior
Disorder in Children*, published by University Press,
New York.

This book has been acclaimed a classic and is a truly
great contribution to the world of behavioural science. It

goes a long way in explaining why children have the individual characteristics they do. It helps explain why some children are easier to raise than others. Why some children are more lovable or easier to handle. Why children raised in the same family or in very similar circumstances can be so different.

Best of all, Chess and Thomas have shown that how a child turns out is determined not only by the home environment, but also by his or her own personal traits. This has had wonderful results in alleviating much unjustified blame toward parents of children with problems. It is an unfortunate habit of many (including professionals) to assume that parents are fully to blame for everything regarding their child. The research of Chess and Thomas proves that some children are more prone to difficulties than others.

Let's look briefly at their research. Nine temperaments that can be identified in a newborn nursery have been described. These temperaments are not only congenital (present at birth) but are basic characteristics of a child that tend to stay with him. These characteristics can be modified by a child's environment; nonetheless, the temperaments are well ingrained in a child's total personality, do *not* change easily, and can persist throughout life. These nine congenital temperaments are:

1. *Activity level* is the degree of motor activity a child inherently possesses and determines how active or passive he is.
2. *Rhythmicity* (regularity versus irregularity) is the predictability of such functions as hunger, feeding pattern, elimination, and sleep-awake cycle.
3. *Approach or withdrawal* is the nature of a child's response to a new stimulus such as a new food, toy, or person.

4. *Adaptability* is the speed and ease with which a current behaviour can be modified in response to altered environmental structuring.
5. *Intensity of reaction* is the amount of energy used in mood expression.
6. *Threshold of responsiveness* is the intensity level of stimulus required to make a response.
7. *Quality of mood* (positive mood versus negative mood): playful, pleasant, joyful, friendly, as contrasted with unpleasant, crying, unfriendly behaviour.
8. *Distractability* identifies the effect of extraneous environment on direction of ongoing behaviour.
9. *Attention span and persistence* is the length of time an activity is pursued by a child and the continuation of an activity in face of obstacles.

The third, fourth, fifth, and seventh temperaments are the most crucial in determining whether a child will be easy or difficult to rear. A child with a high degree of reactivity (highly 'emotional'); a child who tends to withdraw in a new situation (a 'withdrawer'); a child who has difficulty adapting to new situations (cannot tolerate change); or a child who is usually in a bad mood – these children are quite vulnerable to stress, especially to high parental expectations. And unfortunately, they tend to receive less love and affection from adults.

The lesson to learn here is that a child's basic characteristics have much to do with the type of mothering and nurturing he or she receives.

Using these nine temperaments, Chess and Thomas assigned numerical values to evaluate newborn children. From this data they were able to predict clearly which children would be 'easy babies', that is, easy to care for, easy to relate to, and easy to raise. The children who were difficult to care for, difficult to relate to, and difficult to raise were called 'difficult babies'. They would require more from their mothers than would 'easy babies'.

Then Chess and Thomas compared how the children progressed according to the type of mothering they received. Chess and Thomas studied the babies with 'nurturing' mothers (mothers who wanted their children and were able to provide a loving atmosphere where the children felt accepted). The two researchers also studied 'non-nurturing' mothers (mothers who consciously or subconsciously rejected their babies or were not able to provide an atmosphere where the children felt accepted and loved). The graph below summarises their findings.

As you can see, the 'easy' babies and 'nurturing' mothers were a great combination. These children developed well with almost no negative consequences.

The 'nurturing' mothers with 'difficult' babies had some problems with their children, but these situations were overwhelmingly positive. Overall, in the loving atmosphere provided by their mothers, these children did well.

The 'easy' babies who had 'non-nurturing' mothers generally did not do as well. They had more difficulties than the 'difficult' babies with nurturing mothers. Their experiences were somewhat more negative than positive.

Not surprisingly, the 'difficult' babies with the 'non-nurturing' mothers were most unfortunate. These children were in such difficult predicaments that they were

	Nurturing Mothers	Non-Nurturing Mothers
Easy babies	+ +	-
Difficult babies	+ -	- -

aptly called 'high-risk' children. The situations of these children is heartbreaking. They are in danger of everything imaginable from child-abuse to abandonment. They are indeed our high-risk children.

So, as we put all this invaluable material together, some extremely important facts began to emerge. First of all, how a child gets along in the world does not depend only on his home environment and parenting. The basic congenital characteristics of each child have a strong effect on how he develops, progresses, and matures.

These traits also affect and often determine how easy or difficult a child is to care for and how frustrating he might be to his parents. This, in turn, influences the parents' handling of a child. It's a two-way street.

Learning these facts has helped many guilt-ridden parents in my daily practice.

Another important lesson for parents to learn is that despite what type of congenital temperaments a child may possess, the type of mothering (and fathering, of course) is more important in determining how a child will do. Study the graph again. Although a 'difficult' child is, of course, more difficult to rear, the type of emotional nurturing has more influence in determining the final outcome. Parenting can change these congenital temperaments positively or negatively.

That's what this book is all about. It's a how-to book: how to relate to your child so he will grow to be his best; how to give your child the emotional nurturing he needs so badly. It is impossible to cover every aspect of child rearing here. I have therefore included what I feel is the most basic material for effective parenting.

It is a fact that most parents have a feeling of love toward their children and assume that they convey this love to a child. This is the greatest error today. Most parents are not transmitting their own heartfelt love to their children, and the reason is that they do not know how. Consequently, many children do not feel genuinely, unconditionally loved and accepted.

This, I believe, is true in relation to most problems that develop in children. Unless parents have a basic love-bond relationship with their children, everything else (discipline, peer relationships, school performance) is on a faulty foundation and problems will result.

This book provides the crucial basics in establishing a love-bond relationship.

2

The setting

Before we get into the basics of how to genuinely love and discipline a child, it is important to look at the prerequisites of good child rearing. The first and most important of these is the home. We will touch only a few of the essential points.

The most important relationship in the family is the marital relationship. It takes primacy over all others including the parent-child relationship. Both the quality of the parent-child bond and the child's security are largely dependent on the quality of the marital bond. So you can see why it is important to help a husband and wife to have a good relationship before attempting to solve problems they may have in child rearing. The better a marital relationship, the more effective and gratifying will be the application of later information.

However, if you are a single parent, let me assure you that what we discuss in this book applies just as much to you, dear parent. In many ways single parenting is more difficult, yet in some ways easier. But whether two parents or one, the way we relate to our children makes the difference in any home.

We can start by realising that there is a difference between cognitive (that is, intellectual or rational) communication and emotional (that is, feeling) communication. Persons who communicate primarily on a cognitive level deal mainly with factual data. They talk about such topics as sports, the stock market, money, houses, and jobs, keeping the subject of conversation out of the emotional area. Usually they are quite uncomfortable dealing with issues which elicit feelings, especially unpleasant feelings such as anger. Consequently, they avoid talking about subjects which involve love, fear, and anger. Those persons have difficulty, then, being warm and supportive of their spouses.

Others communicate more on the feeling level. They tire easily of purely factual data, and feel a need to share feelings, especially with their spouses. They feel the atmosphere between husband and wife must be as free as possible from such unpleasant feelings as tension, anger, and resentment. Therefore, they want to talk about these emotional things, resolve conflicts with their spouses, clear the air, and keep things pleasant between them.

Of course, no one is completely cognitive or completely emotional. We will all be somewhere on the spectrum this simple graph shows. If a person's personality and communication patterns tended to be almost completely emotional in manifestation, this person would appear on the left side of the graph. If a person exhibited a cognitive pattern of communication, he or she would be on the right side of the graphic. We all fit somewhere between the two extremes. Where do you fit in?

←———————————————————————————————→

Emotional   **Cognitive**

Where would you say men and women tend to be on the chart? Right! As a general rule, women tend to be more emotional in their ways of dealing with other persons, especially spouses and children. Men tend to be more cognitive in their ways of communicating.

At this point, you may believe that being on the right side of the graph is more desirable than appearing on the left. This is a common misconception. The truth is that every type of personality has advantages and disadvantages. A person on the left side of the graph, who shares more feelings, is not necessarily less bright or less intellectual. This person is simply aware of his or her feelings and is usually better able to do something about them. On the other hand, a person on the right side of the graph, who does not display feelings, may simply be suppressing feelings and is therefore less aware of them.

A surprising fact is that the so-called cognitive person (on the right) is controlled by his feelings just as is the so-called emotional person, but *he doesn't realise it*. For example, the stiff, formal intellectual generally has deep feelings also, but uses enormous energy to keep them buried so he won't be bothered with them. But unfortunately they *do* bother him. Whenever someone (like an 'emotional' wife, or child) is around asking him for affection and warmth, he is not only unable to respond, but is angered that his precious equilibrium has been disturbed.

A father's initiative

'My husband, Fred, has been such a good provider and he's so respected,' Mary Davis explained to me in her bewilderment, 'that I feel terrible about how I feel toward him. I get so angry at him; then I feel so guilty I can't stand myself. I try to talk with him about how I feel about him and about the children. He becomes uncomfortable, clams up, then is mad at me. Then I'm upset and angry and get back at him – I even get frigid and can't make love with him. What can I do? I am so worried about my marriage and my children, but I can't even talk with my husband about it. How can our marriage last?'

There's the old story. Fred Davis is competent in the business world. He knows about his business. He has the facts. He is comfortable in a world where emotional factors are omitted and generally not needed. He is 'cognitive' in his communications. But at home he is like a fish out of water. He's married to a normal wife with normal womanly and wifely needs. Mary needs her husband's warmth and support. She needs him to share in her concerns, fears, and hopes. Mary tends to be 'emotional' in her communications. She needs to feel that her husband is willing to assume his responsibility for the family. These needs of hers are normal and do not mean that she is weak, overly sensitive, or that she is not carrying her own responsibilities. I have yet to see a truly happy, warm family where the husband and father did not assume family responsibilities. Again, the wife and mother has her responsibilities, but the husband must be willing to help her and support her in each of these. One reason that this is essential is that a woman has a difficult time initiating love for her husband when she feels her husband is not willing to support her 100 per cent in all areas of family life, emotional and otherwise. Of course, the same is true regarding the husband's family responsibilities. He must know that his wife is ready to help and even step in when needed.

Another way to put it is that when a woman must assume responsibilities because her husband simply won't, it is hard for her to feel secure and comfortable in his love. For example, one wife whom I was counselling complained that she felt insecure in her husband's love and had difficulty responding to him lovingly. As it turned out, she was responsible strictly by default for essentially every aspect of the family life, including the garden and handling the finances. This arrangement may be all right if husband and wife both agree and are happy with it; but even then, the husband must assume these overall responsibilities if needed; that is, he must be ready and willing to take over if the spouse is over-burdened. A husband's 'willingness' to be completely answerable for his family is one of the greatest assets a wife and child can have.

A wife can be wonderful at accepting love initiated by her husband, amplifying it manyfold, and reflecting it to him and the children, filling the home with an inexplicably wonderful climate. But a husband must take the responsibility of initiating love. Husbands who have found this secret are to be envied. The love returned to him by his wife is priceless, in my opinion the most precious commodity in this world. It is difficult to initiate love at first, but as the husband experiences his wife's love in return, he finds it to be multiplied many times, and sees that as this love increases with time, it becomes easier and easier to do.

If there are exceptions, I have yet to find one. The husband who will take full, total, overall responsibility for his family, and take the initiative in conveying his love to his wife and children, will experience unbelievable rewards: a loving, appreciative, helping wife who will be her loveliest for him; children who are safe, secure, content and able to grow to be their best. I personally have never seen marriage fail if these priorities are met. Every failing marriage I have seen has somehow missed these priorities. Fathers, the initiative must be ours.

But, you ask, how can a husband take initiative and responsibility for conveying love in the family when he is essentially cognitive and clumsy in the feelings area, and the wife is more competent in the emotional area? This is one of the most frequent, unrecognised, and difficult problems in marriage today. It is difficult to deal with, because most men, like Fred Davis, are not aware of the problems. Instead of seeing how vital the emotional life of his wife and children is, he sees it as an uncomfortable nuisance which should be avoided. The result, of course, is what we just experienced between Fred and Mary – frustration and bewilderment with a serious breakdown of communication.

It seems that everyone today realises how crucial communication is in family living. Can you see from Fred and Mary's relationship how communication bogs down when a 'cognitive' husband cannot talk on the emotional level, or an 'emotional' wife cannot share her innermost feelings and longings? What a dilemma! Husbands, we must face facts. The chances are overwhelming that our wives are more competent in the area of love, caring, and identifying emotional needs in us and our children. And we generally follow the guidance of experts, right? Then, clearly, we men desperately need our wives' help in leading us in this relatively foreign world of feeling.

Not only must a husband be willing to respect and be guided by his wife's natural know-how in emotional areas, he must encourage his wife and support her daily task of setting the emotional climate in the home. If he is a hindrance to her, insisting on handling matters without regard to her feelings, he will discourage her and eventually break her spirit. Oh, how many wives I have seen in counselling who have been thwarted by their husbands in efforts to feelingly love them and the children. These wives' spirits are broken, and the resulting depression is crippling.

But look at marriages where a husband appreciates his wife's deep feelings and her need to communicate them. He not only listens to her, he learns from her. He learns how rewarding and profoundly fulfilling and satisfying it is to share on the emotional level, whether it is pleasant or unpleasant. This is a marriage that grows over the years. A husband and wife become closer and invaluable to each other. Such a marriage is one of life's greatest gifts.

Is love blind?

'See? John doesn't love me anymore. All he does is criticise me,' complained pretty Yvonne. She and her husband were seeing me 'as a last resort' for marriage counselling. Yvonne continued, 'Isn't there anything good you can say about me, John?' Much to my surprise, John actually could think of nothing with which to compliment his wife. Yvonne was attractive, intelligent, articulate, and talented, but John seemed able only to point out discrepancies. They had been married six years. Why the apparent inconsistency?

It's hard to realise, when we think of the astounding divorce rate, that essentially all marriages begin with great hope, expectation, love, and wonderful feelings between the newlyweds. Initially all seems wonderful, the world is perfect. And the marriage of Yvonne and John began that way too. What a startling change! How could it possibly have happened?

One factor is *immaturity*. But what is immaturity? It does correlate somewhat with age, but not necessarily. Within the scope of this particular problem, immaturity can be defined as the inability to tolerate (or cope with) ambivalence on a conscious level. Ambivalence is simply having opposite or conflicting feelings toward the same person.

This explains the saying 'love is blind'. When we are first in love, and during the first weeks or months of our marriage, we must see our loved one as perfect, and we can tolerate no unpleasant feeling toward her or him. Therefore, we suppress (deny, ignore) anything we might not like in our spouse. We can then be aware of only his or her good points. Then we are oblivious to such things as an imperfect figure or physique, over-talkativeness, quietness, tendency to be fat or thin, over-exuberance, withdrawal, moodiness, lack of ability in sports, music, art, sewing, or cooking.

This hiding of our spouse's undesirable aspects from ourselves works beautifully at first. As we live with our loved one day in, day out, month in, month out, there are new discoveries about him or her. Some good and some not so good. Some even revolting. But as long as we keep suppressing the unpleasant into our uncon-scious, we can continue to see our dear one as a near-perfect model, and everything is fine.

One problem. We cannot keep on suppressing forever. Someday we reach a point of saturation. By that time we may have been married several days or several years. This depends on (1) our capacity to suppress, overlook, and ignore the unpleasant; and (2) our level of maturity, namely, our ability to deal consciously with our mixed feelings.

When we reach this critical point, we cannot continue to support the negative any longer. Suddenly we are faced with days/months/years of disagreeable feelings toward our spouse. Again, because of immaturity (inability to deal with ambivalence), we do a flip-flop. We suppress the good feelings and accentuate the bad. Now we see our spouse in an almost reversed aspect of being all bad with little or no good – overwhelmingly unpleasant or almost nothing pleasant.

And this can happen quickly. Two months ago John saw Yvonne as the epitome of perfection. Now he can barely tolerate her presence. Yvonne has remained essentially the same. John's perceptions of her have almost completely reversed.

How do we cope with this common problem that is plaguing our social structure and threatening the strength of our national fibre? As usual, the answer is easy to give, but difficult to carry out. First, we *must realise* that no one is perfect. It's amazing. We hear that statement every day, but we don't believe it. By playing the suppression game, we show that we want and expect perfection from our loved ones,

Second, we must keep ourselves continually aware of our spouse's assets and liabilities. I must realise and not forget that there are things about my wife for which I am grateful and things about her I wish were different – in this way she is like all other women. It's taken me a long time to learn to think of her delightful traits during times when I'm disappointed with her.

Third, we must learn to accept our spouses as they are, including their faults. The likelihood of finding someone or something better through divorce and another marriage, or in an affair, is remote, especially with the overwhelming guilt and other problems such action would produce. Remember that your wife or husband is truly irreplaceable.

Unconditional love

'Love is very patient and kind, never jealous or envious, never boastful or proud, never haughty or selfish or rude. Love does not demand its own way. It is not irritable or touchy. It does not hold grudges and will hardly even notice when others do it wrong. It is never glad about injustice, but rejoices whenever truth wins out. If you love someone, you will be loyal to him no matter what the cost. You will always believe in him, always expect the best of him, and always stand your ground in defending him' (1 Corinthians 13:4-7, TLB).

This clear statement tells us the foundation of all love relationships. The secret here can be called 'unconditional love' that is not dependent on such things as spouse performance, age, weight, mistakes, etc. This kind of love says, 'I love my wife, no matter what. No matter what she does, how she looks, or what she says, I will always love her.' Yes, unconditional love is an ideal and impossible to attain completely, but the closer I can come to it, the more my wife will be made perfect by God who loves us so. And the more He changes her to His likeness, the more pleasing she will be to me and the more I will be satisfied by her.

This brings us to the end of our discussion on marriage *per se*. We touched only a few points, but there are many fine books on the subject that one can obtain for further study. Now we want to move on to our primary task of learning how to love a child.

As we explore the world of a child, we must remember that the marital relationship remains unquestionably the most important bond in a family. Its effect on a child throughout his or her life is tremendous.

One example from my experience which bears this out involves a Christian family I saw in counselling. Pam, a fifteen-year-old girl, was brought to me by her parents because of sexual misconduct which resulted in pregnancy. The child was a beautiful girl with a delightful personality. She was talented in several areas. Pam had a strong, warm, healthy relationship with her father – a somewhat scarce commodity these days. Her relationship with her mother also seemed sound. At first I was baffled why Pam chose to become sexually involved in the way she did. She had little feeling or concern about the boy who fathered the child. And she was not of a temperament which would inappropriately seek male attention. Pam had always been a respectful, compliant child who was easy for her parents to manage. Then why did she suddenly become pregnant? I was stumped.

Then I saw the parents together and individually. You guessed it. Pam's parents had marital conflicts that were well hidden from others. These strifes were of a long-standing nature, but the family managed to function for years in a fairly stable way. And Pam had always enjoyed a close relationship with her father. As the child grew older, the mother became increasingly jealous of this bond. But other than this jealousy, the mother had a fairly supportive relationship with Pam.

Then Pam reached adolescence. As her physical features began changing into those of a woman, the mother's jealousy mushroomed. By various forms of non-verbal communication (which we will get into later), the mother relayed a message to Pam loud and clear. The message was that Pam was now a woman who could hereafter look after her own emotional needs, especially attention from the male population. As many girls of that age do, she attempted to substitute attention from male peers for her daddy's love. She was acting in accordance with her mother's subconscious, non-verbal instructions.

Pam's mother was aware of her own unhappy marital situation which resulted in a poor sexual life with her spouse. She was also aware of the closeness between Pam and her father. She was *not* aware of the intenseness of her jealousy toward Pam. And she was not aware of her role in Pam's sexual acting out.

In cases such as this, it is fruitless and many times harmful to confront each person (especially the mother in this case) with wrongdoing. Though the surface complaint was the child's behaviour, the basic problem was in the marital relationship. To help this family in the most supportive, loving, sensitive way, as their therapist, I had to help the parents in their marriage bond and not focus on fault-finding and judging their mistakes. I had to bring them to a point of receiving God's forgiveness in Jesus Christ. As the marital bond is mended in a case of this kind and guilt is resolved, this troubled mother-child relationship can be rectified.

This case illustration should show how important the marital union is in the life of a child. The stronger and healthier this bond is, the fewer problems we will encounter as parents. And the more effective will be the information in this book when it is applied.

Let's look now at the second most important relationship in the family.

3

The foundation

Real love is unconditional, and should be evident in all love relationships (see 1 Corinthians 13:4-7). The foundation of a solid relationship with a child is unconditional love. Only that type of love relationship can assure a child's growth to his full and total potential. Only this foundation of unconditional love can assure prevention of such problems as feelings of resentment, being unloved, guilt, fear, insecurity.

We can be confident that a child is correctly disciplined only if our primary relationship with him is one of unconditional love. Without a basis of unconditional love, it is not possible to understand a child, his behaviour, or to know how to deal with misbehaviour.

Unconditional love can be viewed as a guiding light in child rearing. Without it, we parents operate in the dark with no daily landmarks to tell us where we are and what we should do regarding our child. With it, we have indicators of where we are, where the child is, and what to do in all areas, including discipline. Only with this foundation do we have a cornerstone on which to build our expertise in guiding our child and filling his needs on a daily basis. Without a foundation of unconditional love, parenting becomes a confusing and frustrating burden.

What is unconditional love? Unconditional love is loving a child *no matter what*. No matter what the child looks like. No matter what his assets, liabilities, handicaps. No matter what we expect him to be and most difficult, no matter how he acts. This does not mean, of course, that we always like his behaviour. Unconditional love means we love the *child* even when at times we may detest his behaviour.

As we mentioned when discussing unconditional love in the marriage relationship, it is an ideal which we will never achieve 100 per cent of the time. But again, the closer we get to it, and the more we achieve it, the more satisfied and confident parents we will become. And the more satisfied, pleasant, and happy will be our child.

How I wish I could have said when our children were at home with us, 'I love my children all the time regardless of anything else, including their behaviour.' But like all parents, I could not. Yet I will give myself credit for having tried to arrive at that wonderful goal of loving them unconditionally. I did this by constantly reminding myself of the following:

1. They are children.
2. They will tend to act like children.
3. Much of childish behaviour is unpleasant.
4. If I do my part as a parent and love them despite their childish behaviour, they will be able to mature and give up childish ways.
5. If I love them only when they please me (conditional love), and convey my love for them only during those times, they will not feel genuinely loved. This in turn will make them insecure, damage their self-image, and actually prevent them from moving on to better

self-control and more mature behaviour. Therefore, their behaviour and its development is my responsibility as much as theirs.

6. If I love them unconditionally, they will feel good about themselves and be comfortable with themselves. They will then be able to control their anxiety and, in turn, their behaviour, as they grow into adulthood.

7. If I love them only when they meet my requirements or expectations, they will feel incompetent. They will believe it is fruitless to do their best because it is never enough. Insecurity, anxiety, and low self-esteem will plague them. They will be constant hindrances in their emotional and behavioural growth. Again, their total growth is as much my responsibility as theirs.

For my sake as a struggling parent in those years, and, for the sake of my sons and daughters, I prayed that my love for my children would be as unconditional as I could make it. The future of my children depends on this foundation.

A child and his feelings

Remember the simple graph in chapter 2? Where do you think we would find children on it? Right! Way over on the left side. A child comes into the world with an amazing ability to perceive emotionally. An infant is extremely sensitive to the feelings of his mother. What a beautiful thing to see a newborn infant brought to his mother for the first time, if the mother truly wants him. He conforms to the mother's body and the baby's contentment is obvious to all.

But a baby's first meeting with a mother who does not want him presents another picture. This infant is not content and frequently nurses poorly, frets a great deal, and is obviously unhappy. This also occurs when the mother is troubled or depressed, even though there is no discernable difference in the way the mother treats the infant.

So it is important to realise that from birth, children are extremely sensitive emotionally. Since their fund of knowledge is, of course, small, their way of communicating with their world is primarily on the feeling level. This is crucial. Do you see it? A baby's first impressions of the world are through his feelings. This is wonderful yet frightening when we think of the importance of it. An infant's emotional state determines how he sees or senses his world – his parents, his home, himself.

This sets the stage and foundation for almost anything else. For example, if a baby sees his world as rejecting, unloving, uncaring, hostile, then what I consider a growing child's greatest enemy – anxiety – will be harmful later to his speech, behaviour, ability to relate and to learn. The point is that a child is not only emotionally supersensitive but also vulnerable.

Almost every study I know indicates that every child wants to know of his parents, 'Do you love me?' A child asks this emotional question mostly in his behaviour, seldom verbally. The answer to this question is absolutely the most important thing in any child's life.

'Do you love me?' If we love a child unconditionally, he feels the answer to the question is yes. If we love him conditionally, he is unsure, and again, prone to anxiety. The answer we give a child to this all-important question, 'Do you love me?' pretty well determines his basic attitude toward life. It's crucial.

Since a child usually asks us this question with his behaviour, we usually give him our answer by what we do. By his behaviour, a child tells us what he *needs*,

whether it's more love, more discipline, more acceptance, or more understanding. (We'll get into this in
detail later, but let's concentrate now on the irreplaceable foundation of unconditional love.)

By our behaviour, we meet these needs, but we can do
this only If our relationship is founded on unconditional
love. Note the phrase 'by our behaviour'. The feeling of
love for a child in our heart may be strong. But it is not
enough. By our behaviour a child sees our love for him.
Our love for a child is conveyed by our behaviour
toward that child, by what we *say* and what we *do*. But
what we *do* carries more weight. A child is far more
affected by our actions than by our words. More about
this later.

Another critical concept for parents to understand is
that each child has an *emotional tank*. This tank is figura-
tive, of course, but in a sense very real. Each child has
certain emotional needs, and whether these emotional
needs are met (through love, understanding, discipline,
etc.) determines many things. First of all, it determines
how a child feels: whether he is content, angry,
depressed, or joyful. Second, it affects his behaviour:
whether he is obedient, disobedient, whiny, perky, playful, or withdrawn. Naturally, the fuller the emotional
tank, the more positive the feelings and the better the
behaviour.

Now here is one of the most important statements in
this book: *Only if the emotional tank is full can a child be
expected to be at his best or do his best.* And whose responsibility is it to keep that emotional tank full? You
guessed it, the responsibility of the parents. A child's
behaviour indicates the status of the tank. Later we'll
talk about how to fill the tank, but now let's understand
that this tank has got to be kept full, and only we parents
can really accomplish it. Only if the tank is kept full, can

a child really be happy, reach his potential, and respond appropriately to discipline. 'God, help me meet my child's needs as You do mine.' Philippians 4:19 says He will: 'And my God will meet all your needs.'

Children reflect love

Children may be conceptualised as mirrors. As the moon reflects the sun, children basically reflect love, but they do not initiate love. If love is given to them, they return it. If none is given, they have none to return. Unconditional love is reflected unconditionally, and conditional love is returned conditionally.

The love between Tom and his parents (chapter 1) is an example of a conditional relationship. As Tom was growing up, he yearned for a close, warm relationship with his parents. Unfortunately his parents felt that they should continually prompt him to do better by withholding praise, warmth, and affection except for truly outstanding behaviour, when he made them feel proud. Otherwise, they were strict, in that they felt too much approval and affection would spoil him and dampen his striving to be better. Their love was given when Tom excelled, but it was withheld otherwise. This probably worked well when he was very young; however, as he grew older, he began feeling that his parents didn't really love or appreciate him in his own right, but cared only about their own esteem.

By the time Tom became a teenager, his love for his parents strongly resembled that of his parents for him. He had learned well how to love conditionally. He only behaved in a way which pleased his parents when his parents did something to please him. Of course, with both Tom and his parents playing the game, eventually neither could convey love to the other because each was waiting for the other to do something pleasing. In this situation, each one becomes more and more disappointed, confused, and bewildered. Eventually depression, anger, and resentment set in, prompting the Smiths to seek help.

How would you handle that situation? Some would instruct the parents to demand their rights as parents: respect, obedience, and so on. Some would criticise Tom for his attitude toward his parents and demand that he honour them. Some would recommend severe punishment for Tom. Think about it.

Many children today do not feel genuinely loved by their parents. And yet, I've met few parents who do not love their children dearly. This is not just an academic question to think about and then say, 'That's too bad.' The situation is alarming. Dozens of religious cults or other devious organisations are capturing the minds of thousands of our precious young people. How can these children so easily be brainwashed, turned against their parents and all other authority, and controlled by such bizarre doctrines? The main reason is that these young people have never felt truly loved and cared for by their parents. They feel that they were deprived of something, that their parents missed giving them something. What is it? Yes, unconditional love. When you consider how few children really feel properly cared for, loved, and comfortable, it is no wonder how far these cultish groups can go.

Why does this terrible situation exist? I do not believe parents *per se* should be blamed. When I talk with parents, I am gratified to find that most not only love their children, but are genuinely interested in what can be done to help *all* children. I find over and over again that the problem is that parents do not know how to *convey* their love to their children.

I am not pessimistic. As I lecture around the country, I am very heartened that today's parents not only listen, but are willing to expand themselves and their resources on behalf of their children. Many have changed their relationship with their children so that it is founded on scripturally based unconditional love. They have found that once this has been accomplished, their children's emotional tanks are filled for the first time. Parenting quickly becomes fulfilling, exciting, and rewarding. Then these fine parents have guidelines as to when and how to guide and discipline their dear ones.

How to convey love

Let's consider how to convey love to a child. As you remember, children are emotional beings who communicate emotionally. In addition, children use behaviour to translate their feelings to us, and the younger they are, the more they do this. It's easy to tell how a child is feeling and what frame of mind he's in simply by watching him. Likewise, children have an uncanny ability to recognise their parents' feelings by their behaviour, an ability most people lose as they reach adulthood.

On many occasions when my daughter was about sixteen she asked me such questions as, 'What are you mad at, Daddy?' when I was not even consciously aware that I was feeling a certain way. But when I thought about it, she was absolutely right.

Children are that way. They can so finely sense how you're feeling by the way you act. So if we want them to know how we feel *about them*, that we love them, *we must act like we love them*. 'Dear children, let us not love with words or tongue but with actions and in truth' (1 John 3:18).

As you realise, the purpose of the book is to examine how parents can put their feelings of love into action. Only in this way can they convey their love to their child so that he will feel loved, completely accepted, and respected, and able to love and respect himself. Only then will parents be able to help their children love others unconditionally, especially their future spouses and children.

Before we launch into discoveries of how to love a child, there must be one presupposition. It must be assumed that you are willing to apply what you learn. There is a difference between having a vague feeling of warmth toward a child, and your caring enough about him to sacrifice whatever is needed for his best interest. It is rather pointless to continue reading the book if you are not willing to seriously contemplate what it says, understand it, and apply its contents. Otherwise, it would be easy to read it superficially and conclude the information is simplistic and unrealistic.

Conveying love to a child can be broadly classified into four areas: eye contact, physical contact, focused attention, and discipline. Each area is just as crucial as the other. Many parents (and authorities) will focus on one or two areas and neglect the others. The area most overemphasised today, to the exclusion of the other three, is discipline. I see many children of Christian parents who are well-disciplined but feel unloved. In many of these cases the parents have unfortunately confused discipline with punishment, as though the two are synonymous. This is understandable, since I frequently read or hear authorities tell parents to use the rod and physically pinch a child with no mention of loving him. There is no mention of how to help a child feel good toward himself, his parents, or others, and no mention of how to make a child happy.

Every day I see the results of this approach to child-rearing. These children are well-behaved when they are quite young, although usually overly quiet, somewhat sullen, and withdrawn. They lack the spontaneity, curiosity, and childish exuberance of a love-nurtured child. And these children usually become behaviour problems as they approach and enter adolescence because they lack a strong emotional bond with their parents.

So we parents must focus on all areas of loving our children. Let's move on and discuss the first one – eye contact.

4

How to show love through
eye contact

When you first think about eye contact, it may seem relatively unimportant in relating to your child. However, as we work with children, observe communications between parent and child, and study research findings, we realise how essential eye contact is. Eye contact is crucial not only in making good communicational contact with a child, but in filling his emotional needs.

Without realising it, we use eye contact as a primary means of conveying love, especially to children. A child uses eye contact with his parents (and others) to feed emotionally. The more a parent makes eye contact with his or her child as a means of expressing love, the more a child is nourished with love and the fuller is his emotional tank.

What is eye contact? Eye contact is looking directly into the eyes of another person. Eye contact is important in many situations. Have you ever tried to have a conversation with someone who keeps looking in another direction, unable to maintain eye contact with you? It's difficult. And our feelings toward that person are very much affected by this. We tend to like people who are able to maintain pleasant eye contact with us. Eye contact is pleasant, of course, when it is accompanied by pleasant words and pleasant facial expressions, such as smiling.

Unfortunately, parents, without realising it, can use eye contact to give other messages to a child. For instance, parents may give loving eye contact only under certain conditions, as when a child performs especially well and brings pride to his parents. This comes across to a child as conditional love, and as previously mentioned, a child cannot grow and develop well under these circumstances. Even though we may love a child deeply, we must give him appropriate eye contact. Otherwise, he will get the wrong message and not feel genuinely (unconditionally) loved.

It is easy for parents to develop the terrible habit of using eye contact primarily when they want to make a strong point to a child, especially a negative one. We find that a child is most attentive when we look him straight in the eye. We may do this mainly to give instructions or for reprimanding and criticising. This is a *disastrous* mistake, though using eye contact primarily in the negative sense works well when a child is quite young.

But remember that eye contact is one of the main sources of a child's emotional nurturing. When a parent uses this powerful means of control at his disposal in a primarily negative way, a child cannot but see his parent in a primarily negative way. And though this may seem to have good results when a child is young, this child is obedient and docile because of fear. As he grows older, the fear gives way to anger, resentment, and depression. Reread Tom's statements: this is what he is telling us.

Oh, if his parents had only known! They loved Tom deeply, but they were unaware that they seldom gave him eye contact, and when they did, it was when they wanted to give him explicit instructions or when disciplining him. Tom inherently knew that his parents somehow loved him. But, because of this way of using the critical ingredient of eye contact, Tom grew into his teen years confused and bewildered regarding his parents' true feelings toward him. Remember his statement, 'No one cares about me except my friends'? When I replied, 'No one?' he answered, 'My parents, I guess. I don't know.' Tom knew he should feel loved, but he did not.

An even worse habit parents may fall into is actually using the avoidance of eye contact as a punishment device. This is cruel, and we often do this to our spouses. (Come on, admit it.) Consciously refusing to make eye contact with a child is usually more painful than corporal punishment. It can be devastating. It can be one of those incidents in a child's life that he will never forget.

There are several types of circumstances between parent and child which can have lifelong effects, happenings that a child, and sometimes a parent, never forgets. The purposeful withdrawing of eye contact from a child as a way to show disapproval can be such a time and is obviously an example of conditional love. A wise parent will do all in his power to avoid it.

Our ways of showing love to a child should not be controlled by our being pleased or displeased. We must show our love consistently, unwaveringly, no matter what the situation. We can take care of misbehaviour in other ways – ways which will not interfere with our love-giving. We'll talk about discipline and how to do it without disrupting the love-bond. What we must understand at this point is that parents must use the eye contact as a continuous love-giving route, and not merely as a means of discipline.

We are patterns

We all know that children learn by role modelling: that is, patterning themselves after us. Children learn the art and use of eye contact this way also. If we give a child continuous, loving, positive eye contact, he will do the same. If we use eye contact as a way to display our annoyances, he will also.

Do you know a child who seems to be unpleasant or even obnoxious? Most likely he will look at you only briefly when he first sees you, and thereafter only when you have something particularly interesting to say or do. Other than that, he avoids looking at you. This fleeting eye contact is annoying, obnoxious, and aggravating. Now observe the way this child's parents use eye contact with him. Is there a similarity?

Imagine the distinct disadvantage this child has and will have throughout his life. Imagine how difficult it will be to develop friendships and other intimate relationships. How rejected and disliked he will be by his peers, not only now but probably indefinitely because the chances of his breaking this pattern of relating are bleak. First of all, he is not aware he's doing it; and second, changing this pattern is extraordinarily difficult, *unless the parents change their own pattern of eye contact before the child becomes too old*. This is a child's best hope.

A striking example of this tragedy was discovered in a research study on a pediatric ward in a general hospital. The researcher was sitting at one end of the corridor recording the number of times the nurses and volunteers entered each child's room. It was noted that some children were visited many times more often than others. The reasons were startling. It had something to do with the type of seriousness of the child's illness, of course, and with the amount of care required by the child. But this did not explain the great differences in the amount of contact with the patients. You've probably guessed it. The more popular children received more attention. Whenever nurses or volunteers had a free moment or a choice between which room to enter, they naturally picked children who could relate in the most pleasant way.

What made the difference in how pleasant these children were? There were several reasons, such as alertness, verbal ability, and spontaneity, but the most consistent factor was eye contact. The least popular children would initially look at the visitor briefly, then immediately look down or away. Subsequently, the children would avoid eye contact, making it difficult to relate to them. The adults would naturally be uncomfortable with these children. The nurses or volunteers, not realising their roles in initiating communication, would misunderstand them, assuming that the children wanted to be alone, or that the children did not like them. Consequently, they avoided these children, making them feel even more unloved, unwanted, and worthless.

This same thing happens in countless homes. It happened in Tom's. And it could have been corrected with regular, warm, pleasant eye contact (unconditional love) by the parents. If they had known this (and some other basic facts about loving children yet to be mentioned), they wouldn't have had these problems with Tom.

The Failure-to-Thrive Syndrome

Another important finding in our research studies also took place in a pediatric ward in a university hospital.

We were studying the strange phenomenon of the Failure-to-Thrive Syndrome. In this illness, a child, usually between six and twelve months of age, ceases to develop. Often he refuses food and stops growing, becomes listless and lethargic, and may actually die for no apparent reason. All tests and physical examinations are normal.

Why does a child lose his will to live? In most cases we know that the parents have rejected the child, often unconsciously (outside of their awareness). They are unable consciously to deal with their feelings of rejection toward their child, so unconsciously they reject him through their behaviour. In our study we found these parents avoided eye contact and physical contact with their child. Otherwise, they were good parents, providing such necessities as food and clothing.

The Failure-to-Thrive Syndrome is a startling phenomenon, but other findings are even more so. During the World War II Nazi blitzes of London, many young children were removed for their protection from the city and placed with adults in the countryside. Their parents remained in London. These children were basically well cared for physically, in that they were clean, well fed, and comfortable. Emotionally, however, they were severely deprived because there were not enough caretakers to give the emotional nurturing of eye contact and physical contact.

Most of these children became emotionally disturbed and handicapped. It would have been far better to have kept them with their mothers. The danger of emotional damage was greater than the danger of physical damage.

The danger and pitfalls awaiting an emotionally weak child are frightening. Parents! Make your children strong. Your greatest tool is *unconditional love*.

Eye contact and the learning process

In my work with the Headstart Programme, I enjoy teaching those wonderful teachers about eye contact and physical contact and how these affect anxiety and a child's ability to learn.

A teacher will identify a three-to-four-year-old child who is obviously anxious, fearful, and immature by the difficulty he has in making or maintaining eye contact. Mild to moderate emotional deprivation can cause a child to have difficulty with eye contact.

The extremely anxious child will, in addition, have problems approaching an adult (and often his peers). A normal emotionally nourished child will be able to approach the teacher by walking directly up to her, making full non-hesitating eye contact, and speaking what's on his mind – for instance, 'May I have a piece of paper?' The more emotionally deprived a child is, the more difficulty he will have in doing this.

In the average schoolroom it is not hard to find at least one child (usually a boy) who is so anxious and fearful that he cannot make good eye contact, speaks with great hesitancy (and frequently cannot speak without coaxing), and will come to his teacher with a side or oblique approach. Occasionally such a child will be able to approach his teacher only by walking almost backward. Of course these children have difficulty learning because they are so anxious and tense.

When we have found such an unfortunate child, I ask the teacher to teach him something while sitting across the table from him. Then I ask the teacher to hold the child, make occasional eye contact with him (as much as the child can tolerate) while talking with him. After a short while, I again ask the teacher to teach the child something while continuing to hold him. The teacher is amazed, and I am always amazed, at how much easier it is for the child to learn when his emotional needs are cared for first. With eye contact and physical contact, the teacher has eased the child's fears and anxiety, and increased his sense of security and confidence. This, in turn, enables him to learn better. Simple? Of course. Then why don't we do it more? For many reasons, I believe, ranging from a fear that we'll appear unprofessional, or fearing we'll spoil a child, to fearing we'll somehow damage him in some vague way. If there is anything we don't have to worry about, it's giving a child too much love.

In a new place

I am so thankful as a parent that I learned about the importance of eye contact. It has made a great difference with my own children. I'll never forget, for example, when we first moved to a new home. Our two boys were six and two at the time and were happy, energetic, and normally independent.

About a week after moving, we noticed a change coming over both boys. They were becoming whiny, clinging, easily upset, frequently fighting, constantly underfoot, and irritable. At that time, my wife Pat and I were furiously trying to get the house ready before I was to report to my new job. We were both becoming annoyed and irritated with the boys' behaviour, but figured it was because of the move.

One night I was thinking about my boys, and began to try to imagine myself in their place. The answer to their behavioural problems suddenly hit me like a hammer. Pat and I were with the boys night and day and talked to them frequently. But we were so intent on the housework that we never really gave them their rightful attention; we never made eye contact and seldom made physical contact. Their emotional tanks had run dry, and *by their behaviour* they were asking. 'Do you love me?' In their childlike, normally irrational way, they were asking, 'Do you love me now that we're in a new place? Are things still the same with us? Do you still love me?' This is so typical of children during a time of change.

As soon as I understood the problem, I shared my thoughts with Pat. I think she was a bit incredulous at first, but by then she was ready to try anything.

The next day we gave the boys eye contact whenever we could, when they talked to us (active listening), and when we talked to them. Whenever possible, we held them and gave them concentrated attention. The change was dramatic. As their emotional tanks were filled, they became their happy, radiant, rambunctious selves and soon were spending less time underfoot and more time playing with each other and keeping themselves happy. Pat and I agreed that this was time well spent. We more than made up for it when the boys were out from underfoot, but more important, they were happy again.

It's never too early

Now one more illustration regarding the importance of eye contact. An infant's eyes begin focusing somewhere around two and four weeks of age. One of the first images which holds an infant's attention is a human face, but in particular he focuses on the eyes.

After a child is approximately six to eight weeks of age, you will notice that his eyes are always moving and seem to be searching for something. The eyes resemble two radar antennae constantly moving and searching.

Do you know what he's looking for? I think you already know: he's searching for another set of eyes. As early as two months, these eyes lock on another set of eyes. Already he is feeling emotionally, and even at this very early age his emotional tank needs to be filled.

Awesome, isn't it? It's no wonder that a child's way of relating to his world, and his feelings toward it, are so well formed early in his life. Most researchers state that a child's basic personality, modes of thinking, style of speech, and other critical traits are well fixed by the age of five.

We cannot start too early in giving a child continuous, warm, consistent affection. He simply *must* have this unconditional love to cope most effectively in today's world. And we have a simple but extremely powerful method by which to give it to him. It's up to each parent to use eye contact to convey unconditional love.

Though we have alluded to a child's need for physical contact, let's now explore the subject in some depth.

5

How to show love through physical contact

It seems that the most obvious way of conveying our love to a child is by physical contact. Surprisingly, studies show that most parents touch their children only when necessity demands it, as when helping them dress, undress, or perhaps get into the car. Otherwise, few parents take advantage of this pleasant, effortless way of helping give their children that unconditional love they so desperately need. You seldom see a parent on his own volition or 'out of the blue' take an opportunity to touch his child.

I don't mean just hugging, kissing, and the like. I'm also talking about any type of physical contact. It is such a simple thing to touch a child on his shoulder, gently poke him in the ribs, or tousle his hair. When you closely observe parents with their children, many actually attempt to make the least possible physical contact. It's as if these poor parents have the notion their children are like mechanical walking dolls, the object being to get them walking and behaving correctly with the least assistance. These parents don't know the fantastic opportunities they are missing. Within their hands they have a way of assuring their children's emotional security and their own success as parents.

It is heartening to see some parents who have discovered this secret of physical contact along with eye contact.

Scientists have discovered that touch plays a surprising role in our physical and mental well-being, and begins at birth, asserts an article 'The Sense That Shapes Our Future' in *Reader's Digest* for January 1992. The author, Lowell Ponte, points out that researchers at the University of Miami Medical School's Touch Research Institute showed that premature babies who received three fifteen-minute periods of slow, firm massage strokes each day showed forty-seven per cent greater weight gain than their ward-mates who did not get this attention. Premature babies who were massaged also exhibited improved sleep, alertness, and activity. Up to eight months later they displayed greater mental and physical skills.

Dr Michael Meaney, a psychologist at the Douglas Hospital Research Center at McGill University in Montreal, demonstrated that touching baby rats during the first few weeks of life results in development of receptors that control the production of glucocorticoids, powerful stress chemicals that cause a multitude of problems, including impaired growth and damage to brain cells. During his research, the article concluded, Dr Meaney's first child was born and in early childhood he made a point to hug her more than he otherwise would have done. 'Our evidence,' he was quoted as saying, 'suggests that the hugging I give my daughter today will help her . . . lead a happier, healthier life. My touch may be shaping her future.'

The article also pointed out that the caring touch of nurses and loved ones can do wonders for hospitalised patients, relieving anxiety and tension headaches and sometimes reduce rapid heartbeat and heart arrhythmias.

When our son David was eight, he played Peanut League Baseball. During the games I especially enjoyed watching one father who had discovered the secrets of eye and physical contact. Frequently, his son would run up to tell him something. It was obvious that there was a strong affectional bond between them. As they talked, their eye contact was direct with no hesitation. And their communication included much appropriate physical contact, especially when something funny was said. This father would frequently lay his hand on his son's arm, or put his arm around his son's shoulder and sometimes lovingly slap him on the knee. Occasionally, he would pat him on the back or pull the child toward him, especially when a humorous comment was made. You could tell that this father used physical contact whenever he possibly could, as long as he and the boy were comfortable and it was appropriate.

At times, this same father's teenage daughter would come to watch her brother play. She would sit with her father, either at his side or directly in front of him. Here again, this caring and knowledgeable father related to his daughter in an appropriate manner. He used much eye and physical contact but because of her age, did not hold her on his lap or kiss her (as he would have done if she were younger). He would frequently lightly touch her hand, arm, shoulder, or back. Now and then he would tap her on the knee or briefly put his arm around her shoulder and lightly jerk her toward him, especially when something funny happened.

Two precious gifts

Physical and eye contact are to be incorporated in all of our everyday dealings with our children. They should be natural, comfortable, and not showy or overdone. A child growing up in a home where parents use eye and physical contact will be comfortable with himself and other people. He will have an easy time communicating with others, and consequently be well liked and have good self-esteem. Appropriate and frequent eye and physical contact are two of the most precious gifts we can give our child. Eye and physical contact (along with focused attention, see chapter 6) are the most effective ways to fill a child's emotional tank and enable him to be his best.

Unfortunately, Tom's parents had not discovered the secret of physical and eye contact. They misused eye contact. They felt physical contact was all right for girls because 'they needed affection'. But Mr and Mrs Smith believed boys should be treated as men. They felt affection would feminise Tom into being a sissy. These grieving parents did not realise that the opposite is true, that the more Tom's emotional needs were met by physical and eye contact, especially by his father, the more he would identify with the male sex, and the more masculine he would be.

Mr and Mrs Smith also thought that as a boy gets older, his need for affection, especially physical affection, ceases. Actually a boy's need for physical contact never ceases, even though the type of physical contact he needs does change.

As an infant, he needs to be held, cuddled, fondled, hugged, and kissed – 'ooey-gooey love stuff' as one of my sons called it when he was in grade school. This type of physical affection is crucial from birth until the boy reaches seven or eight years of age – and I mean crucial! Research shows that girl infants less than twelve months old receive five times as much physical affection as boy infants. I am convinced that this is one reason younger boys (three years to adolescence) have many more problems than girls. Five to six times as many boys as girls are seen in psychiatric clinics around the country. This ratio changes dramatically during adolescence.

It is apparent then how important it is for a boy to receive just as much or more affection as a girl may need during the early years. As a boy grows and becomes older, his need for physical affection such as hugging and kissing lessens, but his need for physical contact does not. Instead of primarily 'ooey-gooey love stuff', he now wants 'boystyle' physical contact such as playful wrestling, jostling, backslapping, playful hitting or boxing, bearhugs, 'give-me-five' (slapping another person's palm in a moment of triumph). These ways of making physical contact with a boy are just as genuine a means of giving attention as hugging and kissing. Don't forget that a child *never* outgrows his need for *both* types.

As my boys, who are now grown, got older, they became less and less receptive to holding, hugging, and kissing. There were still times when they needed and wanted it, and I had to be alert in order to give it to them every chance I got. These times occurred usually when they had been hurt (either physically or emotionally), when they were very tired, when they were sick, and at special periods such as bedtime or when something sad had happened.

Remember the special moments discussed in chapter 4? Moments that are especially meaningful to a child, so meaningful that he will *never* forget them? These special opportunities to give our children affectionate physical contact (hugging, kissing), *especially as they get older*, are some of these very special times. These are the moments your child will recall when he or she is in the throes of deepest adolescence, when a teenager is in the conflict of rebellion on one hand versus affection for his parents on the other. The more special memories he has, the stronger he will be able to stand against adolescent turmoil.

These precious opportunities are limited in number. A child quickly passes from one stage to the next, and before we know it, opportunities to give him what he needs have come and gone. A sombre thought, isn't it?

Here is one other point about giving physical affection to boys. It is easier to give affection to a boy when he is younger, especially around twelve to eighteen months of age. As he grows older, however, it becomes more difficult. Why? One reason, as mentioned before, is the false assumption that the physical display of affection is feminine. The reason is that most boys become less appealing to people as they grow older. For example, to many people a seven- or eight-year-old boy is unappealing and irritating. In order to give a boy what he must have emotionally, we as parents must recognise these unpleasant feelings in ourselves, resist them, and go ahead with what we must do as mothers and fathers.

Let's now discuss the needs of girls in relation to physical contact. Girls generally do not display as much directness as boys to emotional deprivation during their first seven or eight years. In other words, they do not make their affectional needs so evident. I've seen many, many emotionally deprived children and, generally, it is very easy to tell which boys are suffering – their distress is usually obvious. But the girls seem better able to cope and are less affected by the lack of emotional nurturing *prior* to adolescence. Don't let this fool you. Although girls don't show their misery as much when they are younger, they suffer intensely when not properly cared for emotionally. It becomes quite evident as they grow older, especially during adolescence.

One reason for this lies in this matter of physical contact. Remember that physical contact, especially the more affectionate type (holding, hugging, kissing, etc.), is vital to boys during their younger years. The younger the boy, the more vital affectional contact is to him. While, with a girl, physical contact (especially the more affectionate type) *increases* in importance as she becomes older and reaches a zenith at around the age of eleven. Nothing stirs my heart more than an eleven-year-old girl who is not receiving adequate emotional nourishment. What a critical age!

Sharon's personality change

'I can't believe it! Sharon must be a Dr Jekyll and Mr Hyde,' exclaimed Mrs Francisco in her first visit with me concerning her fifteen-year-old daughter. 'She has always been a quiet, shy girl who never really acted up. In fact, she had to be prompted to do things, especially over the last few months. For a while I couldn't get her to do anything. She seemed bored with life. She lost interest in everything, especially her schoolwork. She seemed to lose all her energy. I took Sharon to her pediatrician, but he couldn't find anything wrong with her. Then I talked with the school counsellor and her teachers. They were also concerned with Sharon's attitude and boredom. Some friends told me not to worry, that it was a stage she'd grow out of. I hoped they were right but had my doubts. Then one day a friend of mine who has a daughter Sharon's age called. She said that her daughter thought Sharon was on drugs. I didn't think Sharon was the type, but I searched her room anyway and found some marijuana.

'For the first time in her life she acted horribly. She yelled and screamed at me, saying I was prowling and I had no right to intrude on her privacy. I was shocked at her defiance.

'That seemed to be the beginning of her personality change. Now she's angry all the time, just hateful. She demands to go out with the worst crowd in school, and it scares me to think of what they might be doing.

'Now all she cares about is being away from home with her gooney friends. What will become of her, Dr Campbell? We can't control her.'

'Is Sharon the same way with her father?' I asked.

'She's much better with him for some reason, but even he is finding it more and more difficult to reason with her. But he's not around much to help anyway. He's so busy. Gone most of the time. Even when he's here, he doesn't give us much time. The children adore him and want to be with him. But he immediately finds something they have done wrong and gets on to them about it. He really cares about the kids. I know he does. But that's his way.'

A tragic story. But a common one. A normal, well-endowed girl who for almost thirteen years was open, docile, easy to love. Like any child, her main concern was, 'Do you love me?' For almost thirteen years her parents had nearly continuous opportunity to answer her question and prove their love to her. As a typical girl, her need for demonstrable love increased over the years and hit a maximum around the age of eleven – that ultra critical age when girls have an almost desperate need for abundant eye contact, focused attention, and notably physical contact, especially from their fathers.

Preparation for adolescence

Why is affectionate love so important to girls around the age of pre-adolescence? The answer: preparation for adolescence. Every girl enters adolescence with some degree of preparation for it. Some are well prepared and some are poorly prepared.

The two most important aspects of this preparation for girls are self-image and sexual identity. At this point, let's look at sexual identity in a growing girl. You have read that a girl's need for affection increases as she grows older. As she nears adolescence she intuitively or unconsciously knows that how she weathers those turbulent adolescent years depends on how she feels about herself. It is vital for her to feel OK about herself as a female. If she is comfortable as a 'woman' when she enters adolescence (usually about thirteen to fifteen years old), her adolescence will be relatively smooth, pleasant, and comfortable with the usual ups and downs. The more stable and healthy her sexual identity, the better she will be able to withstand peer pressure. The less she thinks of herself as an 'OK female', the less stable she will be. She will then be more susceptible to pressure of peers (especially male peers) and less able to hold to parental values.

Sexual identity is self-approval as a female, and a girl gets her sexual identity at that age primarily from her father, as long as he is living and especially if he is in the home. If a father is dead or otherwise removed from relating to his daughter, a girl must find other paternal figures to fill these needs. But when a father has any viable relationship with her, he is the primary person who can help his daughter be prepared in this particular way for adolescence. What a great responsibility!

A father helps his daughter approve of herself by showing her that he himself approves of her. He does this by applying the principles we have discussed thus far – unconditional love, eye contact, and physical contact, as

well as focused attention. A daughter's need for her
father to do this begins as early as two years of age. This
need, although important at younger ages, becomes
greater as the girl grows older and approaches that
almost magic age of thirteen.

One problem in our society is that as a girl grows
older, a father usually feels increasingly uncomfortable
about giving his daughter the affection she needs, especially when she becomes pre-adolescent (about ten or
eleven years old). So as a daughter arrives at the age
when she needs her father's affection the most, a father
feels more awkward and uncomfortable, especially with
physical contact. This is extremely unfortunate. Yes,
fathers, we must ignore our discomfort and give our
daughters what is vital to them for their entire lives.

Our Juvenile Court judge

Like most fathers, I had my difficulties giving my children everything they needed emotionally as they grew
up – especially physical contact and focused attention
for my teenage daughter Carey. Most evenings I came
home from work physically and emotionally exhausted.
After expending myself in my work, how could I find
the energy and resources to give to my family, especially
my daughter, at those times when they needed me? With
my daughter, her need for me occurred when she had a
bad encounter with her peer group, perhaps another girl
being hostile toward her because of jealousy. Sometimes
she didn't understand the cause of the jealousy and tried
to find the fault in herself. On occasions such as this, I
knew what I *should* do. I went to her room, talked with
her about whatever was on her mind at the moment,
gave her all the eye and physical contact she needed at

the time, and patiently waited until she got around to sharing with me her pain and confusion. Then I could clarify her understanding of the whole situation. After a while the fact finally dawned on her that it wasn't anything she had done wrong or should blame herself for. Then she usually saw the situation clearly enough to avoid similar difficulties.

Anyway, that's the way I *liked* it to go, but I was seldom bursting with energy and enthusiasm to carry it out. Usually all I felt like doing was eating supper, sitting in my favourite chair, reading the newspaper, and relaxing.

Here is what helped me overcome this inertia. When my daughter (or one of my sons) needed me, and my whole body was drawn like a magnet to a chair or bed, I thought of a friend, a fine judge of the Juvenile Court. I deeply appreciated and respected the judge. One of the worst, most humiliating and tragic things that could possibly have happened to me or my family would have been to appear in his court with one of my children on, say, a drug charge. I said to myself, 'Campbell, one out of every six kids appears before the Juvenile Court. If you want to make sure one of your kids isn't included, you'd better hop to it and give them what they need instead of looking after yourself.' Just the thought of appearing before the judge with my child on some sort of charge was unbearable. It usually worked. I'd get off my backside and do what I knew I should do as a father.

Back to physical contact. One day in my parenting years, I was thinking how essential physical contact is and yet how most parents seem to consider it so basic and simplistic; we assume we are doing it when, in fact, we seldom do. I was groping for an illustration to point out this problem when my dear wife ran across an article about religious cults, including the Unification

Church (Moonies). A young man who was interviewed told of being brainwashed by the Moonies.

One of the most powerful techniques used was as follows. In an emotionally charged atmosphere and surrounded by several Moonies, the young man was required to think back into his childhood and remember painful moments. He told of an incident when he was three years old. He remembered feeling lonely and distressed, and tried to seek comfort in physical contact from his mother. His mother did not have time for him at that moment and he felt rejected. Then the Moonies embraced him (physical contact) repeatedly, stating that *they* loved him (implying of course that his mother did not).

Frightening, isn't it? The fact that there are dozens of such religious cults and other influences in our country today trying to capture the minds of our children is alarming enough. But even worse, they are able to do so because parents are failing to provide for basic emotional needs of their children by showing unconditional love.

Yet most parents do love their children. Again, the basic problem is that we are not aware that we must convey our love to our children *before anything else*: before teaching, before guidance, before example, before discipline. Unconditional love must be the primary relationship with a child, or everything else is unpredictable, especially their attitudes and behaviour.

But we should not be pessimistic about this. The really encouraging thing is that we know what the problem is and we know how to combat it. These are reasonable answers. I am convinced that most parents, because they love their child, can be *taught* to convey this love. The difficult question is, how can we get this across to all (or at least most) parents? This is something which all concerned parents must consider. The answer will require the input and action of many.

And in addition to learning to use eye contact and physical touch, parents must learn how to make use of *focused attention.*

6

How to show love through focused attention

Eye contact and physical contact seldom require real sacrifice by parents. However, focused attention does require time, and sometimes a lot of it. It may mean giving up something parents would rather do. Loving parents will detect when a child desperately needs focused attention and perhaps at a time when the parents feel least like giving it.

Just what is focused attention? Focused attention is giving a child full, undivided attention in such a way that he feels without doubt that he is completely loved. That he is valuable enough *in his own right* to warrant parents' undistracted watchfulness, appreciation, and uncompromising regard. In short, focused attention makes a child feel he is the most important person in the world in his parents' eyes.

Some may think this is going a bit too far, but take a look at Scripture and see how highly children are regarded. Notice the high priority Christ gave them: 'And they began bringing children to Him, so that He might touch them . . . and [He] said . . ., "Permit the children to come to Me . . ., for the kingdom of God belongs to such as these." . . . And

He took them in His arms and began blessing them, laying His hands upon them' (Mark 10:13-16, NASB).

Their value is also stressed in the Old Testament: 'Behold, children are a gift of the Lord' (Psalm 127:3, NASB) and (when Jacob answered Esau's question, 'Who are these with you?') 'The children whom God has graciously given your servant' (Genesis 33:5, NASB).

A child ought to be made to feel he is the only one of his kind. Few children feel this but oh, the difference it makes in that small one when he knows he is special. Only focused attention can give him that realisation and knowledge, it is so vital in a child's development of self-esteem. And it profoundly affects a child's ability to relate to and love others.

Focused attention, in my experience, is the most demanding need a child has, because we parents have extreme difficulty in recognising it, much less fulfilling it. There are many reasons we do not recognise this particular need. One of the main reasons is that other things we do for a child seem to suffice. For example, special favours (ice cream or sweets), gifts, and granting unusual requests seem to substitute for focused attention at the time. These kindnesses are good, but it is a serious mistake to use them as a stand-in for genuine focused attention. I found it a real temptation to use this type of substitution because favours or gifts were easier to give and took much less of my time. But I found over and over again that my children did not do their best, did not feel their best, and did not behave their best unless I gave them that precious commodity, focused attention.

The tyranny of the urgent

Why is it so difficult to give focused attention? Because it takes *time*. Numerous studies have been done and books written showing that time is our most precious possession. Put it this way. Even if you could give twenty-four hours a day, seven days a week, it is virtually impossible to fulfil all of your obligations. That is a true statement. It is not possible for you to take care of every obligation and every responsibility in your life as you would like it to be done. You *must* face up to that fact. If you do not, you will naively assume that everything will somehow get taken care of, and when you assume that, you will become controlled by the tyranny of the urgent. Urgent matters will then automatically take precedence in your life and control your time. Unfortunately, they usually are not. Take the sacred telephone, for example. I say sacred because it takes precedence over almost all else. The ringing telephone must be answered regardless of time, place, or situation. Your family may be having a few wonderful moments together at supper time. In our home when our children were with us, this was of the highest importance to me. But if the telephone rang, it was given almost a sacred right to interfere with, disrupt, and even destroy our family fellowship. It shows how the tyranny of the urgent wins out over the important things of life once again.

You know, there is just not enough time in our short lives to be controlled by the urgent and be able to look after the important. We can't have our cake and eat it too. So what can we do about it? I'm afraid there is only one answer. And it isn't simple or easy. We must determine our priorities, set our goals, and plan our time to accomplish them. *We* must control our time in order to take care of the important things.

Set priorities

What are the priorities in your life? Where does your child fit in? Does he take first priority? Second? Third?

Fourth? You must determine this! Otherwise, your child will take a low precedence and suffer from some degree of neglect.

No one else can do this for you. A spouse cannot determine your child's priority in *your* life. Nor can your minister, counsellor, employer, or friend. Only you can do this. So what is it, fellow parent? What and who gets priority in your life? – Job? Church? Spouse? House? Hobby? Children? Television? Social life? Career?

In almost all families that have found contentment, satisfaction, happiness, and genuine thankfulness among all family members, the parents possess a similar priority system. Usually their first priority is of an ethical nature, such as a strong religious faith or moral code. In most cases, this is manifested by placing God first in their lives and having a warm, comforting, loving, supportive relationship with Him. They use this stabilising relationship to influence all other relationships. Their second priority is the spouse, as discussed previously. The children take priority number three. As you can see, real happiness is found in family orientation – spiritual family then physical family. God, spouse, children. These are essential. The remaining priorities are important, of course, but these three must come first.

I have talked with many people who sought contentment in such things as money, power, and prestige. But as they experienced life and discovered real values, they sadly realised they were investing in the wrong account. I've seen numerous wealthy persons who spent their better years making it. Tragically, they had to seek counselling when they realised that, despite their wealth and power, their lives were pathetically and painfully empty. Each would weep and consider his or her life a 'failure' because of a wayward child or a spouse lost through divorce. He or she realised only then that the only worthwhile possession in life is someone who loves you and cares what happens to you – God, spouse, and child.

People who are terminally ill, I have noticed, come to the same conclusion. As they look back on life, they too know that the only thing that really matters is whether someone genuinely cares for and unconditionally loves them. If these individuals do have such loved ones, they are content. If they do not, they are to be pitied.

I once talked with the wife of a minister, a most beautiful woman who had incurable cancer. She was such a radiant wholesome person. As we talked, she explained how, since she had known of her illness, her outlook on life had been transformed. With the knowledge of impending death, her priority system was forced to change. For the first time she realised there was not enough time in the life of *any* parent to provide for the needs of spouse and children if less important things were not resisted. The minister's wife gave her husband and children first priority, and what a difference was evident in their lives. Of course, this does not mean we should neglect other areas of our lives, but we must control the time we spend on them and their influence on us.

Fleeting moments

This illustration poignantly points out the importance of focused attention. I read of a father who was sitting in his living room one day. It was his fiftieth birthday, and he happened to be in an irritable mood. Suddenly his eleven-year-old boy Rick bounced into the room, sat on his father's lap and began kissing him repeatedly on the cheeks. The boy continued his kissing until his father sharply asked, 'What are you doing?' The child answered, 'I'm giving you fifty kisses on your fiftieth birthday.' Ordinarily the father would have been touched by this loving act of affection. Unfortunately, because he was depressed and irritable, he pushed the boy away and stated, 'Let's do that some other time.' The boy was crushed. He ran out of the house, jumped on his bike, and rode away. A few moments later the child was struck and killed by a car. You can imagine the grief, remorse, and guilt suffered by this poor father.

These stories tell us several things. First, because life is so unpredictable and uncertain, we cannot know or plan how many opportunities we will have for nurturing our children, especially times to give focused attention. We must take advantage of our timely opportunities because they are fewer than we may realise. Our children are growing up.

Second, these moments of opportunity do not happen every day. Remember those special moments which leave a lasting impression on a child? That moment when Rick tried to kiss his father fifty times was one such priceless moment. If the father had been able to spend those few moments with Rick in a positive way. Rick would have affectionately remembered that time the rest of his life, especially when tempted to act against parental values, as, for example, in the dissident days of adolescence. However, if Rick had not been killed, he would never have forgotten the pain, anguish, and humiliation of that moment.

Let's look at another story regarding focused attention. In the diary of the father of a great humanitarian was found a description of a day spent fishing with his son. The father laments how the day was a 'total loss' because the son seemed 'bored and preoccupied, saying very little.' The father even wrote that he probably would not take his son fishing again.

Many years later a historian found these notes, and with curiosity compared them with the entries of the same day in the son's diary. The son exclaimed what a 'perfect day' it had been, 'all alone' with his father. He described how deeply meaningful and important it was to him.

The goal of focused attention

What is it that defines focused attention? When a child feels, 'I'm all alone with my mummy (or daddy)'; 'I have her (him) all to myself; 'at this moment, I'm the most important person in the world to my mother (father)'; this is the goal of focused attention, to enable a child to feel this way.

Focused attention is not something that is nice to give our child only if time permits; it is a critical *need* each child has. How a child views himself and how he is accepted by his world is determined by the way in which this need is met. Without focused attention, a child experiences increased anxiety because he feels everything else is more important than he is. He is consequently less secure and is impaired in his emotional and psychological growth. Such a child can be identified in the nursery or classroom. He is less mature than children whose parents have taken the time to fill their need for focused attention. This unfortunate child is generally more withdrawn and has difficulty with peers. He is less able to cope and usually reacts poorly to any conflict. He is overly dependent upon the teacher or other adults with whom he comes into contact.

Some children, especially girls deprived of focused attention from their father, *seem* to be just the opposite. They are quite talkative, manipulative, dramatic, often

childishly seductive, and are usually considered preco-
cious, outgoing, and mature by their kindergarten and
infant school teachers. However, as these girls grow
older, this behaviour pattern does not change and
becomes gradually inappropriate. By the time they are
eight or nine they are usually obnoxious to their peers
and teachers. However, even at this late date, focused
attention, especially from the fathers, can go a long way
in reducing the children's self-defeating behaviour,
decreasing their anxiety, and freeing them to resume
their maturational growth.

How to give focused attention

Now that we've seen how vital focused attention is to a
child, how do we accomplish it? I have found the best
way to give a child focused attention is to set aside time
to spend with him *alone*. If you're already thinking how
difficult it is to do this, you are right. Finding time to be
alone with a child, free from other distractions, is what I
consider to be the most difficult aspect of good child
rearing. You might say this separates the best parents
from other parents; the sacrificing parents from the non-
sacrificing; the most caring from the least caring; the
parents who set priorities from those who do not. Let's
face it, good child rearing takes *time*. Finding time in our
hyperactive society is hard, especially when children
often are addicted to television and sometimes would
rather spend time with it. This is all the more reason
focused attention is so crucial. Children are being influenced by forces outside the family more than anytime in
history. It takes tremendous effort to pry time from busy
schedules, but the rewards are great. It is a wonderful
thing to see your child happy, secure, well liked by peers

and adults, and learning and behaving at his best. But believe me, fellow parent, this does not come automatically. We must pay a price for it! We must find time to spend alone with each child.

John Alexander, former president of InterVarsity Christian Fellowship, related at a conference some years ago how difficult it was for him to find time for each of his four children. His solution was to save at least one half-hour every Sunday afternoon for each of his children. Everyone must find his own way of doing this.

My time during our parenting years was also difficult to manage. I tried to conserve it as much as possible for my children. For example, when my daughter was taking music lessons close to my office Monday afternoons, I scheduled my appointments so that I could pick her up. Then we would stop at a restaurant for supper. At these times, without the pressure of interruption and time schedules, I was able to give her my full attention and listen to whatever she wanted to talk about. Only in this context of being alone without pressure can parents and their child develop that special indelible relationship which each child so desperately needs to face the realities of life. It's such moments as these that a child remembers when life becomes difficult, especially during those tumultuous years of adolescent conflict and the normal drives for independence.

It's also during times of focused attention that parents can take special opportunities to make eye contact and physical contact with a child. It is during times of focused attention that eye and physical contact have stronger meaning and impact upon a child's life.

Of course, it is more difficult to find time for focused attention when there are several children in the family. I remember counselling a seven-year-old girl for numerous problems she was having at school and at home –

problems with school work, peer relationships, sibling relationships, and immature behaviour. You've perhaps guessed that her parents had not given her focused attention. She had nine brothers and sisters and her parents couldn't give her the focused attention she needed. Actually, they weren't aware that this girl was suffering from lack of focused attention because all of their other children were quite well adjusted. The parents were farmers, and during the natural course of a day – milking, feeding the animals, and ploughing – they spent sufficient time alone with each child to forestall problems. With this particular child, because of her age, individual chores, and birth order, the natural course of events prevented her from enjoying enough of her parents' attention. She felt neglected and unloved. Her parents loved her dearly, but the child did not feel it and so she did not know it.

Careful planning pays off

This illustration indicates how important it is to *plan* our time in order to provide focused attention for *each* child. This is difficult. In a two-child family, each parent is often able to spend time with one of the children. With more than two children, the problem becomes progressively more difficult. And, of course, in a one-parent family the logistics are more difficult. However, careful planning pays off. For example, on a particular day (say next Friday) one child may be invited to a party, another may be at a relative's, leaving one child free. A careful parent whose children take priority would consider this time a golden opportunity to give focused attention to that child. Of course, our plans must consider the emotional needs of each and every child, or we'll have the same problem as in the ten-child farm family just mentioned.

This is especially difficult when we have both a demanding and a nondemanding child in the same family. We must resist the concept that the loudest squeaking hinge gets the oil. Every child has the same needs whether he demands they be met or not. Especially vulnerable in this regard is a non-demanding, passive child who also is a middle child. And if his siblings happen to be demanding children, his parents will find it all too easy to pass him by until problems develop.

Watching for unexpected opportunities yields additional time. For example, times occur when a parent finds himself alone with a child, a time perhaps when the others are outside playing. Here is another opportunity to fill that child's emotional tank and prevent problems brought on by a dry one. This time of focused attention may be quite short: just a moment or two can do wonders. Every moment counts. It's like making deposits in a savings account. As long as the balance is healthy, a child's emotional life will be sound and he will have fewer problems. It's also an investment in the future, especially the years of adolescence.

Every deposit is assurance that a child's teenage years will be healthy, wholesome, pleasant, and rewarding for both child and parent. The stakes are high. What's worse than a wayward adolescent son or daughter? What's more wonderful than a well-balanced teenager?

Of course, long periods of focused attention are important also. As children grow older, this time of focus needs to be lengthened. Other children need time to warm up, let their developing defenses down, and feel free to share their innermost thoughts, especially anything that may be troubling them. As you can see, if these times of focused attention were begun early in a child's life, he accepts it very naturally and finds it much easier to share emotional things with his parents. On the other hand, if times for focused attention are not provided, how can a child learn to communicate meaningfully with his parents? Again, the stakes are high. What is worse than having a troubled child who can't share his feelings with you? What is more wonderful than for your child to be able to bring anything to you to talk over?

All this is difficult and takes time. But many people I've met have shared with me all sorts of ways they have done this. I remember listening to the late Joe Bayly, a Christian writer and publishing executive, talk about this. He marked off definite times on his appointment calendar to spend with his family, and when someone called and asked him to accept a speaking engagement at that time, he politely told the inquirer that he had another engagement.

Joe Bayly had another good way to give his children focused attention. He had personal flags for each family member. Each flag was designed to suit the personality of the child for whom it was designated and was given to the child on his or her birthday. Thereafter it was flown on the flagpole in front of the house on special occasions, for example, subsequent birthdays, when that child would return home after trips, or going away to university. This is an example of indirect focused attention.

When others are present

We mentioned that focused attention is given when alone with a child, away from other family members. Although this is true, there are times when focused attention must be given with others present. This is especially true when a child is ill, has experienced some emotional pain, or for some other painful reason has regressed. By regressed, I mean he is in poor control of his feelings and/or behaviour.

Here is an example of this. One day, deeply concerned parents sought my advice regarding their twelve-year-old son Tim. The boy's first cousin, also a twelve-year-old boy had come to live with them. The cousin was a very demanding child who had overshadowed Tim by taking almost all his parents' attention. Tim felt displaced by his overpowering cousin, became depressed, withdrawn, and occasionally uncommunicative. Part of my advice to the parents was, of course, to give both Tim and his cousin much focused attention; that is to spend time with Tim alone and the cousin alone. However, the cousin continued to clearly dominate each situation when the two boys were present. Next, I advised the parents to give each boy focused attention whenever the cousin was being overly dominant. The parents were able to do this by turning directly toward Tim when it was his turn to speak, giving him full eye contact, and physical contact when convenient, and responding to his comments. Then when it was appropriately Tim's cousin's turn to speak, the parents repeated the process with him.

This type of focused attention usually works well only if a child is also receiving ample focused attention alone. By the way, I've taught teachers these simple principles which have revolutionised their teaching and perceptions toward each child.

Focused attention is time consuming, difficult to do consistently, and many times burdensome to already exhausted parents. But focused attention is the most powerful means of keeping a child's emotional tank full of investing in his future.

7

Appropriate and inappropriate love

Let's consider the *too-much-love* controversy. Some contend that too much love will spoil a child, while others claim you can't love a child too much. The confusion in this area often causes advocates of both sides to take an extreme position. Many of the former group are severe disciplinarians, and many of the latter group are over indulgent.

Consider the issue in light of the concept of *appropriate love*, which will provide healthy nurturing and foster a child's emotional growth and self-reliance. The picture then quickly becomes clearer. We can then hold to the principle that a child needs a superabundance of appropriate love but no inappropriate love.

Inappropriate love

We may define *inappropriate love* as affection which, when conveyed to a child, hinders a child's emotional growth by failing to meet a child's emotional needs, and which fosters an increasingly dependent relationship upon a parent and hampers self-reliance.

The four most common types of inappropriate love are possessiveness, seductiveness, vicariousness, and role-reversal. Let's take them one at a time.

Possessiveness

Possessiveness is a tendency of parents to encourage a child to be too dependent on his parents. Paul Toumier, noted Swiss counsellor, deals with the subject quite well in his article, "The Meaning of Possessiveness'. He states that when a child is small, dependency is 'obvious and almost complete.' But if this dependency does not diminish as a child grows older, it becomes an obstacle to a child's emotional development. Many parents try to keep their children in a state of dependence upon them. Dr Toumier states that they do this 'by suggestion or by emotional blackmail,' or else by using their authority and insisting upon obedience. The child is theirs. They have rights over him because he belongs to them. Such parents are termed *possessive*. These parents tend to treat their child as an object or property to be possessed or owned, and not as a person who needs to grow in his own right and to become gradually independent and self-reliant.

A child must have respect from his parents to be himself. This does not, of course, mean no limit-setting or being permissive. (Every child needs guidance and discipline.) It means to encourage a child to think to be spontaneous, to realise he is a separate person who must assume more and more responsibility for himself.

If we parents disregard a child's right to gradually become independent, one of two things will happen. He may become overly dependent on us and overly submissive, failing to learn how to live in his world. He may

become easy prey to strong-willed, authoritative personalities or cultish groups; or there will be deterioration
of our relationship with a child as he gets older. He will
become more resistant to our guidance.

Again, as Dr Toumier suggests, we should 'possess as
if not possessing.' Such is the great message of the Bible.
Man can never truly possess anything. He is but the
steward of the goods that God entrusts to him, for 'the
earth is the Lord's, and everything in it' (1 Corinthians
10:26, NIV).

Of course, there is some possessiveness in every parent.
But we must take care to (1) identify it within ourselves;
(2) separate it from true concern for a child's total welfare,
especially concerning his need to become self-reliant; (3)
be as continually aware of it as we can; and (4) resist its
influence.

Seductiveness

The second inappropriate way of expressing love is
through seductiveness. I have to start out by saying this
is a difficult subject to write about because *seductiveness*
is not easy to define. The word seems to be used to
communicate everything from elicitation of sexual experience to pollution.

Regarding our subject at hand, I believe it sufficient to
define seductiveness as attempting consciously or
unconsciously to derive sensual/sexual feelings from an
encounter with a child.

An example of this was discussed at a recent seminar
on child psychiatry. A seven-year-old girl was seen at a
psychiatric clinic for frequent masturbation and poor
school performance. The evaluation disclosed that the
child spent much time fantasising (day-dreaming) her

mother's death and living alone with her father. It was also noted that her father spent much time holding the child, caressing and fondling her in such a way that seemed to bring sensual enjoyment to both father and child. When these facts were gently shared with the father, his response was, 'Oh, my word, I just realised that when I wash the soap off of her when we're showering together, she reacts like a mature woman.' This was a case where the father was obviously seductive. However, he apparently did not fully realise what he was doing. As in almost all cases of this sort, the marital relationship in this family was hurting. In families where the marriage is not healthy, it is not uncommon for seductiveness to exist. In our day the problem is worsening.

What do you think of this letter to Ann Landers which appeared in her syndicated column some years ago?

> Dear Ann Landers: I don't know if I have a problem or not. It's our beautiful twelve-year-old daughter. I've seen girls who are crazy about their fathers, but never anything quite like this.
>
> Donna sits next to (or on top of) her father at every opportunity. They play with each other's hands and act kittenish like a couple of goofy kids. She hangs on her father when they walk or their arms are around one another's waists. Is this normal?
>
> Signed, Me Worried.

Are you a parent of a preadolescent daughter? What do you think? Does this sound good or bad? Would you be worried? What would you do?

Here is Ann Lander's reply:

> Dear W: Sounds to me as if there's entirely too much touching. Today a girl of twelve is more of a woman than

a child. Donna needs to be talked to, but it would be better if the word did not come from you.

Perhaps an enlightened relative or an adult friend could tell Donna it is unbecoming and unhealthy for a young girl to have so much physical contact with her father. (Surely this behaviour has been observed by others.)

If you know of no person you might call on to communicate the message tactfully but firmly, by all means enlist the help of the school counsellor. I believe Donna should be approached rather than your husband. He is apt to be resentful and defensive.

I would like to reply to Ann's reply. I agree that it does sound like there is too much physical contact here, and it does sound seductive. However, this is the mother's viewpoint, and the chances are overwhelming that the marital relationship is poor. In short, neither we (nor Ann) know for sure if there is actually sensual seduction here or not. Perhaps this situation is similar to the one at the end of chapter 2 where the mother is jealous of a good relationship between daughter and father.

Supposing the relationship here is indeed a seductive one, would you go to a twelve-year-old girl and suggest that her own father was sexually improper with her? Genuine respect for parents is hard enough to find today without further undermining it.

But nonetheless there is one principal comment I'd like to make regarding Ann's reply and that is that it exemplifies the general mentality today regarding loving children. Her advice seems to suggest that, because the father was conveying his love to the child inappropriately, he should not show it at all. We have already seen how vital physical contact is to a preadolescent girl. This particular father was not doing it correctly. Is the answer to stop the physical contact completely?

I'm afraid this type of reaction has become generally accepted by our society. It is assumed that because some parents are seductive with their children, physical contact should be held to a minimum or actually be avoided. An analogy would be this: because I saw an obese person today, I should not eat at all, or at least minimally.

Another reason many parents unfortunately avoid physical contact with their children is that they may actually feel some sexual response to them. This can happen to any parents, especially fathers of older daughters. So this is indeed a dilemma. On the one hand, the child desperately needs to feel loved and physical contact is essential for this. On the other hand, the parents feel uncomfortable and fear this would be wrong or perhaps damaging to the child.

I think many loving parents would be greatly helped in this difficult area if they realised that: (1) every child regardless of age needs *appropriate* physical contact; (2) to have some occasional sexual feelings or fleeting sexual fantasies regarding a child is normal; (3) a parent should ignore these inappropriate feelings, go ahead, and give a child what he (or she) needs, including appropriate (non-seductive) physical contact.

With this confusion is it any wonder so few children feel genuinely, unconditionally loved?

Another fear many parents have regarding seductiveness is homosexuality. There seems to be a misconception that too much love expressed from mother to daughter or from father to son will lead to homosexuality, but just the opposite is the case.

It's not infrequent during my work in schools for a teacher to approach me with this concern. A woman teacher recently asked, 'Dr Campbell, I love my daughter so very much that I kiss her a lot and sometimes on the lips. Am I making a lesbian out of her?' After asking for other information to make sure the relationship was healthy, my answer was, 'Keep it up.'

Two examples

Let me give you two other examples. The second example will show what appropriate love, including physical contact, does for a child concerning sexual identity. But the first example concerns what the *absence* of it causes.

The first example is drawn from Rusty, a dear friend of mine who is mean, tough, 'all man', and a drill instructor in the US Marine Corps. He and his wonderfully warm sensitive wife have four boys, 'stair steps'. Rusty decided his boys were going to be like him, tough and rugged men. He treated them like Marine recruits with strict and rigid discipline – no affection, unquestioned obedience, and no questions.

Your reaction to this is important. How do you think his four sons developed? Do you think they are following in their father's footsteps? Do you think they're becoming 'all men'?

The last time I saw these boys each one was extremely effeminate. Their mannerisms, speech, and appearance were those of girls. Surprised? You shouldn't be. I see it every day. Boys with rejecting, harsh, non-affectionate fathers generally become effeminate.

Here's the second example. Several years ago we had a pastor who was a huge man with rugged features. His very presence demanded attention, and he had a warm, loving heart. His boy at that time was three years old, the same age as my David but a head taller and about twenty pounds heavier, a 'spittin' image of his ol' man.' Our pastor loved his son deeply and warmly. He was very affectionate with the boy, lots of holding, hugging, kissing, and wrestling.

How do you think this boy developed? Did he follow in his father's footsteps? You bet he did. That little fellow was just like his father. He had a strong, healthy sexual identification and was secure, happy, lovable, and all boy. He will do all right in this world with a dad like that.

If these two examples don't convince you that a superabundance of appropriate love is not only war- ranted, but needed by every child (girls *and* boys) from *each* parent, let me give you this one fact. In all my read- ing and experience, I have never known of one sexually disoriented person who had a warm, loving, and affec- tionate father.

So, due to these misconceptions we've just looked at (and others), few parents are able to properly nourish their children emotionally. Although there is abundant love in their hearts, there is little in practice. I am con- vinced that once these misconceptions are corrected, and once parents understand what a child needs, most are able to provide the superabundance of appropriate love each child must have.

Vicariousness

The third most common type of inappropriate love is vicariousness. *Vicariousness*, or vicarious love, is living one's life or dreams through the life of a child. One of the most harmful kinds of vicariousness is a mother's living out romantic fantasies or longing through her daughter. A mother does this by steering her daughter into rela- tionships and situations where she herself longs to be. A clue to this phenomenon is a mother's obsessive interests in the intimate details of her child's dating experiences, becoming sensually excited as her daughter reveals them to her. The destructiveness of this process is obvious. A child can be led into situations which she does not have the maturity or experience to handle. Pregnancy is just one possible consequence. Another frequent outgrowth of this is a degrading reputation for the child. Such a reputation can injure a child's self-image and self-respect for life.

This type of vicariousness can also happen between father and son with similar consequences. A father who acts out his own sexual prowess through his son's conquests is harming not only his son but others involved in his life. In this way the boy is heavily influenced to view women primarily as sexual objects. He will find it difficult to relate to women as persons with feelings, and especially as equals.

Of course there are many varieties of vicariousness. The kind just described happens to be the most destructive.

Another example of vicariousness is a father using his son to satisfy athletic longings of his own. To see this phenomenon in action, go to your nearest junior football game. A vicariously oriented parent becomes emotionally involved in the game to such an extent it is as though he himself were the player. You can see him becoming outrageously angry at the referee when the decision is against his son. Worst of all such a parent will reprimand and demean his son when he makes a mistake.

What does this bring to mind? The old problem of conditional love. The more vicarious we are with our children, the more our love for them is conditional upon how well they have performed and have met our own vicarious needs.

But lets face it. We're all vicarious to some extent, aren't we? When our David played junior league football, I considered him a pretty good player. As I sat there watching him, for some strange reason my mind drifted back to my professional football days. I would find myself recalling how desperately I wanted to make it to the major leagues. The pain and disappointment of failing to accomplish this focused before me as I watched David play so well. I wonder why. What a mistake it would have been if I vicariously attempted to fulfil my lost dream through my son.

Vicariousness becomes harmful when it modifies our love so that it is given in relation to a child's behaviour and is, in fact, conditional love. We parents must not let our own hopes, longings, and dreams determine the type of love a child receives.

Vicariousness can be considered a kind of possessiveness if it causes us to view children as possessions to be used to fulfil our own dream. How can a child grow in his own right and think for himself and rely on himself in this situation?

We must keep our love for a child unconditional. We must love him so that he can fulfil God's plan for his life, not our vicarious ones.

Role-reversal

Role-reversal was described some years ago by M.A. Morris and R.W. Gould in their Child Welfare League publications. They define this 'as a reversal of the dependency role, in which parents turn to their infants and small children for nurturing and protection.'

Brandt Steele and Carl Pollock present a description of role-reversal in the book *The Battered Child* (Chicago:

University of Chicago Press, 1974, p 95). They state: 'These parents expect and demand a great deal from their infants and children. Not only is the demand for performance great, but it is premature, dearly beyond the ability of the infant to comprehend what is wanted and to respond appropriately. [These] parents deal with the child as if he were much older than he really is. Observation of this interaction leads to a clear impression that the parent feels insecure and unsure of being loved, and looks to the child as a source of reassurance, comfort, and loving response. It is hardly an exaggeration to say the parent acts like a frightened, unloved child, looking to his own child as if he were an adult capable of providing comfort and love . . . We see two basic elements involved – a high expectation and demand by the parent for the child's performance and a corresponding parental disregard of the infant's own needs, limited abilities, and helplessness – a significant misperception of the infant by the parent.'

Role-reversal is the primary relationship in the frightening phenomenon of child abuse. An abusing parent feels his child must take care of the parent's emotional needs, that the parent has a right to be comforted and nourished by his child. When the child fails in this, the parent feels a right to severely punish him.

Child abuse is the extreme form of role-reversal, but all parents use role-reversal to some extent. Sometimes when we ourselves are not feeling well, either physically or mentally, we expect our child to make us feel better. We may be depressed, physically ill, mentally or physically exhausted. At these times we have little or no emotional nurturing to provide our child. It can then be very difficult to give him eye contact, physical contact, or focused attention. When our emotional or physical resources are drained, we need nurturing ourselves. In this condition its so easy to make the mistake of expecting our child to be comforting, reassuring, compliant, mature in his behaviour, and passively obedient. These are not the characteristics of a normal child. If made to assume this unnatural role, a child will not develop normally. The list of possible disturbances which can result is endless.

We parents must not allow such a situation to develop. We must understand that parents do the nurturing, and a child receives it. During times when we are unable to carry this out, we must not look to our children to parent us. Of course, they can help us as they are able, running errands and getting things for us when we're sick, but they must not be expected to nurture us emotionally.

We should make every attempt to prevent times when we are unable to nurture our children. This may mean better care of our bodies to prevent illness and fatigue, for example – a sensible diet, plenty of rest, and plenty of exercise. It may mean looking out for our emotional health by engaging in hobbies or other refreshing activities to prevent depression or mental exhaustion. It may mean keeping our spiritual life fresh and exciting by allowing ample time for prayer and meditation. Most importantly, it means keeping our marriages strong, healthy, and secure. God should be first and one's spouse second and our children a close third. Remember, we will be able to give more to our child if we keep ourselves emotionally and spiritually replenished. This gets back to setting priorities and planning toward goals.

Don't toss the baby out with the bath water

We have looked at the four most common types of inappropriate love and several common misconceptions. Of course, these are ways of relating which we want to avoid. They are good neither for the child nor the parent.

However, as we avoid these mistakes, let's not 'toss out the baby with the bath water.' Let's not make a worse mistake and withhold *appropriate* love from our child. This is the most common of all child rearing mistakes. Far more children suffer from the lack of appropriate love than from exposure to inappropriate love.

Appropriate love is for the benefit and welfare of the child. Inappropriate love serves the abnormal needs and hang-ups of the parent.

We must face it. Our children have essential needs which only parents can fill. If we find we cannot fill these needs, if we cannot keep their emotional tanks full, if we can't give them an abundance of eye contact, physical contact, and focused-attention appropriately, we had better get help, and fast. The longer we wait, the worse the situation will become.

8

A child's anger

Anger is a natural response with all of us, including young children. Yet handling anger in a child is, in my opinion, perhaps the most difficult part of parenting. And because it is difficult, most parents respond to a child's anger in wrong and destructive ways.

Consider this. When a child becomes angry, he is quite limited in ways to express his anger. He has only two choices – to express the anger in behaviour or verbally. Both ways make it difficult for a parent to know how to respond properly.

If a young child expresses his anger, for instance, by banging his head, throwing toys, hitting, or kicking, such behaviour should be dealt with. On the other hand, if a child expresses anger verbally, it will almost certainly come across to the parent as unpleasant, disrespectful, and inappropriate. And this way of showing anger likewise is intolerable and unacceptable. What can a parent do?

Like steam in a kettle, anger must come out some way. No one, including a young child, can suppress anger and continue to keep it all inside. This is one of the most destructive things we can force a young child to do. If we refuse to allow a child to express anger in any way, he then must push the anger deeper and deeper within, causing destructive problems later in life. If the child is punished for expressing his anger either verbally or behaviourally, he has no other choice but to suppress the anger and bottle it up inside. As a result, this child will never be able to learn to handle anger maturely.

I call this the 'punishment trap'. As parents, we need to understand that punishment in itself is not the way to teach our children how to handle their anger.

Another easy mistake parents make in the face of childhood anger is to explode and dump a load of anger on an angry child. Children are helpless in the face of parental anger. They have no defence against it. A common example is found in such a harsh rebuke as, 'I never want to see you acting that way (or talking that way to me) again! Understand!' When a parent yells and screams at a child, he or she effectively closes off all normal ways for the child to express anger, and, as previously pointed out, the child must keep the anger inside and add the parent's anger to it.

Doubtless, the vast majority of parents today are not doing a good job in handling anger in their young children. If a child's anger comes out behaviourally or verbally, he is either punished or angrily scolded, or both. Again, since these are the only ways a child can express anger, the treatment forces suppressed anger.

Why is this so destructive? Because, as pointed out, the anger eventually must come out some way. If suppressed too much, the anger will come out as 'passive-aggressive behaviour'. Passive-aggressive (PA) behaviour is basically unconscious (out of the child's awareness) and anti-authority. It is an unconscious motivation on the part of the child to upset authority figures (parents and teachers, especially) by doing the opposite of what is expected of them. Once passive-aggressive features start influencing a child's behaviour, discipline becomes a nightmare.

Passive-aggressive behaviour, the opposite of an open, honest, direct, and verbal expression of anger, is an expression of anger that gets back at a person indirectly. A few simple examples of this are procrastination, dawdling, stubbornness, intentional inefficiency, and forgetfulness. The subconscious purpose of PA behaviour is to upset the parent or authority figure and cause anger.

Passive aggressive ways of handling anger are indirect, cunning, self-defeating, and destructive. Unfortunately, since passive-aggressive behaviour is subconsciously motivated, a child is not consciously aware that he is using this resistant, obstructive behaviour to release pent-up anger to upset his parents.

One of the ways a small child can early show PA tendencies is by soiling his pants after he has been toilet-trained – a very effective but unhealthy way to express anger. In most cases, the parents have prohibited expression of any anger, especially verbally. There is little parents can do in such a situation. The parents have backed themselves into a corner. The more the parents punish the child, the more he will soil his pants, to subconsciously upset the parents. What a dilemma, God pity both parent and child in such a situation.

Many school-aged children use PA to express anger by making poorer grades than those of which they are capable. Their attitude is much like 'You can lead a horse to water, but you can't make him drink.' For a PA child who uses poor grades to make his parents angry, its 'You can make me go to school, but you can't make me get good grades.' Again, with PA behaviour the parents are helpless; the child's anger is in control and not visibly showing. The more the parents become upset – the subconscious purpose of all this – the worse the situation becomes.

It is important to again emphasise that a PA child does not do things consciously or purposefully to anger authority figures. They are part of an unconscious process of which he is not aware, and into which he has been forced by the 'punishment trap'.

Passive-aggressive behaviour is very common. Why? Because most people do not understand anger or know what to do with it. They feel that anger is somehow wrong or sinful and should be 'disciplined' out of a child. This is a serious misunderstanding, because the feeling of anger is normal; every human being through the ages has felt anger, including Jesus, who became angry with those who misused the temple. If when your child becomes angry and you spank him or yell at him, 'Stop that kind of talk! I will not allow it,' or as some scream, 'Shut up or I'll smack you!' What can the child do? Only two things – he can disobey and continue to 'talk that way', or obey you and 'stop talking that way'. If he chooses the latter and ceases to express his anger, the anger will simply be suppressed; and it will remain unresolved in his subconscious, waiting to be expressed later through inappropriate and/or passive-aggressive behaviour.

Another mistake some parents make related to the suppression of anger is the inappropriate use of humour. Whenever a situation becomes tense, especially if someone is becoming angry, some parents will tease and try to interject humour to relieve the tension. Of course, humour is a wonderful asset in any family. But where it is consistently used to escape the appropriate handling of anger, children simply cannot learn to appropriately deal with it.

Passive-aggressive behaviour easily becomes an ingrained, habitual pattern which can last a lifetime. If a child into his mid-teen years avoids honestly and openly dealing with anger in an appropriate manner, he may use passive-aggressive techniques in relationships throughout life. This can affect his relationships later with spouse, children, work, associates, and friends. PA behaviour is also the primary force behind drugs, inappropriate sex, school failure, running away, and suicide. What a tragedy! And most of these unfortunate people are hardly aware of their self-defeating pattern of behaviour or their problems with handling anger.

Passive-aggressive behaviour is the worst way to handle anger for several reasons: (1) it can easily become an ingrained tenacious pattern of behaviour which will last a lifetime; (2) it can distort a person's personality and make him/her a quite disagreeable person; (3) it can interfere in all the person's relationships; (4) it is one of the most difficult behavioural disorders to treat and correct.

Scripture instructs parents to train a child in the way he should go. Forcing a child to suppress the anger and not deal with it properly is training him in the way he should not go. It is crucial to train a child in the proper way to handle anger. This is done by teaching him to resolve the anger, not suppress it.

Teaching our children and teenagers to handle anger is what I truly consider to be the most difficult part of parenting. First, it is most difficult because it does not come naturally. As we have discussed, our natural response to a child's anger is becoming more angry than the child and dumping the anger back on the child. Second, teaching the proper way to handle anger is difficult because it is a long, tedious process. As a goal, we want our child to handle his anger maturely by the age of sixteen or seventeen. It is a slow process because the handling of anger is a *maturational* process. An immature adult handles anger immaturely; a mature adult handles anger maturely. Passive-aggressive behaviour is the most immature way of handling anger. The most mature ways of handling anger are *verbally, pleasantly*, and resolving the anger toward the person at whom we are angry if at all possible.

No child can be expected to learn to handle this anger quickly. A wise parent realises that the well-parented child will very gradually learn these critical lessons as he goes from one developmental stage to another. Not until the child becomes six or seven or even older can he be expected to learn specifically how to handle anger maturely. Until that time, we as parents must avoid passive-aggressive behaviour taking root in our child. When the child is able, we can then specifically train our child to handle this anger more and more maturely as he gets older. This subject is far too extensive to cover adequately in this brief chapter. However, it is thoroughly covered in the book *Kids Who Follow, Kids Who Don't*.

Ephesians 6:4 says, 'Fathers, do not provoke your children to anger, but bring them up in the fear and admonition of the Lord.' Study this and also carefully read the following chapters in this book on discipline. Be careful to use punishment as a last resort and refrain from dumping your anger on your child. Parents, please do all in your power to remain pleasant with your child and yet be appropriately firm. If there are two words that sum up Christlike parenting, they are: *pleasant* and *firm*.

Pleasant includes loving kindness, optimism, and refraining from instilling fear or anxiety in the child, especially with our own anger. *Firm* includes fair expectations with consistency. Firmness does not mean rigidity and inflexibility. It considers the child's age, abilities, and maturity level.

Then when your child reaches adolescence, read *How to Really Love Your Teenager*, chapters 6 and 7, which will give you further guidance for that age. This includes how to train your child to handle anger maturely at least by the time he is sixteen or seventeen. Any PA behaviour beyond that age can be permanent.

Yes, teaching a child to handle anger is difficult, but one of the most important responsibilities in parenting today. As parents, we must be serious about this and be quite careful that we truly know what we are doing. Too much is at stake!

9

Discipline: what is it?

Periodically, when I lecture on parent-child relationships for churches and civic groups, we spend three or four hours talking about how to love a child before we deal with discipline. Invariably, after two or three hours, a parent will come up to me and say, 'I've enjoyed the lecture series so far, but when do we get to discipline? That's where I have problems and need answers.'

This poor parent has usually misunderstood (1) the relationship between love and discipline and (2) the meaning of discipline. He has separated love from discipline in his mind as though they are two separate entities. No wonder this parent is confused and has problems controlling his child.

Parents who are confused in this way have usually assumed that discipline means punishment (chastisement according to some).

Both of these assumptions are false. I stress to those parents and I hope to stress to you, fellow parent, that love and discipline cannot be separated, and that punishment is a very small part of discipline.

The first fact parents must understand in order to have a well-disciplined child is that *making a child feel loved is the first and most important part of good discipline.* Of course, this is not all but it is most important.

What you have read thus far in this book is the most important aspect of discipline, and must be applied to expect the best results from disciplining your child. There is no point in reading further at this time if you have not applied what you have already read, and if you have not kept your child's emotional tank full. If you have not made an effort to make your child feel loved with an abundance of eye contact, physical contact, and focused attention in an appropriate way, *please do not read further but go back and reread the previous chapters.* The results will disappoint you. Application of behavioural control techniques without a foundation of unconditional love is barbaric and unscriptural. You may have a child who is well-behaved when he is young, but the results are most discouraging in the long run. Only a healthy love-bond relationship lasts through all of life's crises.

What is discipline?

Now just what is discipline? What is your definition? In the realm of child rearing, discipline is *training* a child in mind and character to enable him to become a self-controlled, constructive member of society. What does this involve? Discipline involves training through every type of communication. Guidance by example, modelling, verbal instruction, written requests, teaching, providing learning and fun experiences. The list is quite long.

Yes, punishment is on this list, but it is only one of many ways of discipline and is the most negative and primitive factor. Unfortunately, we must use it at times and we will discuss its use further. At present, it should be re-emphasised that guidance toward right thought and action is far superior to punishment for wrong action.

With a clear definition of discipline in mind, consider it again in relation to unconditional love. *Discipline is immeasurably easier when the child feels genuinely loved.* This is because he wants to identify with his parents, and is able to do so only if he knows he is truly loved and accepted. He is then able to accept his parents' guidance without hostility and obstructiveness.

If a child does not feel genuinely loved and accepted, however, he has real difficulty identifying with his parents and their values. Without a strong, healthy love-bond with his parents, a child reacts to parental guidance with anger, hostility, and resentment. He views each parental request (or command) as an imposition and learns to resist it. In severe cases, a child learns to consider each parental request with such resentment that his total orientation to parental (and eventually to all) authority is one of doing exactly the opposite of what is expected of him. This type of emotional disorder is increasing at an alarming rate in our country, and children from Christian families are not excluded.

You are by now likely realising how crucial unconditional love is for good discipline (training). The more you keep your child's emotional tank full, the more he will respond to discipline (training). The less full his emotional tank, the less he will respond to discipline (training).

One aspect of appropriate love not yet mentioned is focused (active) listening. Focused listening is listening to a child in such a way that he is sure you know what he is trying to communicate to you. When your child knows you understand how he feels and what he wants, he is much more willing to respond positively to discipline, especially when you disagree with him. Nothing frustrates a child more than to be told to do something when he feels his parents don't understand his position. This does not mean catering to your child's demand or whim; it simply means listening to your child so that he doesn't feel you have ignored his thoughts and feelings, when you use your authority. Is that unreasonable? If you believe it is, you are not regarding your child as a valuable, separate person.

Think about it. When your child feels you have considered his position and feelings, you have assuaged your anger and resentment which would come back to haunt you later. Doesn't your Heavenly Father do as much for you? Christ said, 'Ask, and you will be given what you ask for. Seek, and you will find. Knock, and the door will be opened. For everyone who asks, receives. Anyone who seeks, finds. If only you will knock, the door will open. If a child asks his father for a loaf of bread, will he be given a stone instead? If he asks for fish, will he be given a poisonous snake? Of course not! And if you hardhearted, sinful men know how to give good gifts to your children, won't your Father in heaven even more certainly give good gifts to those who ask Him for them?' (Matthew 7:7–11, TLB).

To give a child focused listening requires at least eye contact, with physical contact and focused attention if possible and if appropriate. Acknowledging that you understand your child (even if you disagree with him) is usually helpful. Repeating your child's thoughts and feelings back to him is a good way to ensure that he understands that you understand. Your child's thoughts and feelings may make a difference in your own understanding and actions also.

I recall an incident with our then 16-year-old Carey. Pat and I gave her permission to go to a wrestling match at her high school on a school night with three of her friends. She was told to come home right after the match. The match was to end around 10 o'clock. It usually takes thirty to forty-five minutes to make the trip. At 11 o'clock I became concerned; at 11:15 I called the parents of one of the boys. They said the group had stopped by there to get a car with snow tyres (bad weather had begun) and the parents offered them a snack. The kids had left home about 11:10. Carey arrived home at 11:40.

I was angry. I sent her to bed after giving her a lecture about responsibility, and placed her on one week's restriction (she was grounded). Why did I react without listening to what Carey had to say? I was thinking more of myself than the actual situation. I wasn't feeling well that night and wanted to get to bed early. I had a busy schedule the next day. Secondly, my daughter was later than I expected, and she did not call to tell us that she would be late. I assumed she was totally negligent in the whole situation.

I have a wise daughter. She waited until the next day when I had recovered my composure and loving ways before giving me all the facts. She also knew that I listen better when I am not angry. As it turned out the kids took a longer but safer way home. Ice and snow were making the roads slippery. She was telling the truth; it all checked. Where she had been negligent was failing to call us when she saw that she would be later than we expected. After apologising to her for over-reacting, I decreased the restriction to be commensurate with what she had done.

There are two lessons we can learn from this experience. The first is the importance of really listening to a child when he or she is communicating. I could have saved myself frustration and my daughter's pain and possible anger and resentment toward me by listening to her before acting.

The other lesson is the importance of controlling our emotions at such times. I do believe that a mother or father's worst enemy in raising a child is uncontrolled feelings, especially anger. As in my experience, this can cause a parent to say or do things he or she will regret later. Too much anger, especially uncontrolled anger, will frighten a child initially. It may even seem to help a child's behaviour, but this is only temporary. As a child grows older, parental expression of too much anger (temper outbursts) will instill increased disrespect for the parents along with kindling a child's own anger and gradual resentment. When you stop to think about it, uncontrolled feelings draw disrespect from anyone. Why should we expect otherwise from our spouse or child?

You know as well as I that we all lose our cool at times. One thing to remember is that when we do, we shouldn't be afraid to apologise later after things have calmed down. It's very possible to make something beautiful out of something bad. It's amazing how pleasant communication can become when a family member is big enough to apologise when he is wrong, and losing one's calm inappropriately (over-reacting) can be such an occasion. Believe it or not, the times of warmness and closeness that usually follow this are among those special moments that a child (and parents) never forgets. They are priceless.

Emotional overreactions, however, can only be tolerated in a family to a limited extent, especially if no apology takes place. They should be kept to a minimum. How is this accomplished?

Control your anger

It's important to remember that anger is difficult to control under certain conditions. Some of these are (1) when a person is depressed; (2) when a person is afraid; (3) when a person is physically not well; (4) when a person is fatigued mentally or physically; and (5) when a person's spiritual life is not healthy.

A book could be written on coping with each of these problems. For now it must suffice to warn each parent to look out for himself mentally, emotionally, physically, and spiritually. Unhealthiness in any of these areas can hamper the parent-child relationship, the marital relationship, in fact, all relationships, primarily by hurting our ability to control our anger. Lets get in shape. Uncontrolled anger is detrimental to good discipline.

Discipline and punishment

I hope you are realising that you may have much to do before you can expect your child to respond well to discipline. Anyone can beat a child with a rod as the primary way of controlling his behaviour. That takes no sensitivity, no judgement, no understanding, and no talent. To depend on corporal punishment as the principal method of discipline is to make that critical error in assuming that discipline equals punishment. Discipline is *training* the child in the way he should go. Punishment is only one part of this, and the less the better. Please remember this statement: *the better disciplined a child is, the less punishment will be required.* How well a child responds to discipline depends primarily on how much the child feels loved and accepted. So our biggest task is to make him feel loved and accepted.

There are several reasons why so many parents fall into the punishment trap, why they somehow get the idea that their greatest responsibility in discipline (training a child) is to spank (punish) him.

One reason parents fall into this trap is because so many books, articles, seminars, institutes, radio programmes, sermons, and papers advocate corporal punishment while glossing over or bypassing all other needs of a child, especially love. Few plead for a child and his real needs. Too many today are dogmatically calling for children to be punished, calling it discipline, and recommending the harshest, most extreme form of human treatment. Most perplexing of all, many of these advocates call this a biblical approach. They quote three verses from the Book of Proverbs (13:24; 23:13; 29:15) to totally justify beating a child. They neglect to mention the hundreds of Scripture verses dealing with love, compassion, sensitivity, understanding, forgiveness, nurturing, guidance, kindness, affection, and giving, as though a child has little or no right to these expressions of love.

Proponents of corporal punishment seem to have forgotten that the shepherd's rod referred to in Scripture was used almost exclusively for *guiding* the sheep, not beating them. The shepherds would *gently* steer the sheep, especially the lambs, by simply holding the rod to block them from going in the wrong direction and then gently nudge them toward the right direction. If the rod was (or is) an instrument used principally for beating, I would have a difficult time with Psalm 23, 'Thy rod and Thy staff, they comfort me' (v 4, KJV).

I have not noticed one of these advocates state that there might be times when punishment may be harmful. So many parents have come away from these gatherings or readings with the idea that corporal punishment is the primary, or even the only way to relate to a child.

The results of this approach

I have seen the results of this approach. Children who were passive, compliant, very quiet, withdrawn, and easily controlled when they were young, lacked a strong, healthy, love-attachment to their parents, and gradually became defiant, resentful, difficult to control, self-centred, nongiving, nonaffectionate, insensitive, nonforgiving, noncompassionate, resistant to authority, and unkind as adolescents.

I think Scripture is quite helpful here. The Apostle Paul instructed, 'And, fathers, do not provoke your children to anger; but bring them up in the discipline and instruction of the Lord' (Ephesians 6:4, NASB). What has happened to these dear children just described? Yes, they were provoked to anger by mechanical, harsh discipline (primarily punitive) without the foundation of unconditional love. I like *The Living Bible* paraphrase of the Ephesians passage: 'And now a word to you parents. Don't keep on scolding and nagging your children, making them angry and resentful. Rather, bring them up with the loving discipline the Lord Himself approves, with suggestion and godly advice.'

Have you noticed that one deceptive trait of a young child who is disciplined primarily with punishment? Yes, he is easily controlled. That is the other reason so many parents fall into the trap. When a child is young, his behaviour can usually be well controlled by corporal punishment alone. That is, if you consider good behaviour as submissive compliance, lack of spontaneity, lack of self-confidence, and anxious docility.

You may be surprised, but I have seen many young children who were raised with much punishment especially corporal punishment, but who were unmanageable. These unfortunate children would be spanked severely, but the spankings would have no effect, and the children often would not even cry. Of course before coming to me, many parents have tried every piece of advice given to them, from trying to give even more punishment (like pinching the trapezius muscle), to not giving sweets, to putting the children in certain types of rigidly structured nursery schools. In every case, one of the problems was a lack in the parent-child love bond. These children just didn't feel genuinely loved and accepted. At that early age, resentment and defiance can develop to such an extent from a lack of unconditional love that not even corporal punishment can subdue these responses.

Put the horse before the cart

First things first, fellow parents. Practice uncontrolled love, *then* discipline. Putting the horse before the cart will create a positive relationship between parents and child and will keep *negative* interactions such as corporal punishment to a minimum. Notice that I did not say unconditional love will abolish the need for corporal punishment. How I wish it could, but it won't. The more genuine and unconditional the love-bond from parents to child, the more positive is the relationship, minimising the need for punishment. Unfortunately, punishment is required at times, and we'll explore that together later.

To summarise, in order for a child to respond well to discipline (training), we parents must give him what he needs. A child can learn (train) well only if he is happy, feels safe, content, confident, secure, accepted, and loved. Expecting a child to learn, namely, be disciplined, without our giving him what he needs is cruel enough.

But then to beat him for not living up to our expectations? We treat our pets better than that.

Consider this: An aggressive junior high school football coach once threatened to beat my then thirteen-year-old Carey with a paddle for what he considered an infraction in the school cafeteria. I called a school official and asked him if his school system actually allowed children to be beaten (especially teenage girls by male teachers with all the sexual connotations connected with such an act). He answered yes. When I asked him if he beat his dog he said he didn't. We wonder why children are becoming more and more disrespectful and resistant to authority. Can you figure it out?

The corporal punishment trap

One important reason why using corporal punishment as a principal means of behavioural control is dangerous is that it drastically alleviates guilt. Corporal punishment degrades, dehumanises, and humiliates a child. As a result, a child may feel the beating is punishment enough in itself. If the corporal punishment is instituted with enough frequency and severity, there will not be sufficient guilt provocation to enable a child to develop an adequate conscience. Without the foundation of unconditional love, the required developmental phases, especially proper parental identification, will fail to evolve, further crippling the development of a healthy conscience.

Many forget the important positive factor of guilt and consider it to be an unwanted feeling. Too much guilt is harmful, but a proper amount is vital in the formation and maintenance of a normal conscience. A normal, healthy conscience which keeps a child's behaviour within normal boundaries is far better than control by fear, and preferable to poor control or no control at all. What do you think enables a happy, well-adjusted teenager to control his behaviour? Right – his conscience. If you want your child to develop a normal responsive conscience which will enable him to *control himself*, then refrain from building your relationship with him on a punitive basis – by controlling his behaviour primarily by spanking and scolding, especially spanking.

Another tragic consequence of corporal punishment is called *identification with the aggressor*. It is also a guilt-escaping mechanism. A child identifies (sides with) the punishing parent, coming to the place where he feels being aggressive and punitive is right. Then, of course, this child grows up, has children, and treats them as he himself was treated. This is why abusing parents were themselves usually ill-treated by their parents. This use of corporal punishment (or the threat of it) as the main way of handling a child is passed on from generation to generation. This in itself is bad enough. With the frightening advent of violence in all modes of mass communication, especially television, is it any wonder that child abuse and all other forms of violence have become a national disgrace? Until we parents begin to proclaim the indispensable needs of a child, namely, unconditional love and loving discipline, the situation will continue to become worse. We must stand against the avalanche of demanding critics who insist that beating a child (confusing punishment with discipline) should be the primary way of relating to him. Are you aware that some of the critics do not have children themselves? Until we give a child what he desperately needs, he (and we) will suffer.

Dear parents, look at every statistic regarding children and adolescents in our nation today – academics, attitudes, respect for authority, emotional disturbance, motivation, drugs, crime, and so on. The situation is horrible. I maintain that the principle reason for our national dilemma with youth today is that our children do not feel genuinely loved, accepted, and cared for. With the deafening roar of disciplinarians (actually punishment-oriented) on one side and advocates of vague, difficult-to-follow programmes on the other, parents are confused.

Using designed programmes, such as those based on behaviour modification techniques, as the *primary* way of relating to your child is also a mistake. Like punishment, these programmes do have a place in child rearing and can be a very helpful, *but not as the principal way of relating to a child*. Some of these programmes are quite good, but usually their techniques are used in place of unconditional love and loving discipline (training). Here is the error. These designed techniques can be of great value in certain situations (which we will mention later), but we parents must first make sure that our child's emotional tank is as full as possible before we resort to punishment or designed techniques. In most cases, if a child receives his required amount of unconditional love and loving discipline, the parents seldom need to resort to punishment or programmes. Yes, punishment and techniques are at times necessary, quite helpful, and often good, but let's face it; they are not the best – appropriate love and guidance are.

We want the most positive, pleasant, loving relationship we can possibly have with a child. At the same time, we want him to develop self-control and act appropriately to the extent that he is able (considering his age, development, etc.) In order to see these two priceless happenings come to pass, parents must give their child two things. First, give him unconditional love, and give it appropriately. Second, give him loving discipline –

that is, training in the most positive way possible. Train by all available means, in such a way that enhances a child's self-esteem and does not demean him or hurt his self-concept. Positive guidance to good behaviour is far superior to negative punishment for poor behaviour.

But no matter how well we do our jobs as parents, a child will sometimes misbehave. This is inevitable. There are no perfect parents and there is no perfect child.

So how should we handle a child's misbehaviour? We will consider this in the next chapter.

10

Loving discipline

Up to this point we have explored how to convey unconditional love to a child by proper use of eye contact, physical contact, focused attention, and discipline (training). We have found how important it is to make sure we keep a child's emotional tank full for only then can he develop to be his best. Only then can he develop full self-control and self-discipline. We found in chapter 8 that guidance toward right action is better than punishment for wrong action. Then we ended that chapter with the fact that every child will misbehave at times. Let's now consider how to deal with misbehaviour.

In order to understand how to deal with a child's behaviour, we must understand the irrational way in which all children think. This crucial area must be carefully considered. All children need and want love. They know they need love and they know they want it, but the way in which they seek it is immature and irrational.

First, let's look at a rational way to obtain love. Say a man named Jim loved a woman named Carla. How would Jim be likely to win Carla's love? Acting immaturely, putting his worst foot forward, whining, pouting, being argumentative and demanding? Of course not. If

Jim were mature, he would be at his best. He would put his best foot forward, remain calm, pleasant, helpful, kind, and considerate. When he was not sure of Carla's love, he would not resort to immature behaviour; rather he would try to earn Carla's love. He would try to deserve it in her eyes. That's a rational way to obtain love.

But that is not the way a child does it, folks. The younger a child, the less mature he is. That makes sense, doesn't it? And the less mature he is, the more irrational he is. A child knows by nature how desperately he needs love. But he does not by nature try to deserve it or win it. This logic is beyond his inherent understanding. Eventually, he may (or may not) learn this, but he is not born with this capability.

What does a child do then, especially a younger child? A child communicates primarily with his behaviour. He continually asks the question, 'Do you love me?' How we answer that question determines many things. It determines a child's self-esteem, attitudes, feelings, peer relationships, and so on. If his emotional tank is full, you can see it in his behaviour. If it is empty, it is manifested by his behaviour. Put it this way. Most behaviour in a child is determined by how much he feels loved.

This is the irrationality of a child. Instead of winning our love and affection by good behaviour, a child by nature continually *tests* our love by his behaviour. 'Do you love me?' If we answer that all-important question, 'Yes, we love you,' great! The pressure to seek love is then off a child and his behaviour can be more easily controlled. If a child does not feel loved, by nature he is compelled more earnestly to ask, 'Do you love me?' through his behaviour. We may not like this behaviour because there are only a limited number of ways a child may act, and many of these ways may be inappropriate for the occasion. It stands to reason that when anyone is desperate enough, his behaviour may become inappropriate. Nothing makes a child more desperate than the lack of love.

This is the primary cause of misbehaviour in a child. When his emotional tank is empty, he cries out behaviourally, 'Do you love me?'

Is it fair then, or wise, to demand good behaviour from a child without first making sure he feels loved? Without first filling his emotional tank?

What does this child need?

Here's an example. When our daughter Carey was sixteen, she went to summer camp. Our nine-year-old David was then the oldest child at home, and he liked it. He acted more maturely, and sought more responsibility. David liked being the oldest. It was great.

The problem was that eventually Carey had to come home. Well, on the day she returned, David's behaviour regressed. He suddenly became whiny, discontented, pouty, somewhat angry, moody, and withdrawn.

What happened? Why the sudden, drastic change in David? What should I do as a parent? Punish David for his poor behaviour? Send Carey back to camp? Tell David his five-year-old brother Dale acts better than he? What would you do?

Well, let me explain what I did and why. Of course, Carey's coming and again becoming the oldest kid was hard on David. That's difficult for a young boy to handle. His behaviour was the pleading question, 'Do you love me? Do you love me now that Carey is home and I'm not the oldest anymore? How does your love for me compare to your love for Carey? Is she more important?

Can she take away your love from me?' Oh, the heartache of children at these times!

If I punished him at that time, how would David think I was answering his question, 'Do you love me?' As soon as I could, I took David off by himself, held him close, and we talked for some time. Occasionally I told him in boy ways how much I loved him. I gave him eye and physical contact. As his emotional tank was filled, his mood changed back to his happy, outgoing self. It took about fifteen to twenty minutes before he was off to play. David was happy and his behaviour was fine. That was one of those special moments we talked about before. I think he will never forget that precious time together. I won't.

Please don't get the idea I have been the perfect father. I have not. I've made many mistakes. But here was one situation I think I handled all right.

All this leads us to the realisation that when our child misbehaves, we must ask ourselves, 'What does this child need?'

The tendency is for parents to ask, 'What can I do to correct this child's behaviour?' Unfortunately, all too often this question leads initially to punishment. It is then difficult to consider the real needs of a child, and we may end up spanking him or sending him to his room. A child will not feel loved if we approach the handling of his misbehaviour this way.

We should always begin by asking ourselves, 'What does this child need?' Then we can proceed *logically* from there. Only then can we take care of the misbehaviour, give him what he needs, *and* permit him to feel genuinely loved.

The next step is to ask ourselves, 'Does the child need eye contact? Does he need physical contact? Does he need focused attention?' In short, does his emotional tank need filling? We parents must make sure that if the misbehaviour is in any way caused by a need for any of these, we must first meet these needs. We as parents should not continue to correct a child's behaviour until we have met his emotional needs.

This reminds me of a situation with our Dale when he was five. I had been out of town for a few days and had returned home. Dale was acting in a way which irritated me (and everyone else). He was doing all sorts of antics designed to aggravate the rest of the family, especially his nine-year-old brother, David. You see, Dale knew exactly what to do or say to make David climb the wall. And, of course, David could do the same to Dale. In fact, one son annoying the other was one of the first clues my dear wife and I had that an emotional tank needed filling.

Anyway, on this certain day, Dale was especially aggravating. He would needle his brother, pout, and make unreasonable demands. My first reaction, of course, was to really get on to him. Perhaps send him to his room; perhaps put him to bed; perhaps spank him. Then I stopped to think. 'What does he need?' The answer came in an instant. I had been out of town. He had not seen me in three days, and I had not really paid him much attention (no focused attention). No wonder Dale was asking the old question, 'Do you love me?' Actually he was asking, 'Do you still love me after being gone so long and acting as though it didn't affect me?' Suddenly his behaviour made sense. He desperately needed his daddy, and his daddy was not giving him what he needed. If I had done anything other than give him what he needed, *me*, his behaviour would have become worse. (Yes, even if I had spanked him.) He would have been deeply hurt, resentful, and I would have lost the opportunity to give him one of those special moments.

I can't tell you how thankful I am that I didn't goof on that one. I took Dale to our bedroom, held him close, and said nothing. That normally active fellow was so still and quiet against me. He just sat there and absorbed that intangible nurturing. Gradually, as his emotional tank was filled, he came to life. He began talking in his confident, easygoing, spontaneously happy way. After a short conversation about my trip, he jumped down, and ran off. Where? To find his brother, of course. When I walked into the family room, they were playing contentedly together.

So we can see how vital it is always to be asking ourselves, 'What does this child need?' If we do not, we will most assuredly skip prematurely into handling misbehaviour inappropriately. We will miss chances, to have those extremely important special moments with him. And we will punish a child at times which will hurt him in such a way that will create anger and resentment.

Fellow parents, if you miss this, you've wasted your time reading this book. Misbehaviour should not be condoned, but if it is dealt with in an inappropriate way, that is, too harshly or too permissively, you're going to have problems with that child. Yes, we must check misbehaviour. We *must* not tolerate misconduct. But the first step is *not* punishment. Punishment is occasionally necessary, but because of its negative effects from overuse, punishment should be used *only as a last resort*. It is far, far better to handle misbehaviour positively, especially with genuine love and affection, than to punish a child, especially with corporal punishment. So the first step in any situation is to make sure a child's emotional needs are met. Once again, *a child's emotional tank must be full before caring parents can take any other action*.

Is there a physical problem?

The next question to ask in the face of misbehaviour is, 'Does a physical problem exist which is precipitating this behaviour?' The younger a child, the more behaviour is affected by physical needs. Is my child hungry? Is he tired, fatigued? Is he ill? Is he coming down with something, like a cold or flu? Is he in some kind of pain or other discomfort?

This does not mean misbehaviour could be condoned if such a physical reason exists. (Misbehaviour, in my opinion, should *never* be condoned.) It means that we parents must make sure we are taking care of what is *causing* the misbehaviour as well as the misbehaviour itself. It is certainly better to correct the misbehaviour by giving a child what he needs – eye contact, physical contact, focused attention, water, food, a nap, relief of pain, or treatment of an illness – rather than punishment. Punishment may be appropriate, but we must make sure that a child has all his physical and emotional needs met first.

How can we tell when punishment is appropriate and when it will be destructive? An excellent question. It brings us to the next step in our logical way of handling misbehaviour.

Learn to forgive

In my experience, the most destructive time to punish a child for misbehaviour is when a child feels genuinely sorry for what he has done. The key word here is *genuinely*. If a child is genuinely remorseful for a wrong act, punishment (especially corporal punishment) would be harmful. The harm could come about principally in two ways.

First, if a child is already sorrowful for his inappropriate act, his conscience is alive and well. That's what you want! He has learned from his mistake. A good, healthy conscience is the best deterrent to repeating misbehaviour. Punishment, especially corporal punishment, would remove the feelings of guilt and remorse and enhance the possibility for a child to forget the discomfort of these feelings and to repeat the misconduct.

Second, punishing a child under these circumstances could provide feelings of anger. When a child already feels genuinely contrite and remorseful for his act, his conscience is dealing severely with him. He is punishing himself. He needs and is seeking comfort and reassurance that, even though his deed was bad, he is a good child. He desperately needs this assurance at such a time. So if you make the mistake of spanking him at a time when he painfully needs affection, he is deeply hurt. Under such circumstances a child will then feel that he is bad as a person and that you, the parents, believe this to be true. The result is feelings of anger, hurt, resentment, and frequently bitterness that a child will carry with him indefinitely.

What should we parents do when a child commits a wrongful act and is genuinely sorry and remorseful about it? Scripture is a real help at this point. When we do wrong and are sorry for our wrongdoing, what does our Heavenly Father do? He forgives us. Look at this writing of the psalmist: 'Just as a father has compassion on his children, so the Lord has compassion on those who fear Him' (Psalm 103:13, NASB). With the tenderness, compassion and forgiveness that our Heavenly Father gives to us under these circumstances, how can we then turn right around and punish *our* children?

The Apostle Paul warned of this mistake when he wrote, 'Fathers, do not exasperate your children; instead, bring them up in the training and instruction of the Lord' (Ephesians 6:4). I personally know of no surer way to provoke a child to anger, resentment, and bitterness than to punish him, especially physically, when he is genuinely sorry for his behaviour. At these times we must learn to forgive.

Another reason it is essential to forgive a child under these circumstances is that he must learn how to feel forgiven during childhood or he will have problems handling guilt. Consider how many people are guilt-laden today (including Christians) because they have never learned to feel forgiven. These poor persons may actually be truly forgiven by God and others. But they still *feel* the guilt even though they know that they are forgiven. We can save a child untold problems with guilt if we will teach him how to deal with it – namely, by the feeling of forgiveness. And we can do this by forgiving him when he is genuinely sorry for a misconduct.

A broken window

I remember an experience I had in this regard, but again please remember, just because I am picking out an example of a time when I did something right as a father doesn't mean I'm a perfect father. It just means that there are advantages to being a writer. I can pick out an example to illustrate a point.

One time I came home after a long, difficult day. I was exhausted and certainly not feeling my best. As soon as I got out of the car, David, who was nine then, ran to me. Usually David had a great big smile on his face and would jump up to give me a big bear hug. This time he was different. His face was so long and forlorn. There was a look of sadness in his beautiful blue eyes as he said, 'Dad, I have to tell you something.'

Because of my state of mind, I didn't feel I could handle a big problem very well right then. So I said, 'Let's talk about it later, OK, David?'

David looked at me very intently and replied, 'Can't we talk about it now, Dad?'

Just then I reached to open the back door of our house and noticed that one of the windows was broken. Somehow I figured out what was on David's mind.

Because I was in an irritable state of mind, I decided I had surely better handle this matter after I had relaxed. But David had followed me to my bedroom and pleaded, 'Please, let's talk about it now, Dad.'

With that pleading look on his face, what could I say? I said, 'OK, David, what would you like to talk about?' (As if I didn't know.)

David told me how he and his friends were playing ball close to the house and how a ball had hit a window and broken it. He knew he had done wrong and was obviously sorry about it. He was, through his behaviour, asking, 'Do you love me after what I did?'

So I took my son on my lap and held him dose for a little while, and said, "That's OK, David. That was an easy thing to do, and we can get the window fixed. Just play further from the house, OK?'

That was a special moment. David was immediately filled with relief. He cried briefly and just rested in my arms for a few moments. I could just feel the love flow from the child's heart. It was one of the most wonderful moments of my life. Then David was his old happy, radiant self. He jumped up and was off.

I've learned so much from this type of experience. This was one of those opportunities that do not come every day. A child does not always feel genuinely sorry for his misconduct, so we must be constantly looking for this type of opportunity to actually do what we say we should do. At these times we are able to convey to a child that, although we do not like his misconduct, we do love him no matter what. We love him unconditionally.

When a child is forgiven a misconduct, this does not mean he should not assume responsibility for its consequences. Restitution may be indicated. In the case of David's breaking the window, it may have been constructive to have had him pay for the broken glass in an appropriate way, like working it off. But again, we must make sure that the restitution is in line with the child's age, level of development, and ability to handle it.

We mustn't be manipulated. I am sure you have heard a child say, 'I'm sorry,' when he wasn't. Quite frequently a child says, 'I'm sorry' whenever he thinks he may be punished. Of course this is not being genuinely sorry or remorseful, and we must be able to distinguish the difference.

Fortunately, it is seldom difficult to tell if a child is really sorry or not. The most obvious indication is his repeating the misbehaviour. If David continued to play ball near the house after the incident, I could conclude that I had been manipulated and other measures should be taken.

If a child frequently attempts to manipulate his parents in this manner, I would be quite concerned. It could be indicative that a child's sense of right and wrong are developing in a twisted way. He could be learning to use untruthful statements to gain an advantage, saying, 'I'm sorry' simply to escape punishment. This particular behaviour is a good example of what placing the cart before the horse will develop. When parents relate to a child primarily by using punishment to control behaviour instead of first meeting a child's emotional needs, a child will develop all sorts of gimmicks to escape punishment.

One of these is 'I'm sorry' when the parents become angry or upset over a child's behaviour.

This is a dangerous situation. A child is then learning to be insincere, dishonest, calculating, manipulative, and insensitive. There is one commodity which cuts straight across this mistake and reverses the trend. It is unconditional love.

In such a situation good judgement on the part of the parents is imperative. Parents are in the best position to discern whether a child is being truthful and sincere. If a child is frequently manipulative and untruthful, trouble is ahead and help should be sought.

However, any child can do this occasionally, just as any child occasionally will feel real sorrow and guilt for misbehaviour. Wise, careful parents will realise there is a difference, discern the difference, and handle each situation appropriately.

In short, forgive a child when he is genuinely sorry, remorseful, and repentant for a misconduct. These infrequent opportunities are priceless ones and let him know beyond a doubt that you understand him, are genuinely concerned about him, and deeply love him regardless of anything else. This is unconditional love.

11

Discipline – requests, commands, rewards and punishment

What we have considered thus far are by far the most important and crucial aspects of child rearing. If these principles are applied properly, most problems of raising a child will be alleviated or averted. Meeting a child's emotional needs and applying loving discipline will permit a healthy, strong, positive love-bond between parents and their child. When any problem with a child occurs, parents must re-examine the child's needs and fill them before doing anything else.

Please remember the material in the preceding chapters because I am now going into the part of discipline which I do not like to put into print. Why? Because there are some parents who read a book such as this to glean from it only the material which they need to justify preconceived notions about child rearing. They are likely to apply only this section of the book and completely miss the fact that punishment should be used only as a last resort.

I hope you will apply the principles in the first ten chapters before trying to apply rules relating to discipline. Please love your child unconditionally and give him a superabundance of eye contact, physical contact, and focused attention. Please be careful not to love your child with possessiveness, seductiveness, vicariousness, or role-reversal. Please discipline (train) your child in *positive* ways such as guidance, example, modelling, and instruction. When your child misbehaves, ask yourself if he needs eye contact, physical contact, focused attention, rest, or water, and fill these needs first. When your child is sorry, remorseful, and repentant for a misbehaviour, please forgive him, and let him know he is forgiven.

Fellow parents, if you are diligently doing these things, and other factors such as marriage and home environment are satisfactory, things should be going fairly well with your child. Your child should be happy, responsive, well-behaved, doing what you ask him to do (according to his age and level of development) without too much difficulty. I'm not saying everything should be *perfect*, but you should be satisfied with your child, your relationship with him, and the way he is progressing.

I am saying all this now because it is a tragic mistake to expect punishment *in itself* to provide anything but negative results. Punishment without a firm foundation of unconditional love and loving discipline (training) cannot but create a poor relationship between parents and their child. Unfortunately, this is a common type of child rearing today. This is one reason children are generally having unprecedented problems today in every area, from academics to personality problems.

Requests

Proper behaviour from a child is required first by requesting it. This is the most positive way of achieving good behaviour. More importantly, requests instill a sense of personal responsibility in a child. A child feels that proper behaviour is just as much his responsibility to do as it is his parent's responsibility to see that it is done. A child knows by nature that he had a choice in how to act. When parents *request* good behaviour, a child knows his parents understand that he has ability to think and make decisions himself, has control over his behaviour, and must learn to take responsibility for it. When requests instead of commands are used as much as possible, a child will consider his parents in alliance with him in helping him to mould his own behaviour. This is so important.

If commands are primarily used in requiring proper behaviour, a child may be obedient and well behaved. But his tendency will be to act properly only because Mummy or Daddy says so, not because proper behaviour is best for him. He will not see his parents in alliance with him primarily for his own best interests. He will see them as requiring proper behaviour for the sake of good order, quietness, and their own social acceptance, in fact, for their own interests.

It is crucial to understand that making requests is a very effective way of giving instructions. It does not make us permissive or less firm. Using requests is simply a more thoughtful, pleasant, considerate way of giving instructions to a child. This is especially true when you want your child to enjoy doing things without resenting it.

For example, once when I was taking a bath, I noticed there were no towels in the bathroom. Dale, then five, was passing by, so I asked, 'Dale, would you go down and get your daddy a towel, please?' Dale was very happy to do so and was back with a towel before I could say 'Jack Robinson'.

Another example. The teacher of my son David's Sunday School class was having a problem with rowdiness from the boys. I had a choice of being very authoritarian and demanding that nine-year-old David 'behave himself, or talking over the problem with him, clarifying the issues, and then requesting his cooperation. I chose the latter, and ended the conversation with, 'I want you to pay attention to the teacher, join in the discussions, and learn all you can. Will you do that, David?' So far so good.

Direct instruction

The fact must be faced, however, that requests will not always suffice. Occasionally, parents must be forceful and give directions not by requests but by direct instruction (commands). This usually happens when a request is given to a child and he fails to carry it out. Before parents do anything else they must make sure that their request was appropriate, that it was suitable to the child's age, understanding, and ability to carry it out. The most frequent mistake in this regard is asking a child to do something which seems to be within his ability and actually is not.

A classic example of this is asking a four-year-old child to pick up his things by himself. Unless there are only two or three things to pick up, this request is unreasonable. A parent must help the child with the task. Frequently, a parent mistakenly will believe a task such as this is appropriate, gets angry when his child refuses or fails, and punishes him instead of helping him to accomplish the task.

Another real value in using requests whenever possible is to help you determine when a task is reasonable or not. You know your child better than anyone else. If on countless previous occasions your child would very willingly do a task when requested, but on one occasion he suddenly refuses, it is harmful to get angry and punish him. Obviously, because he has had no problems with this request in the past, *there is something wrong now.* Don't you want to know what it is? I believe you would. You would do your best to find the problem, because it might be extremely important. You would certainly rather take care of the problem and see your child proceed to do the task willingly than force him to do it before understanding the situation. If the reason for your child's behaviour was legitimate, then you would be the one who should be punished for forcing him to perform the task.

As a parent you have the responsibility and authority to see that your child behaves properly, but you are also responsible for your child's total welfare. You are responsible for seeing that your child is not hurt by misuse of your power and authority over him. His future happiness and welfare are heavily dependent on how you use parental authority over him.

At this point I would like to insert a very important piece of advice and warning. The more parents use such authoritative techniques as commands, scolding, nagging, or screaming, the less effective they become. It is like the boy who yelled, 'Wolf, wolf!' so many times that it lost its effect. If parents normally use pleasant requests, the occasional use of direct commands will be quite effective. The more parents use authoritative ways of telling a child what to do, the less response they will have. This is especially true if they are also angry, hostile, or hysterical when they do it.

For example, have you been in a home where the tension level is high? In these homes the parents have used essentially all their authority and reserve force just to discipline (train) their children in routine, daily events. When real forcefulness and authority are needed for unusual and really important situations, these poor parents have nothing in reserve to handle the situations. Their children then react as they usually do to their parents' wishes. They are no more responsive to emergency situations, for example, than they are to such mundane matters as tying a shoestring.

Parents, we must save the big salvos for the important situations. We must have reserve ammunition to handle critical situations. It is important to maintain pleasantness with a child by considerate, reasonable requests as much of the time as possible.

Once I made the mistake of using a forceful order when a simple request would have sufficed. The two boys and I were home, and I wanted to have the house clean before Pat came home from a weekend conference. I started out pretty well. I asked the boys to start cleaning up their bedroom while I made the beds. When I returned in a few minutes, they were busy doing their chores. But I noticed that they had thrown some clothes on the floor of their closet instead of hanging them up. David and Dale were usually obedient, easy-to-handle boys, and a short word of explanation and simple request would have sufficed. But I was somewhat annoyed and I overreacted. I barked out some orders to hang up the clothes which they were 'ruining'. See the error I made? I should not have used such forcefumess when a simple explanation and request would have been sufficient.

I should have saved forcefulness for a time when I would really need a rapid response under difficult circumstances. For example, one Sunday after we parked in our church's parking lot, Dale was walking around the car when another car pulled out. It was a dangerous situation. I yelled at Dale to run to me. Thank goodness he understood the urgency in my voice and responded immediately. If it had been my habit to yell at Dale, I know he would have responded routinely.

Another example occurred when our David and I were playing basketball with several friends. We all got carried away because we were having so much fun and we had played much too long. Consequently, we were all extremely tired. Then David fell when someone ran into him. He hurt his ankle slightly, but this pain in a very fatigued young boy was more than he could handle at that particular moment. He became angry at the person who knocked him over and began telling him about it. I saw this as inappropriate behaviour on David's part but also as a good learning experience for him.

First, I was convinced that David's emotional tank was full. He had had much affection, eye contact, physical contact, and focused attention that weekend. Second, I made a request. I asked David to go with me to a place where I could talk to him. He was too angry to respond. That is where I needed enough force to control him. The next level of use of force is to give direct instruction (command). I said, 'David, come with me,' in a firm tone. He immediately responded. When we were alone, and as he calmed down, we talked about getting so angry we lose control of our behaviour, and how to prevent it. It was a very profitable time for David because he learned much about self-control over inappropriate anger.

Suppose David simply would not have responded as I wanted him to do and could not calm down or gain control over his anger even after I commanded him to do so. The next step would have been to take him to a place where he could be by himself. If I could not get him to do this by verbal instruction, then I would have had to go to the next level of forcefulness, the use of physical force. But even here I would have used the least harsh method. I would have taken him by the hand, perhaps have one arm around his shoulder, and lead him to a quiet place. I call this 'gentle physical manipulation'. The point is to control a child's behaviour in the most gentle, most considerate, and most loving way possible.

Defiance

It is entirely possible that David could have remained unresponsive to any verbal approach. He could have refused to do as I wanted him to do in that situation. It could have developed into a battle of the wills. This could then be called *defiance*.

Defiance is openly resisting and challenging authority – parental authority. It is stubbornly refusing to obey. Of course, defiance, as well as any misbehaviour, cannot be permitted. At these times, punishment is often indicated, and such times occasionally occur no matter what we do. However, parents must attempt to avoid such unpleasant encounters – not by catering to a child's unreasonable whims or wishes, but by constantly re-examining their own expectations of their child, making sure their expectations are reasonable, considerate, and are in accordance with their child's age, level of development, and ability to respond. Yes, times which require punishment will come, but if parents find themselves punishing their child frequently, they had better re-examine their relationship with that child and what they expect from him.

But a child's defiance does not automatically mean that punishment is indicated. In fact, punishment at the wrong time can worsen the situation greatly. Punishment, especially given often at the wrong time, can permanently harm the parent's relationship to the child. For example, if the misbehaviour is passive-aggressive in nature, punishment may cause the child to use this particular behaviour to an even greater extent as a way to upset the parent. The child's behaviour will then worsen as the child is repeatedly punished for it. Please reread the chapter 'A Child's Anger' if this is unclear to you. Misapplying punishment, especially corporal punishment during such times, can rapidly snare the parent into the 'punishment trap', where the more the child is punished, the worse the behaviour becomes.

A wise parent can avoid the punishment trap by using punishment as the last resort. A loving parent can use pleasant means of controlling a child's behaviour first with requests, explanations, and 'gentle physical manipulation'. Next the parent can use commands in a pleasant tone of voice. If unsuccessful, a parent can use a 'time out' chair where a child can sit for a reasonable length of time until he can calm down and be reasonable. These measures should be effective the vast majority of the time. However, if the parent has diligently and pleasantly tried the above ways to control a child's behaviour, then the parent can assume that the behaviour is not passive-aggressive in nature, that the punishment trap has been avoided, and punishment must now be considered.

Imagine that the child becomes obviously defiant and his defiant behaviour does not respond to filling his emotional tank, and there are no physical problems. He does not respond to requests nor to 'gentle physical manipulation', nor to explanation, nor to commands (firm instructions). He remains defiant (again, let me say this situation should be quite rare: when it occurs, make sure you have tried everything before considering punishment). He must be punished, but how?

Appropriate punishment

Determining the appropriate punishment is seldom easy. Why? The punishment must fit the offense. A child is sensitively aware of fairness and consistency. He knows when parents have overreacted or have been too harsh with him. He also knows when parents are too accepting of poor behaviour. He detects inconsistency, either with him alone or in comparison with other children, especially siblings. This is the reason parents must be firm with their child, always demanding appropriate behaviour and not being afraid to love and discipline (train) him simultaneously. But parents must remain flexible, especially regarding punishment.

Parents make mistakes. If you feel parents should not make changes in their disciplinary actions once a decision is made, you are going to back yourself into a corner. Of course, parents can change their minds, and lessen or increase the punishment. (Remember that this is a disadvantage to corporal punishment, for once done, it can't be changed.)

Naturally, parents don't want to change their minds so often that they are wishy-washy and confuse the child. For instance, if a punishment is set forth – say confinement to the bedroom for one hour, and later parents discover extenuating facts which show this punishment to be too harsh, it is logical and proper to explain this to the child and lessen the punishment. If the child has already been punished or for some other reason has suffered inappropriate punishment, it is perfectly all right for parents to apologise to the child and attempt to make the situation right.

Parents must be flexible in order to change their approach to their child when indicated. Parents must also be flexible to be able to apologise. The need occasionally to change decisions and the need to apologise occur in every home.

Being flexible in order to appropriately change our approach to handling discipline (training) and being firm are two different things. Both are essential. Firmness first of all includes what our expectations are regarding a child and his response to requests. If our expectations are too rigid (for example, expecting a two-year-old to consistently respond to first requests), we are being unreasonable. A normal two-year-old will naturally be negative most of the time and seem to be quite disobedient and defiant. But this is a normal stage of development – let's call it 'two-year-old negativism'. Punishment for this is unwarranted. Loving parents of a two-year-old will, of course, be firm, but firm in *limit setting*, not in punishment. These parents will control the child's behaviour by gently manoeuvring the child physically, for example, picking him up, turning him around, guiding him, or placing him in the correct place or position – 'gentle physical manipulation'.

This 'two-year-old negativism' is crucial for normal child development. The child will eventually do what we ask but he must say 'no' first. This is one of the ways each of us had to separate ourselves psychologically from our parents. It may appear to be defiance but it is distinctively different. One difference between two-year-old negativism and defiance is belligerence. Two-year-old negativism is normal and should not be punished. Belligerent defiance on the other hand cannot be tolerated and must be dealt with quickly. Incidentally, 'two-year-old negativism' can occur in any age child.

As a child becomes older, his ability to respond to verbal requests increases, and by the time he reaches four and one-half (this varies from child to child), parents can expect him to respond to first requests. I fully expected my children to respond to first requests. If they did not, they knew that action would be taken. Of course they were free to make an appropriate statement regarding the request, if they had any question about it. But unless I changed the request, they knew they must carry it out.

It is so important to remember that being firm does not mean being unpleasant. We must be firm in our expectations and enforcement of these expectations, but we will be just as effective by doing it pleasantly. Loving firmness does not require us to be angry, loud, authoritative, or otherwise unpleasant.

Every child needs to experience all the ways of loving simultaneously. He needs eye contact, physical contact, focused attention, *and* discipline *simultaneously*. A child must have a parent's love and firmness together. None of these things are mutually exclusive. Being firm does not negate affection. Showing affection does not lessen firmness or foster permissiveness. *Lack of firmness and limit setting foster permissiveness, but love and affection do not.*

When parents have conscientiously provided all of the preceding means of loving and disciplining a child, and the youngster remains belligerently defiant, the parents must punish him. This type of defiance must be broken. The punishment must be severe enough to break the belligerent defiance, but it must also be as mild as possible to prevent the problems we have already discussed. If a command or explanation to a child is sufficient to break the defiance, why be more punitive? If sending a child to his room for a period is required and will suffice, fine. If taking a privilege away from a child is necessary to crush the defiance, proceed to do so. Let's face it, corporal punishment is sometimes necessary to break a pronounced belligerent defiance, but only as a last resort.

Another problem with punishment is that punishment for one child may mean little to another. For example, one of my boys was more sensitive than the other. The most severe punishment for him was to send him to his room. This rejection was far more devastating to him than corporal punishment. Yet, my other boy didn't mind going to his room at all. Each child is unique.

One other problem with punishment is that the type and severity of punishment usually depends on the parent's feelings at the time. At times when the parent is in a pleasant, upbeat, loving mood, the punishment will most likely be quite different and less harsh than when the parent is in a negative mood. This, of course, leads to inconsistent discipline which has its own unhealthy effects on the child. For these reasons, I suggest that parents confer with each other or with a friend and determine appropriate punishment for each child in each situation. This decision-making should be done, of course, when the parent is calm, rational, and is able to think the matter completely through.

Be careful

When physical punishment is used, we must be careful in several respects. First, the child must understand exactly why he is being punished. Explain to him in terms of his behaviour exactly what he has done wrong. Words such as 'bad boy' or 'bad girl' can hurt the child's self-esteem and should not be used.

Second, parents must be careful not to inflict any physical damage on the child. For example, it is easy to hurt a finger or another part of the body inadvertently.

Third, immediately after the punishment, as the child is crying, he should be left alone. Parents should stay nearby, however, listening for the crying to stop. When a child's crying has subsided and he is looking around, a child is again asking, 'Do you love me? Do you still love me?' Parents should then give the child an abundance of eye contact, physical contact, and focused attention to reassure him that he is indeed loved.

Behaviour modification

Finally, I believe it appropriate to mention *behaviour modification*. This is a system of thought which is in wide use today concerning the handling of children. Behaviour modification utilises positive reinforcement (interjecting a positive commodity into a child's environment), negative reinforcement (withdrawing a positive commodity from a child's environment), and punishment (interjecting a negative commodity into a child's environment). An example of positive reinforcement is rewarding a child for an appropriate behaviour by giving him some sweets or fruit. An example of negative reinforcement is withdrawing television privileges from a child for inappropriate behaviour. An example of punishment (sometimes called aversive technique) is pinching him on the trapezius muscle for inappropriate behaviour.

It is beyond the scope of this book to speak on this subject in depth. However, a few important points should be made.

First of all, such emphasis has been made concerning behaviour modification that such techniques are frequently substituted for emotional nurturing. If behaviour modification is overused by parents in relation to a child, a child will not feel loved. Why? First of all, the very foundation of behaviour modification is *conditional*. A child receives a reward only if he *behaves* a certain way.

Second, behaviour modification is not concerned with feelings or the emotional needs of a child (love). Consequently, parents, using behaviour modification as the primary way of relating to your child, cannot convey unconditional love.

For instance, consider the example I used in the last chapter regarding filling Dale's emotional tank when he misbehaved following my three-day absence. A strict behaviourist would say I was rewarding Dale for his misbehaving by giving him affection at that time. See the difference? Parents cannot *primarily* use behaviour modification in relating to their child and love their child unconditionally.

Another problem with relating to a child primarily by behaviour modification is that a child will derive an inappropriate value system. He will learn to do things primarily for a reward. A 'what's-in-it-for-me?' orientation will develop. An example of this occurred at the home of a dear friend of ours. He happens to be a strict behaviourist and was raising his children as closely to the behaviour modification concept as he could. One evening, when we were eating at their home, he said, 'Jerry is just three and he can count to a hundred already. Watch this.' He went up to his son and said, 'Jerry, count to a hundred and I'll give you some sweets.' Jerry instantly replied, 'I don't want any sweets.' If we want our child to do things for the satisfaction of doing them or for the pride of a job well done, we should not use behaviour modification. The end result is inappropriate motivation.

One other problem with the use of behaviour modification is this. If parents overuse these techniques, a child will learn to gain what he wants by using the same method on the parents. He will behave as the parents wish *in order to get something he wants*. Most persons would call this manipulation. One of the surest ways of encouraging your child to become cunning and manipulative is to use behaviour modification techniques too often.

Now that I've expounded on the negative aspects of behaviour modification, let me express the positive. There is a place for these techniques in child rearing, but not as the primary way of relating to a child (the primary way must be unconditional love).

Behaviour modification should be used for specific, recurring behavioural problems for which a child is neither sorry nor defiant. This type of problem must also be specific enough to be easily defined and understood by a child.

Here is an example of this type of problem which we encountered in our home. When our two boys were nine and five years of age, they were at stages during which they frequently fought with each other. Of course, neither one was remorseful about this. Forgiveness was certainly inappropriate. And neither one was defiant about it. Requests did not work. Commands had effect only for a few hours. Punishments also had brief effects and were quite unpleasant for everyone. You know what worked? You've probably guessed it, a reward system.

We used a chart-with-stars technique. One star for every fifteen minutes of peace, gradually increasing the time interval until the fighting was extinguished. We gave each boy an appropriate reward for a certain number of stars. It worked beautifully and we had 'peace in the valley'.

However, one word of warning about this type of technique. It takes time, consistency, real effort, and persistence. Don't start something like this unless you are prepared to stick with it and be consistent. Otherwise it will fail.

There are numerous good books on behaviour modification to tell you more about specific techniques.

This has been a long chapter, but one more point. As you can tell, good child rearing requires balance. A child needs everything we have discussed; eye contact, physical contact, focused attention, discipline, requests, firmness, flexibility, commands, forgiveness, punishment, behaviour modification, instruction, guidance, example, and active listening. But we must give our children these things in *proper measure*. May our discussions help you to do this in a way that will enable your child to feel unconditionally loved.

12

Children with special problems

Why do children with special problems such as diabetes, learning disabilities, deafness, hyper-activity, or mental retardation generally have markedly greater emotional and behavioural problems? The answer to this question is extremely complex. To explain why children in each of these problem areas are more prone to emotional and behavioural disturbance is more than can be dealt with in this book.

However, a few very pertinent points would be helpful to every parent of such a child. Some of these facts are closely related to conveying love to our children.

Perceptual problems

First, let's look at the general area of perceptual problems. To perceive is difficult to define, but let's try. It can mean to grasp or take in information through the senses to the mind, in which case a child with perceptual problems has difficulty taking in information from his environment and transmitting it to his mind. Consequently, when such information as visual images, sound, and touch is processed in a child's mind, he has difficulty understanding it clearly. His understanding of his environment is distorted in those areas where his misperceptions lie.

Using this very broad and simplified definition of perceptual problems, we can see that many special problems can be included. Visual problems, hearing problems, certain neurological diseases, and many type of learning disabilities have one thing in common: each child suffering from one of these disorders has a distorted conception of his surroundings. In one or more ways his incoming stimuli or information are distorted to him.

Do you see the great significance of this beyond the perceptual disability *per se*? Every way you have to convey your love to your child requires the use of one or more of the perceptual senses? Eye contact requires the perceiving of visual imagery. Physical contact requires the use of the sense of touch, which in itself is overwhelmingly complex. Focused attention requires the use of all of your senses. So if there is enough perceptual distortion in any of these areas, your child's understanding of how you feel about him can be distorted. This makes it more difficult to convey your love to this particular child.

This difficulty in a child's feeling loved is one big reason perceptually handicapped children generally have less than adequate self-concepts. It is one reason they usually become increasingly depressed as they grow older, frequently resulting in rather severe emotional and behavioural disorders, especially in early adolescence.

The common story of a perceptually handicapped child with resultant learning disabilities is that this unfortunate child cannot keep up academically or in other ways with his peers. He makes poor grades or is in other ways forced to endure continual degrading experiences. Even in nongraded situations he realises his deficiencies. As he goes into the pre- and early adolescent years, he becomes increasingly depressed. Depression in this age group is unlike any other. Generally these children do not look or act depressed unless the depression has reached severe depths. Typically young teenagers manifest their depression by difficulty in paying attention in the classroom (decreased attention span and ability to concentrate) with a resultant dropping of grades. Subsequently, prolonged boredom sets in with decreased interest in wholesome activities. At this stage the youngster is profoundly miserable.

If the boredom continues, eventually the teenager will act out his depression and misery. A severely depressed and bored girl in this predicament may then become promiscuous, use drugs, run away, or may try other antisocial behaviours. A boy in a comparable situation will be prone to behave similarly but is usually more inclined to such actions as stealing and fighting.

If we know that perceptually handicapped children are almost predisposed to poor self-concept feelings of being unloved and unacceptable, and of depression, how can we help them? I firmly believe that the area where they require the greatest help is the area which is largely over-looked. You guessed it, these children need most of all to feel genuinely, unconditionally loved. They will then be better able to overcome their handicaps.

How do we do this? The same way we give our love to all children, except that we must remember that, though their perceptions are distorted in some areas, they are seldom distorted in all sensual modalities. These children almost always need more affection and other means of conveying love in order to feel loved. In addition, they need our love to be given to them in more direct, simplified, straightforward, and accentuated ways. We must also give it to them in a somewhat more intense manner. All of this is necessary to make sure that these children do not misunderstand our feeling toward them. Our love-communications with such children must be clear and strong.

Other medical problems

Children with chronic (long standing) medical problems are also prone to emotional and behavioural problems. This is especially true of medical problems which require close supervision and continual attention such as juvenile diabetes. Taking care of young children with this disease requires tremendous time and effort by parents. So much so that it is difficult not to devote one's full attention to treating the disease and overlooking other needs of the children. This is exactly what happens concerning the emotional needs of most of these children. The caring parents become so intent, for example, on giving the right doses of insulin, regulating the diet, doing glucose determinations and the like, that these necessary procedures replace the natural giving of love. As essential as they are, these medical duties are no substitute for unconditional love given through eye contact, physical contact, and focused attention. As children grow older, especially during adolescence, they become increasingly angry, resentful, and bitter about their disease. Because of the aforementioned substitution of medical care for love, the children resent the disease and their parents. They become hostile and defiant not only toward parental authority but all authority. They are inclined to depression and all of its consequences. Worst of all, they frequently use the seriousness of their illness to defy parents and express anger and frustration. This may be done by taking too much insulin, eating too many carbohydrates, and so on. Some actually kill themselves as an angry defiant act.

Of course, there are other reasons in this complex illness which contribute to young patients' bitter and destructive attitudes. In my experience, however, there are two principal reasons why these unfortunate children become so intensely resentful and defiant. The first is as we just discussed, substitution of medical procedures as a manifestation of love. The other is poor limit-setting and lack of behavioural control by the parents. The parents may feel pity for the children in their illness. They may also feel guilt, fear, or depression. If the parents cannot control the children's behaviour in the same manner as they would other children, namely with firmness, the children will be able to manipulate the parents. This is especially easy for chronically ill children to do. They can use their illness to control their parents by taking advantage of the parents' guilt and pity, by making the parents fearful that the children's condition may worsen, and even by using the outright threat of purposely succumbing to the illness.

These dynamics may occur to some extent with any children with a prolonged disability, illness, or other problem. Examples include asthma, chronic bronchitis, heart defects, physical deformity, mental retardation, seizure disorders, neurological diseases, muscular diseases, dental problems, and even learning disabilities. The list goes on and on.

So, dear parents, if your child has a handicap, a problem of any kind, do not become so wrapped up with the problem that you neglect the child. He needs your unconditional love far more than anything else. Far more than braces, far more than tutoring or other academic remediation, far more than any exercise, and far more than any medicine. The most indispensable ingredients in your child's life are you and your giving unconditional love to him. With that, your child can derive the strength and will to overcome and develop.

The resistant child

Now, let's consider help for the resistant child, namely, one who is resistant to receiving affection. Yes, believe it or not, many children are naturally (congenitally) resistant to the natural ways of giving affection and love. They resist eye contact, they do not want to be touched, and they do not care for focused attention.

This may occur in varying degrees. Some children are only mildly resistant whereas others are quite uncomfortable with the conveying of love. Some children may be comfortable with one way of conveying love but not another. Each child is unique.

The resistant child is invariably an enigma to his parents. Caring parents instinctively know that their child needs affection and other forms of emotional nurturing; but when they try to meet this need, the child finds innumerable ways to avoid receiving love. What a dilemma. Many parents eventually resign themselves to what they conclude is 'what the child wants'. They assume that the child does not need their attention, love, and affection. This is a disastrous mistake.

Even the extremely resistant child needs everything we have talked about concerning unconditional love. However, since he is uncomfortable accepting it, we parents must gradually teach this child to receive love comfortably.

We can begin by understanding the five periods during which a child is able to receive love. During these periods the child's defenses are down, and he is able to relate closely enough on the emotional level to be receptive. Of course, every child is different. One child may be more receptive during one period and less receptive during another. It behoves parents to know when their child is most receptive to love and affection.

The first receptive period is when a child finds something to be quite humorous. For instance, a child may be watching television and see a funny scene. At this time parents have the opportunity to make eye contact, physical contact, and focused attention while commenting on the humorous subject. Parents must usually be quick in doing this because the defenses of a truly resistant child are down only briefly. We've got to 'get in and get out' or a child may defend against similar tactics in the future.

The second period of receptivity is when a child has accomplished something for which he is justifiably proud. It cannot be just anything. The accomplishment must be something a child feels genuinely good about. At these times, parents can make eye and physical contact (and focused attention if appropriate) while praising a child. Again, we must be careful not to overdo it, especially by prolonging it; again 'get in and get out'.

The third receptive period is at such times when a child is not well physically. A child may be ill or hurt, and his receptivity at these times is somewhat unpredictable. Sometimes illness or pain may increase a child's ability to receive affection, but at other times a child's resistance may increase. We parents should continually monitor this in order to take advantage of opportunities to give love at these times of illness or pain. A child will never forget special moments such as these.

The fourth period of receptivity occurs when a child is

hurt emotionally. This frequently happens when he has a conflict with peers and the peers have taken unfair advantage of him. At these times of emotional pain, many resistant children become able to accept our showing love to them.

The fifth receptive period largely depends upon previous experiences of a particular child. For example, one child may have had many pleasant, meaningful experiences while going on long walks with his parents. Such a child will quite likely be more receptive to parental conveying of love while on walks. Another child may have had pleasant experiences at bedtime when his parents would read, pray, and talk with him. He will naturally be inclined to be more receptive at bedtime. This is why providing routine times of pleasant, warm experiences for a child is very important and pays large dividends to child and parents. Bedtime routine, for example, is a good investment.

In a nutshell, all children need the natural ways of conveying love – eye contact, physical contact, and focused attention. If a child is not receiving an ample amount, we should find out why and correct the situation.

13

Helping your child spiritually

One of the chief complaints we hear from teenagers today is the failure of their parents to give them ethical or moral standards to live by in formative years. This yearning is expressed by older children in many ways. One adolescent says he needs 'meaning in life'. Another wants a 'standard to guide her'. Other seeking youngsters long for 'something to hold on to' or 'someone to show me how to live'.

These desperate cries do not come from a few unhappy, discontented teenagers. Most adolescents are feeling and expressing these yearnings. They are confused – terribly confused – in this existential area of living. It is quite unusual to find young people who have 'got it together' in regard to a meaning and purpose in this life, who are at peace with themselves and their world, and who have perspective and understanding about living in this confused, changing, fearful world today. And much goes back to their childhood.

A child first looks to his parents for direction that enables him to develop healthy values. Whether he finds what he needs from his parents depends on two things. The first is whether the parents have it themselves. The second is whether a child can identify with his parents in such a way as to incorporate and accept parental values. A child who does not feel loved will find this difficult.

The first requirement

Let's look at the first requirement that is necessary in giving a child that longed-for meaning to life. We parents must possess a foundation upon which to base our lives and which can withstand the test of time – something that will support us through every phase of living: adolescence, young adulthood, middle age, old age, marriage crises, financial crises, children's crises, energy crises, and especially, a rapidly changing society in which spiritual values are swiftly eroding. We parents must have that crucial foundation upon which we base our lives in order to give it to our child. In my opinion, it is the most valuable treasure we can pass on to our offspring.

What is this indispensable possession which gives purpose and meaning to life and is transferable to our child? Many have sought after it since the beginning of civilisation but few have really found it. Philosophers have been struggling with these questions and answers for centuries. International diplomats have occasionally claimed some answers. Government planners are claiming to have answers even now, and their diligently planned legislation will leave hearts just as empty and longing as before, but more dependent upon man's (government's) control. The field of mental health offers help concerning emotional problems, mental disturbances, psychophysiological disorders, adaptational problems, and marital disharmony.

But this treasurable, peace-giving possession which every heart craves is God Himself. He is intimately personal, yet can be shared with another. He is strengthening in times of conflict, yet is comforting in times of distress. He gives wisdom in times of confusion, yet gives correction in times of error. He provides help in times past and present, yet promises even more in the future. He gives direction and guidance at all times, yet does not send us out alone – He stays closer than a brother.

He gives directions to be carried out, yet gives amazingly wonderful promises to those who are willing to obey. He allows loss and pain at times, but He always heals and replaces the loss with something better. He does not force Himself upon us, but patiently waits to be accepted. He does not coerce us into doing His will, but is deeply distressed and hurt when we follow the wrong path. He wants us to love Him because He first loved us, but He gave us a free will to choose Him or reject Him. He wants to take care of us, but refuses to force Himself upon us. His greatest desire is to be our Father, but He will not intrude. If we want what He wants, a loving, caring, Father-child relationship with Him – we must accept His offer. He is too considerate to force it. He is waiting for you and me to open our lives to Him and become His children. Of course, as you have guessed. He must be a personal God.

This personal, intimate relationship with God through His Son Jesus Christ is the most important thing in life. This is the 'something' which our young people are yearning for: the 'meaning in life,' 'something to count on,' 'higher guidance,' 'something to bring comfort when everything seems to be falling apart.' It is all there.

Do you have it? If you do not, seek help from a minister or Christian friend; or write me through the publisher, and I will send you helpful material.

The second requirement

The second requirement necessary in order to give a child what we have is that a child identify with his parents so as to accept and incorporate the parents' values.

As you recall, if a child does not feel loved and accepted, he has real difficulty identifying with his parents and their values. Without a strong, healthy love-bond with his parents, a child reacts to parental guidance with anger, resentment, and hostility. He views each parental request (or command) as an imposition and learns to resist it. In severe cases, a child learns to consider each parental request with such resentment that his total orientation to parental authority (and eventually to all authority, including God's) is doing the opposite of what is expected of him.

With this type of attitude and orientation, you can see how difficult it becomes to give your child your moral and ethical value system.

In order for a child to identify with his parents (relate closely with them) and be able to accept their standards, he must feel genuinely loved and accepted by them. To give a child the close relationship with God which they possess, parents must make sure that a child feels unconditionally loved. Why? Because this is the way God loves us – unconditionally. It is extremely difficult for persons who do not feel unconditionally loved by their parents to feel loved by God. This is the greatest and most common obstacle to many people in establishing a personal relationship with God. Parents must prevent this from happening to their own children.

How do parents ensure that their child is prepared and ready to accept God's love? By ensuring that they fill his emotional needs and keep his emotional tank full. Parents cannot expect a child to find a close, warm, *rewarding* relationship with God unless they have cared for him emotionally and he has such a relationship with them.

Yes, I have seen children who were raised by corporal punishment become Christians. But because they were raised primarily by inflicting physical pain instead of unconditional love, these unfortunate people seldom have a healthy, loving, warm relationship with God. They tend to use their religion punitively against others under the guise of 'helping' them. They use biblical command-ments and other scriptural statements to justify their own harsh, unloving behaviour. They also tend to set them-selves up as spiritual magistrates dictating the propriety of others. It is possible, of course, for any child eventu-ally to find his way into God's loving arms and to accept His love. With God anything is possible. Unfortunately, a child's chances are markedly diminished if his parents have not given him a loving foundation.

So there are two requirements essential to helping a child spiritually: A parent's personal relationship with God, and a child's assurance that he is unconditionally loved.

A child's memory

The next important thing to know about a child is how his memory operates. Remember that a child is much more emotional than cognitive. He therefore remembers feelings much more readily than facts. A child can remember how he felt in a particular situation much eas-ier than he can remember the details of what went on.

Let me give you a very pertinent example. A child in a Sunday School class will remember exactly how he felt long after he forgets what was said or taught.

So, in some ways, whether a child's experience was pleasant or unpleasant is much more important than the details of what a teacher taught. By pleasant, I do not mean that a teacher need cater to a child's desire for fun and frolic. I mean treating a child with respect, kindness, and concern. Make him feel good about himself. Do not criticise, humiliate, or otherwise put him down. Naturally, what a child is taught is extremely important, but if it is a degrading or boring experience for a child, he is very likely to reject even the very best teaching, especially if morality and ethics are involved. It is from this type of situation that a child develops a bias against religious matters, and tends to consider church people as hypocrites. This attitude is difficult to rectify and can continue with him for a lifetime. On the other hand, if the teaming experience is a pleasant one, a child's memories of spiritual teaching will be pleasant and can then be incorporated into a child's own personality.

As an illustration, friends of ours had an eight-year-old son, Michael, who used to enjoy Sunday School and being taught about spiritual things. There was no problem getting him to go to the Lord's house. Sadly, one Sunday morning, Michael and another energetic boy were talking and laughing during a presentation by the teacher. In anger, the teacher put Michael and his friend in a small room by themselves and made them write 'Thou shalt honour thy mother and thy father' over and over until Michael's parents came to get him. The unreasonableness and insensitiveness of that unjust and humiliating punishment had dramatic effects. It induced such anger, hurt, and resentment that Michael began holding animosity toward anything spiritual. He didn't want to return to his church, and, of course, his conception of God was severely damaged. Only after several months were his loving parents able to help Michael again trust spiritual truths. This type of thing, in greater or lesser extremes, happens when the importance of a teacher's teaching is placed before the emotional welfare of a child. Emotionality and spirituality are not entirely separate entities. One is quite related to and dependent upon the other. For this reason, if parents want to help a child spiritually, they must care for him first emotionally. Because a child remembers feelings much more easily than facts, there must be a series of pleasant memories upon which to accumulate the facts, especially spiritual facts.

A popular misconception

At this point, let's examine a popular misconception. It goes something like this: 'I want my child to learn to make his own decisions after he is exposed to everything. He shouldn't feel he has to believe what I believe. I want him to learn about different religions and philosophies; then when he has grown up he can make his own decision.'

This parent is copping out or else is grossly ignorant of the world we live in. A child brought up in this manner is indeed one to be pitied. Without continual guidance and clarification in ethical, moral, and spiritual matters, he will become increasingly confused about his world. There are reasonable answers to many of life's conflicts and seeming contradictions. One of the finest gifts parents can give a child is a clear, basic understanding of the world and its confusing problems. Without this stable base of knowledge and understanding, is it any wonder many children cry to their parents, 'Why didn't you give me a meaning for all this? What's it all about?'

Another reason this approach to spirituality is grossly negligent is this. More and more groups, organisations, and cults are offering destructive, enslaving, and false answers to life's questions. These people would like nothing more than to find a person who was brought up in this seemingly broad-minded way. He is easy prey for any group offering concrete answers, no matter how false or enslaving.

It is amazing to me how some parents can spend thousands of dollars and go to any length of political manipulation to make sure their child is well prepared educationally. Yet, for the most important preparation of all, for life's spiritual battles and finding real meaning in life, a child is left to fend for himself and made easy prey for cultists.

Every child loves a story

How do parents prepare their children spiritually? Organised religious instruction and activities are extremely important to a developing child. However, nothing influences a child more than his home and what he is exposed to there. This holds true regarding spiritual things as well. Parents must be actively involved in a child's spiritual growth. They cannot afford to leave it to others, even superb church youth workers.

First, parents themselves must teach their children spiritual concerns. They must teach not only spiritual facts, but how to apply them in everyday life. This is not easy.

It is quite simple to give a child basic scriptural facts such as who different Bible persons were and what they did. But that is not what we are ultimately after. A child needs to understand what meaning biblical characters and principles have for him personally. We can only teach this at somewhat of a sacrifice to ourselves, as with focused attention. We must give focused attention and be willing to spend time alone with a child in order to provide for his emotional needs as well as his spiritual. In fact, whenever possible, why not do them simultaneously?

Bedtime is usually the best time to accomplish this, for most children are then eager to interact with their parents. Whether it is because their emotional tanks need filling or because they want to delay bedtime makes little difference. The point is that it is a great opportunity to meet the emotional needs of a child, give him spiritual training and guidance, and do it in an atmosphere which a child will remember fondly. By what other means can parents give so much to a child in such an economical way?

Every child loves a story. When our children were growing up, Pat and I would often read to an individual child, sometimes a secular story, at other times a story from a Christian book. I even got requests for stories that I made up – 'Bing Bing and Bong Bong', 'The Great Rutabaga', and other fanciful tales.

We also made it a point to read short devotional stories. My boys especially loved to answer questions about the stories, and books with questions after each story were good for our purpose. Most of the books we used when our children were young are likely out of print, but a visit to a Christian bookstore will acquaint you with many good books you can use with your children.

As a child answers questions following the reading of a story, there are always similarities and applications to what is going on in his own life. The hard part is getting the message across to a child and, because many parents feel awkward and inept at this, they usually give it up, especially if a child doesn't contribute much. Don't let these things stop you! Whether a child appears to be responding or not, you can rest assured that you are strongly influencing him. Your time spent with your child in this way will have far reaching effects. If you don't influence your child in the area of the supernatural now, someone else will do it later.

Share your spiritual life

One more point about helping a child spiritually. With the factual knowledge gained from church, Sunday School, and home, a child only has the raw materials with which to grow in his spiritual life. He must learn to use this knowledge effectively and accurately to become a mature person spiritually. To do this, a child must have the experience of walking with God daily and learning to rely on Him personally.

The best way to help a child with this is to share your own spiritual life with him. Of course, this depends on the quality of what you have to share, and how much you share depends on the child, his age, level of development, and ability to comprehend and handle it.

As a child matures, we parents want to gradually increase sharing with him how we ourselves love God, walk daily with Him, rely on Him, seek His guidance and help, thank Him for His love, care, gifts, and answered prayer.

We want to share these things with our child *as they happen*, not afterward. Only in that way can a child get on-the-job training. Sharing past experiences is simply giving additional factual information, not letting a child learn for himself through his own experience. There is a lot of truth in the old statement, 'Experience is the best teacher.' Let him share in yours. The sooner a child learns to trust God, the stronger he will become.

A child needs to learn how God meets all personal and family needs, including financial. He needs to know what his parents are praying for. For example, he needs to know when you are praying for the needs of others. He should (again, as appropriate) know of problems for which you are asking God's help. And don't forget to keep him informed about how God is working in your life, how He is using you to minister to someone. And, of course, a child should certainly know you are praying for him and for his individual, particular needs.

Finally, a child must be taught by example how to forgive and how to find forgiveness both from God and people. Parents do this first of all by forgiving. Next, when they make a mistake, they apologise and ask for God's forgiveness. I cannot overstress how important that is. So many people today have problems with guilt. They cannot forgive and/or they cannot feel forgiven. What can be more miserable? But the fortunate person who has learned how to forgive those who offend him and is able to ask and receive forgiveness, demonstrates a mark of mental health and finds peace as a result.

As we end our discussion, I hope you will seriously consider the principles stressed in this book. It was written especially for you by a parent who himself has learned by experience at home and in his profession that parents must truly love their children to see them grow into strong, healthy, happy, and independent adults. Now, perhaps you will want to go back and reread this volume and underline principles that you determine to put into practice as you seek to really love your child. I challenge you to do so.

How To Really Know
Your Child

Ross Campbell

Contents

In this book . . .

. . . identify your child's true personality

. . . enabling your child to grow spiritually,
emotionally and intellectually

. . . what you are like as a parent

. . . learning to handle conflict positively

. . . helping teenagers to express their
feelings

. . . disciplining your child with wisdom

. . . making the most of your relationship

. . . and more

To my children

CAREY, CATHY, DAVID and DALE, who have been my best teachers.

The stories told in this book are based on real case histories. However, names and details have been changed to prevent identification. If you think you see yourself or your neighbour herein, you are really seeing the problems and challenges faced by all parents.

Preface

1 first met Dr Ross Campbell six months ago, and during the ensuing weeks as his co-writer, I became the first parent to benefit from *How to Really Know Your Child*. However, I am not the first to benefit from his wise and understanding counsel, for Dr Campbell has spent many years as an internationally known child psychiatrist helping parents and children. And after working with him on this project, I know his work has been a labour of love.

Putting in writing his beliefs and experiences has taught me more about myself and my children than I thought possible. The most important lesson I learned was that in order for a child to develop as a Christian, he must first develop as a *whole* individual. As Dr Campbell puts it, 'Develop the *whole* child. Don't just zero in on the spiritual area of his life and expect everything else to fall into place – it won't.'

Dr Campbell obviously loves children. By patiently and clearly explaining their basic needs, he teaches *us* how to love *our* children. From experience, he knows that the first and most basic need in a child is the need for love – unconditional love.

In this book, Dr Campbell shares two decades of knowledge in a simple, straightforward way. He gives you no pat answers; he has no tricks. Instead he offers good, common-sense advice. He never tells you child-rearing is easy; he only knows the challenge is of infinite worth.

I have met few people who care as deeply for the welfare of children as Dr Ross Campbell.

Pat Likes, Co-writer, 1986

Foreword

Mention 'Christian parenting' and the chances are that, like me, you'll think of those familiar Bible verses that talk about training children up in the way that they should go, and not exasperating them.

They are, of course, wise words that have often encouraged, advised and corrected me in turn as I strive to be the kind of parent that I long for my children to remember in their adult years.

But only recently have I really come to see the most fundamental way in which we can seek to become godly mothers and fathers – not by concentrating on 'parenting skills', but simply by growing more like Jesus.

When he said 'Anyone who has seen me has seen the Father', I believe he was doing more than hinting at the mysteries of the Trinity. He was telling us that if we look closely at him and his life, we'll see the quality of the father – parenthood – we should replicate.

Suddenly 'Christian parenting' becomes more than only a set of guidelines for living that we try to pass on. It becomes discipleship – and we look to drawing our children to follow, freely, in our faithsteps. Discipline, teaching, leisure . . . they take on a new light in the context of Jesus' relationship with the twelve.

I've met many Christian parents whose admirable and burning desire for their children is to come to faith in Jesus. This has been the very thing – suffocating in its intensity and rigidity – that has made that increasingly unlikely as the years go by.

Ross Campbell's simple but profound message to all of us who long to see our youngsters become Christian is: 'Ease up!' Concentrate on making sure that they know you love them – in the same way that Jesus poured his life into his inner circle.

How to Really Know Your Child asserts the human parallel of the fact that it's easier to pull a piece of string along the road than to push it. It's a task that I value greatly, and commend to you – and *for* your children.

Andy Butcher
Former Editor Christian Family *magazine,*
now Parentwise

1

The way things are

> 'After that whole generation had been gathered to their fathers, another generation grew up, who knew neither the Lord nor what he had done for Israel' (Judg. 2:10).

The smartly dressed middle-aged couple stepped nervously into my office.

I glanced at their names on my appointment schedule: John and Mary Perkins. The notes underneath said they had a fifteen-year-old unmarried, pregnant daughter.

They took seats across from my desk. Mary, a stunning blond, looked familiar. 'We've met somewhere. More than once, haven't we?' I asked.

She managed a tight smile, 'I've shown you to a table several times at the Sailmaker Restaurant.'

'You're the hostess there at lunch. I was there last Tuesday.'

I turned to John and asked about his work. 'I'm an accountant,' he said.

'That figures,' I punned, trying to lighten the air.

We spent another minute or two on small talk and found we had mutual friends at the Presbyterian church where they were members.

I glanced down at my appointment notes, then looked up at Mary. 'You came in to talk about your daughter, Ann. Tell me about her.'

Tears welled up in the mother's eyes. 'Oh, Dr Campbell, she's only fifteen. The youngest of our four. And she's pregnant! What are we going to do?'

The words were gushing now and she kept dabbing at her eyes. 'We did everything to be good parents to Ann. We've both worked for years to give her and our other children the good things in life. We took her to Sunday School and church. We gave her piano lessons and sent her to summer camp. She's so talented and beautiful. But how are we going to handle *this*?' Her voice trailed off in sobs as her husband twisted in his chair.

'I just don't know where we went wrong, John Perkins added. 'Why did she get herself into this mess? Why has she become so defiant? She goes against anything and everything her mother and I try to do for her.'

After spending about an hour with John and Mary, I realised that they really loved Ann, but communicated their feelings to her by giving her material things. They honestly felt that this would make up for not being able to spend time with her or share in her life.

Then I spoke to Ann. My suspicions were confirmed. Ann did not feel her parents loved her. She did not feel she was important to them.

'I don't know why I got pregnant; I just did. I could have kept from it. I knew how,' Ann stated defiantly. 'Maybe I wanted to be somebody too, like my mother. Maybe I thought if I was a mother, then I would be important – *somebody* would love *me*.'

For the next month, John, Mary and Ann came for counselling on a weekly basis. At first, the sessions were reserved; few feelings were openly stated. Ann usually had little to say; she was obviously angry and frustrated. But after two or three weeks, she began to open up.

'Remember the night of the mother-daughter banquet, Mum?' Ann asked. 'You couldn't be there because you had to go with Daddy to that accountant's seminar or whatever it was. I was the only one there without a mother!'

'But, Ann,' Mary interrupted, 'we talked about it, and I bought you that lovely yellow dress for the banquet. I thought you didn't mind that I went with Daddy.'

'Well, I did! You just never seem to be around when I need you. My friends' parents always drive us to games and stuff; you never offer to drive. I'm always hitching lifts with someone. You never take me and my friends anywhere.'

'Now wait a minute, Ann,' her father retaliated. 'You're talking as if we never do anything for you. I happen to know that you're quite an accomplished pianist. Who took you to all those lessons? Who paid for all of them?'

'Big deal, Daddy. Anyway, how would you know whether or not I can play the piano? The last time you attended one of my recitals I was ten years old!'

During outbursts like these, John would often leave the room. But gradually both he and Mary began to understand their daughter's feelings. They realised that the *things* they had given Ann could not begin to replace the love and personal attention she really needed from them. They had left Ann with an empty emotional tank.

Fortunately, John and Mary worked hard to gain insight into Ann's problem and found ways to share in her life. As Ann heard her parents express their love and concern, and experienced it daily at home, she began to loosen up and communicate with them in a more positive way.

It has been a slow and painful process, but Ann and her parents are really getting to know each other for the first time. Their sincere desire to develop a loving family is the key to the success of their counselling sessions. Ann's anger has gradually subsided as she has realised that her parents love her. This knowledge, and the feelings of self-worth that Ann is experiencing, will sustain and strengthen her in the trying days ahead.

Taking Ann to church camp, giving her piano lessons, and buying her new clothes all the time in no way filled her emotional needs. She became an angry, frustrated teenager who sought emotional fulfilment outside her home. If John and Mary thought that two hours every Sunday and church camp would fill Ann's spiritual needs, they were wasting their time. She was too angry to accept spiritual teaching, and she was too anti-authority to adopt any attitudes suggested by her parents.

Do we really know our children?

Ann's story, with minor changes, typifies far too many of today's families. Parents become so involved in their own problems, in the stress and strain of everyday life, that they forget to stop and talk or listen to their children. As a result, many children are angry and depressed because their emotional needs are not being met.

These young people simply turn outside their homes for need satisfaction. This is not totally undesirable because young people *do* need friends, but if parents are not aware of who these friends are, trouble often rears its ugly head. A damaging involvement in drugs, sex, lying, cheating, or stealing is almost certain for teenagers who feel unloved by their parents.

Some statistics might be helpful at this point. According to a survey made in the USA of 8,000 Protestant young people aged ten to fourteen, 87 per cent of the fourteen-year-olds believe that Jesus Christ is the Son of God who died on the cross and rose again. Now that's a positive picture, isn't it? Unfortunately, by the time these young people are eighteen, only 20 per cent will say they are committed to Christ or will define themselves in any way as Christian. The remaining 80 per cent will have lost their faith in the church and in the Lord of their parents.

Why is this happening? Why are fewer and fewer young people continuing in the faith? I feel very strongly that the answer lies in the way we are raising our children. We do not really *know* our children. We are not communicating our true feelings to them; we are not letting them know that we love them – unconditionally.

Once you are able to love your child unconditionally, you will be able to guide him successfully to adulthood. Unconditional love is real love. It should exist in *all* love relationships.

Unconditional love

If you love your child unconditionally, you love him *no matter what*. You love him if he is tall or short, fat or skinny, moody or happy. In short, you love him no matter what his handicaps, assets, or liabilities. Unconditional love means you love your *child*, but you do not always love his behaviour. A perfect definition of unconditional love is given in 1 Corinthians 13:4–7: 'Love is patient, love is kind. It does not envy, it does not boast, it is not proud. It is not rude, it is not self-seeking, it is not easily angered, it keeps no record of wrongs. Love does not delight in evil but rejoices with the truth. It always protects, always trusts, always hopes, always perseveres.'

Any child who has less than unconditional love from his parents will be an angry, frustrated child. He will not be happy in any area of his life, including the spiritual area.

Let's go back and look at Ann's reaction to feeling unloved. What did she do? She sought love elsewhere and became pregnant. She was angry with her parents and went against them. She also went against their spiritual values. And this is a point I want to emphasise: *spirituality is not something which should be kept separate and apart from all other aspects of your child's life.*

Spirituality is just *one* part of the whole person, and it is very much influenced by the rest of the personality. Your children are physical beings, emotional beings, psychological beings, and spiritual beings. These components are all related, each to the others.

The way you help your child handle anger, frustration, and his natural anti-authority behaviour during the teen years will affect him spiritually in exactly the same way it affects him physically, emotionally, and psychologically.

The formulation and the dynamics, the cause and effect, the reasons why teens lapse in faith are exactly the same dynamics, exactly the same situations, and exactly the same reasons why teens have all the other problems in their lives. If your child is anti-authority about academics, about staying out late, about any area in his life, he will be anti-authority about spirituality too. I stress this to all parents who come to me for counselling. If you can keep as much anger as possible out of your child's life, his chances of becoming a strong Christian adult are greatly improved. And the way to keep this anger to a minimum is unconditional love.

The survey mentioned earlier reveals that 54 per cent of parents of ten-year-olds display little positive physical and verbal attention daily to their children. Only 32 per cent of parents of fourteen-year-olds give their children positive physical and verbal attention. This abrupt drop in affection and caring comes just when young adolescents need it most. It comes at a time when they have an increasing need to feel self-confident, and yet, ironically, are instead feeling threats to their self-esteem because their parents pay so little attention to them. Again, look at Ann. She just wanted someone to stop and talk to her for a minute. New designer jeans couldn't fill her emotional tank.

All you need to do is pick up a newspaper or watch any television news bulletin, and you will see that anti-authority attitudes are running rampant in our world today. Divorce, family conflict, a breakdown of moral values – all of these are anti-authority, and all are major influences in the lives of our children.

This same anti-authority attitude can show itself in the spiritual life of your child. I repeat: if he is anti-parent, anti-academics, anti-anything, he will also be anti-spiritual. He must have his emotional needs met and feel unconditional love so that he will not develop damaging anger and anti-authority attitudes.

You cannot force your child into accepting spiritual values if he does not feel your love and concern. Many Christian leaders in the U.S.A. are telling parents to administer harsh disciplinary actions (e.g., use corporal punishment often) and break the stubborn wills of children who misbehave. The results of such authoritarian teaching are angry children, rebelling from the faith with which they were brought up.

If this practice continues, the future of Christianity is gloomy. The only way to ensure that the next generation will be Christian is for parents to practise love and spirituality daily in the lives of their children. The children from these homes will want to follow the faith of their parents.

Almost every day, I talk to children and teenagers who are hurting because they do not feel loved. And the sad thing about it all is that Christian parents think they are doing the right thing. They are following the advice of certain Christian child-rearing 'experts', but the results are not what they expected.

In their book *What Are They Teaching Our Children?* Mel and Norma Gabler remind us that absolutes are not being taught in schools.

The only absolute truth in modern humanistic education is that there are no absolute values. All values must be questioned – especially home- or church-acquired values. Discard the experience gained from thousands of years of Western civilisation. Instead, treat the students as primitive savages in the area of values. Let them select their own from slanted, inadequate information. Nothing, absolutely nothing, is certain. There are no universal rules – absolutely none.

Unfortunately, today's society does not provide the standards needed to support our youth. Society does not produce emotional or spiritual growth. This is the sole responsibility of loving, Christian parents with the help of the church. Society's alternatives are less than attractive, as the following counselling episode illustrates.

Glen Andrews, a respected medical doctor, sat slumped in his chair, as though the weight of the world were on his shoulders. 'If anybody had told me six months ago that I would be sitting in a psychiatrist's office discussing my son's drug problem, I would have laughed in his face,' he said. 'I always reckoned Andy was a pretty good kid. At least he usually seemed happy and contented to me.'

Peg Andrews sat next to her husband, folding and refolding her handkerchief. Her face mirrored the pain I knew she was feeling. 'Where did we go wrong, Dr Campbell? Do you think Andy could have a physical problem that caused him to take drugs? Should he have a physical check-up? Could he have inherited a tendency towards using drugs? Oh, I'm so confused. I don't know what to think!'

I turned to Glen. 'You said earlier that Andy always seemed happy and never gave you much trouble. Had you noticed any change at all in him before you found he was using drugs?'

'I guess it was about a year ago that I mentioned to Peg that Andy's grades at school were down a little. It was about that time too that he began to stay in his room a lot. I didn't think much about it. Just thought it was a passing thing. We didn't make any particular issue of it.'

'About eight or nine months ago, I noticed that he had a different group of friends,' Peg added. 'They weren't the kind of kids we would have chosen for him, but we didn't want to interfere. We have always prided ourselves in letting Andy make all his own decisions, and that includes choosing friends.

'But in the last two or three months, we've hardly seen him at all. When he is in the house, he's in his room. We thought we were raising him in a fair, open-minded way, but since finding those drugs in his room, I wonder if we've done anything right.'

Glen dropped his head as Peg fell silent and waited for me to speak. 'I'll tell you what. Why don't I talk to Andy for a while, and then the three of you together can come back into my office. Don't give up; we'll do all we can to get you through this.'

Glen and Peg left the room, and I motioned for Andy to come in. He shuffled across the floor, his long, unkempt hair matching his faded, tattered jeans. I managed some small talk for a few minutes, gradually drawing him into a conversation, and then we discussed his use of drugs.

'Why do you think you started using drugs, Andy?' I asked.

'Just bored, I guess,' he replied. 'Curious. There's nothing much else to do. Nobody at home cares where I am or what I'm doing anyway. They never know or ask where I'm going or who I'm going with or when I'm coming back.'

As Andy began to feel comfortable with me, he confided that he would like to spend time with his dad, but his dad was always too busy. 'He doesn't want to spend time with me; he has too many more important things to do.'

This kind of situation always puzzles me. I know that Glen and Peg are good parents. They have tried to give Andy all the basic needs of life. They have a good marriage. They truly love and respect each other and yet, somewhere along the way, something went wrong. They didn't realise that they had neglected to show or tell Andy that they also loved and respected him.

I met regularly with Glen, Peg and Andy, and gradually they became aware of the feelings they felt but were unable to show. It will take time for Andy to put things back together, but I have hopes for this family because they are not afraid to ask for help, and they have a basic foundation of love.

The bored generation

I'm a parent too, and I know all the pressures that leave us little time. But I can't stress enough the importance of time spent with your child. When we become too busy to let our children know how much we love them, we are doing them great harm. If we leave them out of our lives more than we include them, they will become angry, depressed, and bored. It is when they are experiencing these feelings that they become the most vulnerable to negative influences.

In a lecture on adolescent drug abuse, Sergeant Bud Hulsey, youth officer with the Kingsport, Tennessee Police Department, declared: 'I have asked many parents why they think their children get involved with drugs, and I get two answers – peer pressure and escape from reality. But of the 4,000 to 5,000 kids I have asked, not one of them said they take drugs due to peer pressure or for escape. Almost everyone said it was because they were bored, and that they like the feeling – they liked the buzz.'

In speaking to youth groups, Sergeant Hulsey tells teens that they are not just physical beings. 'You are spiritual beings, emotional beings, intellectual beings, and physical beings. And if you satisfy only your physical being, you are going to be retarded spiritually, emotionally, and intellectually!'

He is so right. But society is screaming at our children to satisfy their physical desires. Society and parents are standing empty-handed when it comes to helping them grow spiritually, emotionally, or intellectually. So it is up to parents to become aware of these needs and meet them at home. And the first step in this is to offer your child unconditional love. Only then will he develop into a whole child; not a bored and depressed teenager, but a self-confident, capable young adult ready to adopt the lifestyle of his parents, including their spiritual values.

National morality in Britain and the USA has reached an all-time low in the last twenty-five years. In that short span, we have heard educators tell teens that their bodies are their own – they can do what they want with them, including having premarital sex. The only precaution is that the people involved should be responsible; pregnancy should be avoided.

Swearing is commonplace on television. Sex and obscenity are the norm in films. Such films used to be prohibited in family cinemas, but now they are available to anyone, anywhere.

Teens today are bombarded with information that teens in the 1960's hardly knew existed. And with today's economic conditions forcing both parents to go out to work, teens are receiving unheard-of freedom and less and less parental guidance.

I know that what I am saying sounds dismal and hopeless, but facts must be faced. The attitudes of today's teenagers, if allowed to continue, will cause an even further decline in church and family life. It is up to us parents to look deeply into our relationships with our teenage children. It is up to us to admit our weaknesses, try to understand them, and begin to work towards improvement. A strong, Christ-centred, love-based relationship with our children will make the difference between Christian and non-Christian adulthood.

I recently attended a conference in the USA of leaders in a national youth ministry. Most of them seemed pessimistic and disillusioned and many were leaving the ministry. The general opinion of these leaders was that teens today lack spirit, are depressed, and possess a strong anti-authority attitude. Little progress is being made toward reaching these young people.

These youth leaders felt that most youth groups are made up of young people who are forced to attend church, not by youngsters who sincerely want to follow their parents' spiritual attitudes and develop spiritual values of their own. Of the teenagers in youth groups, most are under fifteen – only 1 in 30 are over that age. What are these numbers telling us?

They are saying that we just can't raise our youngsters as they were raised twenty-five or thirty years ago. We cannot *make* them go to church, knowing that many will rebel during some of their teen years, and then depend on society gradually to guide them back. The basic moral values are just not there any more.

What can Christian parents do?

Christian parents are searching for help in developing their children into spiritual adults. The problem is that they are receiving wrong information. Some Christian writers are so over-zealous about helping parents to get their child into church that they tend to overlook the whole child.

They deal only with disciplining the child about spiritual matters. Parents are told to *force* their children to do their bidding, and all else will fall into place, including spirituality. Exactly the opposite is true. When you *force* a child, you will make him angry, and an angry child will become anti-authority and will go exactly opposite the desired direction.

Another problem which occurs when parents seek advice about raising children is that they read only what they want to read: they derive from their reading only that information which agrees with their preconceived ideas on the subject. Many parents feel that they already know all there is to know about child-rearing. These are the parents who are difficult to reach. These are the parents who need to question their ideas honestly and weed out those that are unbiblical.

The advice I am offering in this book is based on eighteen years of working with children. It is offered because of my sincere and anxious concern for the future of the church and the family. The sad truth is all around us. Young people are not adopting their parents' spiritual values. They are going in exactly the opposite direction.

On a television programme dealing with teen pregnancies, a doctor made the following statement: 'To combat this terrible problem of teenage pregnancies effectively, we must see to it that the *whole child* is developed. Even before kindergarten, when children are still toddlers at home, parents must see to it that their kids feel loved and respected. Only in this way can these children develop self-esteem. Then and only then will we begin to solve the awesome problem of the teen pregnancy rate of today.'

That's the key. We must lovingly help our children develop as whole beings. We cannot zero in on one area of their life, and expect the rest to take care of itself.

The purpose of this book is to guide you through helping your child develop as a whole being, so that when he is a young adult, he will adopt your spiritual values. I suggest that you set a goal of Christian adulthood for your child, and then lovingly guide him towards that end.

It won't be easy. I'm not offering you twelve simple steps to raising spiritual sons and daughters. I'm offering advice to sincere Christian parents who want for their children the meaning and fulfilment which only Christianity can provide.

2

What are we like as parents?

'This is what the Lord Almighty says: "Give careful thought to your ways"' (Hag. 1:7).

Knowing who you are and how you feel about yourself plays a very important part in how you interact with your children. Ellen's story, shared just as she told it to me, will enable you to understand more fully the importance of self-knowledge – especially self-esteem.

'I was born into a family of twelve children. It would seem that any parents who already had twelve children would not be particularly pleased about the arrival of the thirteenth. But my parents were not just any parents. I always felt their love and concern for me, so they must have been happy about my arrival.

'My problem didn't develop because I was unloved; it developed because I was so quiet. Oh, I did my share of making noise and I caused my share of arguments. By quiet, I mean I always wanted everyone to be peaceful. I was for ever trying to settle disputes which occurred daily in our large household. Even when I was the cause of the argument, I was always the first one to back down – the first one to say, "Oh, just forget it; it was my fault."

'For as long as I can remember, I really felt awful if I couldn't settle an argument, if I couldn't restore calm. Sometimes, I would blame myself if one of the other kids got a spanking, thinking, "If I had tried just a little harder, maybe I could have talked him out of misbehaving."

'Then another problem attitude developed within me. Maybe it was because I was the baby of the family, but I felt that no one really took me seriously, neither my older brothers and sisters nor my parents. I was just the "cute little baby sister" and if I didn't complete an assigned task, somebody else would. My parents were probably so glad that I was such an easy kid to get along with that they saw no need to create problems which could easily be avoided. After all, there were plenty of other able bodies around to get things done.

'Anyway, regardless of why it happened, it happened. I gradually began to realise that my actions or lack of actions did not have the same impact as those of my siblings.

'And so I went into adulthood, carrying these odd notions in my mind – feeling worse and worse about not keeping constant peace among my siblings, and feeling less and less that anything I did was important.

'In retrospect, I realise that that was the image I projected to my peers. I was the peacemaker who felt terrible if she failed, but on the other hand, I didn't amount to all that much anyway, so nothing really mattered. That is the way my peers reacted to me. They learned to depend on me to settle arguments, but they walked on me whenever they didn't need a peacemaker, and I let them do it.

'Now, here comes the bad part. I took these attitudes with me into marriage and parenting. When my husband and I disagreed, I would always be the first to want to restore peace. I taught him very quickly that his word was much more important than mine – that I really didn't amount to all that much.

'And our first two children – what did I do to them! Without realising it, I gave them the "peace at all costs" and "low self-esteem" messages, and tried to train them to act the same way. And I topped it all off by setting their dad up as the total authority figure. What a burden I placed on him!

'Our little family struggled along for about twelve years, and then one day I started crying. I knew I had to have professional help.

'It wasn't an overnight thing, but gradually I learned who I was. Then came the tedious task of helping the children pull out of the mould I had built for them – just as they were going into adolescence. It left some pretty bad scars on them, and it almost destroyed my marriage, but we did make it.

'The two older children have now moved away from home, but maybe their little brother will be able to reap some of the benefits of my newly established self-worth. I know for sure that things will be different for him.

'Shortly after he was born, my oldest daughter said, "You know, Mother, I think God gave TJ to you and Daddy because He knew all along that you were a good mother. He knew that you would get your thoughts straightened out. But don't ever worry, you didn't do all that badly with the two of us."

'I am one of the lucky parents. I finally got to know myself in time to salvage my family and my marriage. I know now the only way to be an effective parent: you really have to know and love yourself.'

In my years of counselling, I have heard various renditions of Ellen's story. Many times, I have seen how the personal problems of parents can cause serious damage to their children. As a general rule and depending on the personalities of the children, parents with low self-esteem will affect their children negatively, both as they are raising them and when they reach adulthood.

It is extremely important for a mother and father to take an honest look at themselves and discover who they are. Self-confidence and self-worth must be evident at all times so that the children can learn to develop these same traits. And parents must be able to love themselves so that they can give their children the unconditional love so necessary to their full development.

After you have determined whether you are a submissive, quiet person like Ellen (and that's not all bad – it just has to be handled properly) or a more aggressive, 'look out world, here I come' person, let's take a look at how you apply yourself in daily life.

Assessing our attitudes

Consider your attitudes at home, work and religion. Answer the following questions and think, 'Do I do this always, sometimes or rarely?'

At home, if you are a married parent, do you have and exhibit respect for your partner? If you are both employed, do you share the workload at home? Do you nag and complain about everything your partner does that is wrong? If you are a single parent, do you constantly belittle your ex-mate to your children? Do you try to show some respect for your ex-mate? Do you have a good attitude to members of the opposite sex?

At work, do you give your employer a full day's work? Do you do as little as possible and then demand full pay? Do you pattern your workday after the axiom,

'Anything worth doing is worth doing well'? If you are an employer, are you fair and honest with your employees, giving them the best working conditions possible?

Thinking lastly about religion, do you try to cultivate Christianity in your marriage? Do you try to do things *for* God? Do you spend some time every day alone with God? And is your interaction with the general public Christ-centred?

Honestly answering these questions will help you ascertain your strengths and weaknesses. Then you can begin to build the positives and correct the negatives.

Remember: all that you do and all that you say are the examples on which your children will pattern their lives. They are either going to want to do the same things you do, or they are going to feel so sorry for the people whom you have mistreated that they will lose their respect and love for you.

It is essential for you as a parent to maintain a positive and optimistic attitude. It is essential that you maintain an attitude of responsibility and fairness, because the very best way to teach a child is by example. If you are constantly pessimistic and exhibit negative, irresponsible behaviour, you are promoting an anti-authority lifestyle to your children. You are showing them that they don't have to be responsible for their actions. Teenagers constantly influenced by anti-authority parents are placed in double jeopardy because they are already, by nature, anti-authority.

The question of divorce

It is very difficult to make a generalised statement about divorce. However, in most cases, if the parents will try to work out their problems, the children are far better off.

In well over 80 per cent of the cases I have seen, I have strongly encouraged both partners to try to resolve their marital difficulties.

Let's get back to Ellen's story. Now, there is a marriage that could easily have ended in divorce. But counselling revealed that Ellen and her husband had too much to lose to separate. They had two fine children and a lot of respect for each other even though Ellen had some serious problems to work through. I encouraged them to wait until Ellen got a grip on things before they made up their minds about getting a divorce.

Obviously, both partners in that marriage worked very hard to resolve the problems. I was glad that they took my advice and gave it some time. They now have a great marriage, and their family has increased by a son, a son-in-law, and a beautiful granddaughter.

However, there are marriages in which one partner is so sick that the other is in danger. In these cases, I do not recommend reconciliation. My main consideration is to offer support and help on an individual basis.

Unfortunately, in many marriages, the basic problem is selfishness. And no wonder, for the prevailing attitude of today is 'me-ism'. What's more, the absence of moral values in society makes it very easy to become involved with someone else and simply walk out of a marriage.

Many couples get married because they have low self-esteem, thinking the marriage will solve the problem. The fact is, just the opposite occurs, because it takes an awful lot of 'self to make a marriage work.

For a while, Ellen's marriage contained only one confident self, and that was her husband. It must have been very frustrating for him to be the only real partner in a marriage of two people. An ideal marriage is a union of two strong, self-confident people who know themselves and exhibit their feelings from the onset of the relationship.

Getting to know yourself and developing high self-esteem will help you to look at any problem from a different point of view. If, for example, your marriage is in trouble, an honest, different view of the situation could just put it on the road to recovery.

Craig Reid sat defiantly across from me, his body slightly turned away from his wife, Fran. They were both bright young people, but they were seriously considering a divorce.

'I have my work and a couple of interesting hobbies,' Craig said. 'Fran never wants to do anything with me. She just stays at home with the boys. We don't have anything in common any more. I keep telling her that she can get a weekend sitter for the boys and we can go boating or climbing. We can afford it. She works too.'

'And I keep telling him that we don't have much time to spend with the boys as it is,' Fran interrupted. 'I think he is being just plain selfish. Not only does he want to do just what he enjoys, he insists that I do what he enjoys too. After working all week, I need a little time just for me, and the boys need us too.'

Fran turned directly toward her husband. 'Craig, you are a very selfish person. I wish we could all go climbing together once in a while. I could stay in the foothills with the boys while you go on to the top, and we could be waiting for you when you return. I am so tired of saying no to you, and watching you storm out of the house never considering why I said no. And then you come home on Sunday evenings and don't bother to tell us anything about your weekend.

'We'll be better off without you because we won't have to look forward to those hateful home-comings you always give us.'

'Craig,' I interjected, 'how do you feel about being called selfish? Do you see yourself as a selfish person?'

'No. I never thought I was selfish. I make a good living and give Fran and the boys a lot. I don't think that's being selfish. I even ask Fran to come along with me. Is that selfish?'

'But I want to include the boys. They're old enough now to be with us, and they need us. That's the part I've never been able to get you to understand.' Fran seemed to be pleading now. 'Craig, you give plenty of things to them, but so little of yourself. I just can't bear to see them hurt any more.' Fran covered her face with her hands and cried.

'Fran, don't cry. You know I hate it when you cry. Why didn't you tell me all of this before? Why didn't you tell me the boys needed me? I thought they had all they needed. They have you, and I'm home once in a while.'

'I never could get you to listen until now. Now that we're sitting here in Dr Campbell's office where I can talk without you yelling at me, I finally feel brave enough to tell you how I feel.'

'Is Fran being honest, Craig?' I asked. 'Do you yell at her and refuse to listen to her suggestions?'

Craig fell back in his chair. 'I guess she's right, Dr Campbell. I don't pay much attention when she tries to rearrange my weekends. I usually just slam out of the house. I don't like to have people telling me what to do and what not to do with my time.'

It took a few months of counselling, but Craig acquired a different perspective of himself. Often a third party can be the answer; that's why it's good to seek professional help when you have problems. Craig and Fran were able to sort out a lot of little things that had been bothering them. I felt all along that theirs was a marriage that could be saved. It just needed a different point of view. I am happy to report that even the boys do a little hill climbing with their dad now.

A troubled marriage is very damaging to children, who usually experience problems with their ability to think rationally, logically, and sequentially because of the troubled home front. As a consequence, their school work suffers. Craig and Fran's boys were experiencing these things. They were fighting with their friends. In time, their spirituality would have suffered because even spirituality requires the possession of a certain amount of logic to be understood.

A marriage based on Jesus Christ is a beautiful, strong marriage. Craig and Fran now have that marriage. Obedience to Christ in a marital relationship means a lifelong, selfless commitment to each other and the children of that marriage.

When we put the needs of our spouse and our children before our own desires, our needs are met by God and family members. It is a beautiful circle. No marriage is always easy and perfect, but when problems do arise, a Christian marriage has the power of God at its disposal.

This kind of home offers much for the children to copy and carry into their own homes as adults. They will easily learn by example how to make Christ the centre of the household. Preaching, threatening, and demanding will not be necessary, because the child from this home will want to follow parental examples.

What we teach our children

Later in this book, I will devote an entire chapter to discipline, but here I want to make a point about teaching a child right from wrong.

There is a big difference between discipline and education. Discipline is used in determining a child's behaviour, while education deals with morality. A child cannot be disciplined in morality; he must be taught morality by word and example. In other words, you must teach a child what is right and what is wrong; you do not discipline him into it.

This is one area in which you should really know yourself and give careful thought to your ways. It is the one in which parents make the most flagrant mistakes, causing their children to rebel against parental ideas of right and wrong. Parents try all too often to *discipline* their children instead of to educate them by example.

When children are punished for the wrong reasons and under wrong conditions, they rebel. They have to see proper behaviour lived out in front of their eyes before they can understand and copy it. The sad fact is that far too many parents follow the old axiom, 'Do as I say, not as I do, and then don't understand why their children rebel against what they say.

It is hard to educate your children in matters of right and wrong if you are doing one thing and saying another.

How can parents hope to instil any kind of values in their children, including spiritual values, if they are having affairs, being fraudulent, doing lousy work for their employers, being deceitful, cheating – in short, doing what far too many people are doing today? Look at the parent who cheats on his income tax returns every year, and then becomes totally irate when he finds that his child has cheated on a test at school. What a confused child! He was just doing what his father taught him to do.

And what in the world is this same child going to do about spirituality if his parents preach it, but don't live it? Probably very little. I think Titus 1:16 aptly describes the situation: 'They claim to know God, but by their actions they deny him.'

It is the action of denial that your children will copy. The verbal demands that you make in trying to discipline

them into a Christian lifestyle will only create in them feelings of rebellion and confusion, and will move them away
from Christianity. What you speak must come from your
heart and be evident in your daily life.

Is our Christianity evident?

Let's go back to the questions we asked at the beginning
of this chapter and discuss religion. What is your attitude towards God? Spending time with Him each day –
not a rigid, set time, but a quiet, unscheduled time to be
alone with Him and get to know Him – is a must for
every Christian.

And the people with whom you come in contact every
day – bank clerks, shop assistants, people to whom you
can be nice or not nice – is your interaction with them
Christ-centred? Do you try to present Christ to them by
the way you treat them, not necessarily in witnessing,
but at least in your attitude towards them?

How do you interact with the leaders in your church?

Do you sit in church Sunday after Sunday and tune
out the sermon? Your mind drifts to thoughts of
why the building committee didn't take your advice.
Or why the stewards don't make the building warmer.
And then, do you discuss these thoughts in a negative
way at Sunday dinner? Do you criticise other Christians?

Again, all these things are examples to your children.
And since they pertain directly to the church, they will
have a strong influence on the way your children view
Christianity. So it is imperative that you become completely honest about how you feel about your own spirituality, and correct the areas which are detrimental to
both your children and yourself.

We all go through phases in our spiritual growth. When we first become Christians, we are excited and on fire for the Lord. We experience strong, vibrant emotions because we feel so good. This is the time we are wide open for teaching, and we grow by leaps and bounds in our Christian knowledge.

Then we enter what I call the 'either-black-or-white phase'. We become very rigid and feel that everything pertaining to our faith has to be only one way – either totally black or totally white. This is a stage of spiritual immaturity, but everyone goes through it. It's like learning how to drive a car.

In fact, this learning pattern – dealing first with the concrete realities and then with the 'grey areas' – is true in almost all phases of life, but few people apply it to their spirituality. As we mature and learn that choices are not always black and white, and exact answers are not always available, one of two things will happen. We either learn to become more reasonable and flexible in our thinking without losing our faith, or we lose our faith.

More and more people today are simply rejecting their faith. In our counselling practice, my colleagues and I are seeing fewer and fewer people over the age of forty-five who are still practising Christians. And if they are Christians, they are not growing spiritually. Many have become discouraged because the rigid things, the pat answers they learned during their either-black-or-white stage do not always apply to all of life's experiences.

A perfect example of this is trying to cope with the complexities of raising teenagers. There are simply no nice, pat answers for every problem that arises.

Try to determine your current phase of spiritual growth. If you are still in the rigid phase, you will adversely affect your children, especially if you have a tendency to be unbending when dealing with them. One of the most important traits a parent, especially of teenagers, must possess is flexibility. Flexibility does not mean permissiveness. It means not being rigid in your expectations, but remaining pleasant, positive, and firm as you guide your children in the decision-making process.

For example, one young mother recently told me how proud she was that all three of her daughters were taking dancing lessons. 'I absolutely insisted that they all take dancing,' she said. 'I took ballet and I want the same for my children. I think it's important for their physical well-being, plus it's very character-building.' Unfortunately, she didn't ask the girls if they really wanted to dance.

I just happened to know that the oldest one wanted to take swimming lessons instead, but went dutifully to dance class every Saturday morning. How much happier this girl would have been if she could have been dropped off at the pool while her sisters danced. But the mother wasn't flexible. She had made up her mind that all of her daughters would take dancing lessons, and that's what they did.

The chances are this is not a particularly happy home. It is most likely a home where Mother 'rules the roost'. And that is unfortunate, for above all we must make our homes havens for our children. They must be places where our sons and daughters feel secure, relaxed, and loved. It is very hard for a parent in the either-black-or-white phase of his spirituality to achieve such an atmosphere.

When many Christians emerge from the either-black-or-white stage and realise no absolute answers exist for most problems, they are faced with the danger of becoming cynical. They may see a Christian hero perform a non-Christian act. They begin to realise that living a Christian life is difficult. They see that they must use their own minds to think, and that they must spend time with the Lord and daily ask for His leading.

The danger at this point is that one can become very disillusioned. Unfortunately, this occurs for most parents about the same time that their children are teenagers – the time when their children need the most stability in their lives. And here we are as parents, having a hard time with many of our own thoughts and beliefs. It is during times like these that we must hang ferociously to our faith. Remember the words of Solomon: 'My son, do not forget my teaching, but keep my commands in your heart, for they will prolong your life many years and bring you prosperity' (Proverbs 3:1–2).

We must seek time to pray, to read Scripture and, above all, we must not let the mistakes, lies, and frailties of other Christians undermine our spiritual foundations. I have seen that happen again and again. Whatever the inner turmoils, we must be careful not to show a visible, cynical attitude toward spirituality at this time, because it will be directly reflected in our children.

During these episodes when we feel our faith is weakening, we should step back and review our spiritual life as it was during the either-black-or-white stage. We should try to grasp some of the positive attitudes we had then, and hang on until our feelings of cynicism weaken and our spirituality becomes strong again.

It is like saying, 'Stop the world; I'd like to step off for a few minutes and get a different view of life.' Or it's like stepping out of the cloudy water and letting the mud settle to the bottom. Soon you'll be able to see things clearly again.

Don't worry; it is perfectly normal for your teenagers to see you struggle, as long as you don't choose anti-authority, cynical solutions to your problems. Adopting that kind of attitude will immediately kill the spiritual growth of your children. They need to see you working towards positive, biblical solutions to your problems.

The same advice applies to a troubled marriage. As long as your children see that you are struggling to improve the situation, they will have hope and will not be damaged. The damage occurs when cynicism overrides the struggle for improvement and a constant state of turmoil develops.

When you finally get through this difficult phase of your spirituality, you then enter your spiritual adolescence. It's a real questioning time in your life. You question churches and, in a healthy way, question your own faith. This is real growth.

It is healthy to question your authorities and what has been handed down to you through the years. Sometimes, when you get into thoughtful examination, you find that some of your presuppositions are wrong. I found, for example, that God does not have a detailed, pinpointed plan for my life. Instead, His plan for my life is based on my own decision making, as I prayerfully seek to follow His leading.

This is the time when you really begin to find out things on your own. You begin reading Scripture in a new light. You begin interpreting it against your own experiences, and not the experiences of others. Be careful, though, for there is a danger in this phase.

The danger is that we tend to forget that our children have not gone through this or any other phase of Christianity. If you try to explain your attitude towards your spiritual life to your children now, you will really confuse them. Incidentally, this holds true in relating to other newer Christians as well.

So, what you must do is make your spiritual attitudes continually obvious to your children in your daily life. Again, I stress, I know these suggestions are not always easy, but I do know that they will pay off in the long run for both you and your children.

And so, if you always give careful thought to your ways, and present them in a Christ-centred manner, you are giving your best to your children. Equally as important as getting to know yourself, and giving careful thought to how you present yourself, is getting to know your children. I don't just mean that you should recognise their appearance and the sound of their voice; I mean you must get to know your children as whole individuals. Understanding each child's specific personality is of the utmost importance. Let's discuss this next.

3

Children and their personality

'See that you do not look down on one of these little ones. For I tell you that their angels in heaven always see the face of my Father in heaven. In the same way your Father in heaven is not willing that any of these little ones should be lost' (Matt. 18:10, 14).

Children who want to please

If I had to tell you that you could read only two chapters in this book, I would choose this one and the next. I would choose these two chapters, because becoming totally aware of your child's personality is the most crucial thing you can do in order to help him develop into a strong Christian adult.

I have found it practical to separate people by the way they respond to authority, and place them into two categories – approximately 25 per cent are basically pro-authority; about 75 per cent are generally anti-authority (i.e., they usually consider their own opinions above those of others).

I have two sons, David and Dale. Dale is my 25 per-center and David is my 75 percenter. Dale was born asking, 'Dad, is there anything you and Mum would like me to do?' and David arrived with an order to all in hearing distance: 'Would you people please step out of the way; I have a life to live, and I would like to get on with it with as little interference as possible!'

However, nobody is perfect. Each of the boys has his pros and cons, and each possess a little of the good and the bad, which offers both problems and joys in raising them. These next two chapters will be a discussion of 25 percenters and 75 percenters.

The personality factor

Every child in the world is born with a unique personality. Parents can damage that person or enhance his development, but his basic personality is congenital. That is to say, the parents did not create the personality *after* the child was born. They supplied the genetic traits upon conception, and the personality developed from there.

Now, considering that there are millions of people in the world, the fact that I place them into only two categories may surprise you. However, after working with parents and children for about twenty years, I have found that this procedure is both legitimate and practical.

I realise this sounds too simple, but just imagine memorising all the different characteristics of each type of personality, and trying to apply them, all sorted out, on a minute-by-minute, day-by-day basis. It would be utterly impossible. So, I am offering the practical simplification of describing two basic facets of personalities. I have used this in raising my own children, and also in professionally working with children. *I want to stress again that I don't consider either facet all good or all bad; I just recognise that they exist.*

Basically, how a child responds to almost anything depends on his attitude towards authority, and his attitude towards authority depends on his personality. So, dividing personalities into just two groups is of tremendous value when dealing with the problems of children.

I have shared this division of personalities with many people, and it worked as beautifully for them as it does for me. When we understand the personalities of our children, we can better understand our children's behaviour and emotions, and possibly keep from making some tragic mistakes in raising them. Of course, we are only human. Regardless of the amount of information we gather in an effort to do a perfect job of child-rearing, we are still going to make mistakes. So don't feel guilty when things go wrong, because all that God expects of you is your best, not infallibility.

Twenty-five percenters

Twenty-five percenters are born with a need to be under authority. They want approval and praise. They want somebody to tell them what to do and to structure their time for them. They want someone to make decisions for them. So, to the casual observer, the 25 percenter would seem to be an easy child to raise. All you have to do is tell him what to do, set the time for him to do it, tell him when to stop doing it, and then praise him for doing it.

Sounds simple, doesn't it? Well, it's not. Twenty-five percenters are just as difficult to raise as 75 percenters. Where the 75 percenters strike out on their own and begin thinking for themselves almost from day one, the

25 percenters have to be taught to think for themselves. They love to follow; therefore, they are subject to joining cults, to being used, and to being unable to stand on their own two feet as adults. In fact, they have a terrible handicap as adults, because they are always expecting somebody else to tell them what to do.

Twenty-five percenters can be easily controlled with guilt, because they are so prone to guilt. Most parents of 25 percenters control their children in exactly this manner without realising it, and then take great pride in the fact that they have such wonderfully disciplined children.

Julie Hyde, fourteen-year-old daughter of Evelyn and Richard Hyde, is a perfect example of a 25 percenter controlled by guilt. And Evelyn and Richard are not even aware they are doing it.

Julie is the oldest of the five Hyde children. She is a quiet, obedient 25 percenter. A few weeks ago, a friend invited her to a swimming party. 'Mum, Carla is having a swimming party this afternoon and evening and wants me to come. Is it all right with you?'

'Oh, I'm sorry, Julie. I had planned to go shopping this afternoon and then have dinner with your dad. I was looking forward to it. I had hoped you could watch your brothers and sisters for me. Oh, well, never mind. I'll do it another time.'

Julie knew that her mother rarely got out of the house, but she really wanted to go to that swimming party. However, she would have felt terrible being the one to keep her mum from some much-needed time away from the children. 'Go ahead, Mum. My swim-suit's faded anyway. I'd rather wait until I get a new one before I go to a swimming party. Why don't you go on and meet Daddy for dinner? I can stay here.'

It began to be easy for Evelyn Hyde to ask her eldest daughter to baby-sit because Julie never complained.

She was so convincing that her mum thought she actually enjoyed it. And she did once in a while, but there were many times when she would have liked to have done anything but stay home with her brothers and sisters. It was her guilt that kept her home.

When 25 percenters are very young, they're really good children; they are so easy to manage. And the parents of these children are envied, especially in church and especially by parents of 75 percenters. Parents of 25 percenters are usually overheard saying to parents of 75 percenters: 'If you would just become more firm with your child, he would be just like mine.'

All parents compare their children, not realising they simply cannot compare a 25 percenter and a 75 percenter. As a consequence, many children are damaged by this seemingly innocent action of comparison.

Parents who are controlling their children with guilt, as Evelyn and Richard Hyde did Julie, are controlling them in the worst way possible. Even though such control is totally unintentional, it still occurs. Twenty-five percenters are so eager to please that they are easily crushed. They take everything too personally and too seriously. Imagine how Julie would have felt at the swimming party. She would have had a terrible time, because she would have felt personally responsible for denying her mother a pleasant afternoon and evening.

Twenty-five percenters are always afraid they are going to hurt someone or do something wrong. They are perfectionists, and want to do everything exactly right. Even a bit of criticism will smash their egos and make them feel so guilty that they cannot develop as individuals.

The parents of very young 25 percenters do not see this. These mothers and fathers just enjoy having a nice little child who always does exactly what he is told to do, never giving anyone a hard time.

What these parents don't realise is that 25 percenters are keeping all their feelings to themselves. They are extremely self-critical. Being perfectionists doesn't mean that they expect everything to be perfect. It just means that they expect everything to be much better than they, in reality, can make it.

A 25 percenter has such high expectations of himself that every day is a disappointment to him, because every day something goes wrong. Even if ninety-nine good things happen and one bad, he will see only the bad thing. Such a child is obviously prone to depression.

A typical day for a 25 percenter might go something like this: Brett is fifteen. He started this particular day by getting an A on his maths test and an A on an English test. At this point, he is feeling great. Then he is handed back an essay – another A. What a day!

That afternoon, he scored the winning goal for his football team. After walking home from school, he discovers a note from his mum on the kitchen table. She's shopping and won't be home until 6 o'clock. Never mind – he has to go bowling anyway. He can tell her later about his perfect day.

He goes to his wardrobe and reaches for his red bowling shirt, but it's not there. Then he discovers it in the laundry basket with streaks and stains. His mother didn't wash it. His day is ruined. His team is bowling in a tournament, and he doesn't have his shirt! Everything good about the day leaves Brett.

This story may sound extreme, but this is the way a 25 percenter can think. He can very easily become depressed over one seemingly insignificant happening. And depression causes anger. Keeping in mind that a 25 percenter wants above all to please, he will keep that anger inside, causing even deeper depression. And deeper depression causes more anger, which the 25 percenter is directing inward, towards himself.

Just look at the plight of the 25 percenter when his parents are not aware of his personality. He suffers from years of guilt manipulation. He has not been taught how to think for himself or express his feelings outwardly and verbally. As a consequence, he is going to be a depressed and angry adult.

The natural need of all humans to be loved and feel self-worth is multiplied in the 25 percenter personality. So, when his parents do not realise his low self-esteem and unintentionally leave him with an empty emotional tank, he goes outside his home for need satisfaction.

By the time he becomes a teenager, he may become involved with drugs, lying, cheating, stealing, and sex. The list of all the pain a 25 percenter can cause himself and his parents is endless.

The story of Denise

Tall, slender Denise came to see me about eight months ago. A nursing student in her early twenties, her expression gave away her depression. She sat fidgeting in a chair in my office, trying to find the words to discuss her problem with me.

Finally, she blurted it out. 'I'm anorexic, Dr Campbell. I attended a lecture on anorexia this afternoon, and it made me realise that I am anorexic and bulemic.' She began to cry. 'I don't want to tell my parents because they don't think I've done much of anything right in my life as it is. Now they'll be sure to hate me when they hear this.'

I looked into her tear-filled brown eyes. 'What are you doing that makes you think you are anorexic, Denise?'

'Well, I starve myself for as long as I can stand it. Then I eat everything in sight, take a laxative, and purge.'

'How long have you been doing this?'

'About four months, now, I think.'

I was glad to see that Denise recognised her problem as early as she did. She had not yet reached the point of physical damage, so I felt we had a good chance of helping her through it. What we needed to discover was why she felt so negative about herself that she would hurt herself in this way.

As I began to counsel Denise, her problem unfolded. Her older brother, Bill, was outgoing and aggressive. Denise was the quiet one.

'Ever since I can remember, Bill had Mum's or Dad's attention about something,' Denise began. 'When he was about seven years old, he developed a very serious, life-threatening illness. I stayed with my grandparents while he was in the hospital. I really got lonely there, but I hated to bother Mum and Dad because I knew that they were upset about Bill.

'Finally, when Bill came home from the hospital, he had to stay in bed for a month. I did everything I could to make him happy. I was glad that we were all home together, but I remember that Mum hardly noticed me. I don't remember feeling that she should notice me, because I knew Bill needed her so much, but I realise now that I did miss her attention.

'When Bill and I were eight and ten, Mum and Dad built a new house. That was really a hectic time. Once, Bill and I got into a fight. We were arguing about some work that Mum had asked us to do. Actually the fight happened when Bill began to tell me what to do. I already knew what to do; Mum had told me. So I punched him in the stomach. He hit me back – right in the mouth – and cut my lip. I really got mad then, and grabbed for his hair.

Just as I got a big handful of hair, he jerked away, leaving me with a wad of his hair in my hand.

'Dad came in about then, and spanked both of us. Afterwards, Bill ran out into the garden, but I finished the job that Mum had asked us to do. I was so scared. I was afraid that Bill would have a bald spot on his head that would never grow back.'

So went Denise's life. She told me that she almost always gave in – not just to her brother and her parents, but to anyone who crossed her. However, when she started secondary school, she changed.

'Oh, I still tried to keep peace at home, but I was a real character at school. I went out with a boy who didn't amount to anything. He was just plain trouble. I didn't tell Mum and Dad that I was going out with him, but they found out. Boy, was I in trouble. They lectured me for two weeks. I never went out with him again. I didn't know what in the world Mum and Dad would do to me if I did it a second time.

'Again, I felt very guilty because I did something that displeased my parents so. I thought I was probably the worst person in the world.'

Denise went on to college and failed her course. 'I did quite well my first year, but after that I failed everything. I didn't even attend lectures. I lied to Mum and Dad, telling them that my results must have been lost in the post.

'I was feeling worse and worse, but I didn't know how to get out of it. Then one day, Mum surprised me and came to visit me at college. She and I visited all my tutors, and I tried to make them all think that I had been attending lectures: they just had been negligent in marking my attendance.

'Finally, I couldn't stand it any longer. I broke down and cried and cried and told Mum the truth. I hadn't been attending lectures. Mum didn't yell at me. She just called Dad, and he came down with the truck and moved me back home. They told me I would have to get a job and pay them back the money I had wasted on my education, or lack of education, as the case was.

'I held two or three different jobs, finally succeeding in paying back the money, but feeling worse and worse about myself. I had no particular direction. I never completed anything I started. Even a relationship I developed with a man who asked me to marry him failed.

'All this time, Mum was directing my life. I didn't think she had done such a great job with her own life, and I resented her interference in mine. But I couldn't afford to move away from home, so I had to put up with her direction.

'When I told her that I was going to finish my education, she was genuinely pleased and offered to lend me the money. I refused the loan. I knew that I was either going to have to do something on my own soon, or I never would. So I borrowed the money and moved out of my parents' house and went back to college.

'I fell into the same old trap of trying to settle everybody's arguments. I felt I was always there for everyone else, but they never seemed to be there for me. I even had one friend who wouldn't let me tell her about my dates because she hadn't been dating. I didn't want her to feel bad, so I didn't tell her. I gave no thought to what I was denying myself.

'As time for graduation drew closer and closer, I panicked. I had never completed anything of importance before, and 1 was afraid I probably wouldn't complete this.

'I had always been slightly overweight (at least I thought I was), so I started on a diet about the same time that I was beginning to panic about graduation. And soon I discovered that I could lose weight easily – at last

I was doing something right! The only problem was that it became an obsession with me.'

After about six weeks of intensive counselling with Denise, she began to understand what kind of person she was – a 25 percenter. Being a 25 percenter didn't make her hopeless. Twenty-five percenters are wonderful people. It's just that Denise's type of personality was not recognised by her parents, and they hadn't interacted with her accordingly.

Just think of the suffering Denise and her parents could have avoided if they had understood her personality. Her parents always loved her. They just didn't realise that her quiet ways were, in essence, deceiving. She didn't demand any attention; as a consequence, she didn't get any extra attention. Her parents just assumed her emotional tank was full, and tended instead to the natural demands of her 75-percenter brother, Bill.

Fortunately, the story of Denise has a happy ending. She graduated third in her year, and is now working in a large hospital. She and her parents have a real relationship these days. It is based on love and understanding and knowledge. Her parents now realise that just because she is quiet and demands little attention doesn't mean she needs no attention from them.

You can see how simple it was for Denise's parents to control her. She wanted approval and praise, so she tried to be the perfect little girl. But it finally became more than she could handle. Her lack of emotional fulfilment resulted in anger and frustration which turned inward, and manifested itself as anorexia.

And what about Denise's spirituality? As an adolescent, Denise attended church and youth meetings and made a profession of faith in Christ as her Saviour. She became the exemplary child, but as soon as she reached secondary school, she rejected her spiritual training, considering it 'baby stuff'. However, she kept attending church because she wanted the approval of her parents, and *they* wanted her to attend.

We must be very careful about the spiritual lives of our 25 percenters, but in the process not ignore their emotional, physical, and psychological health. We must recognise the times when they feel anger and teach them to express it openly. We must keep their emotional tanks filled with unconditional love, especially during the anti-authority period so natural to the teenage years. By doing these things, we can be assured that our quiet little 25 percenters will mature into strong, healthy adults who love the Lord as we do.

4

Children who kick against authority

'Peacemakers who sow in peace raise a harvest of right-eousness' (Js. 3:18).

I knew when David was about two that he was a 75 per-center. He was definitely one of those I'd-rather-do-it-myself children, and I knew how I was going to have to handle him. We've never had to wonder whether or not David was angry; he has always been able to let us know, but Dale, our 25 percenter, is different. My wife, Pat, and I try to be watchful and help Dale to express his anger when we know something is bothering him. Again, I reiterate, this doesn't make one boy better than the other; it just means that we sometimes handle situations differently, depending on the personality involved.

Seventy-five percenters want to do their own think-ing. They want to make their own decisions. They want to learn the hard way and to control their own behav-iour. They can become angry when someone tries to tell them what to do. They feel that if they are going to learn anything at all, they are going to have to do it them-selves.

On the surface, the 75 percenter appears much harder to raise than the 25 percenter, but he is not. Even though he is born with an anti-authority attitude (not necessarily grossly anti-authority, just generally anti-authority), he takes the same amount of patience, love, and understanding as the 25 percenter.

He may seem more difficult because he already has an inborn desire to think for himself, and he is going to practise that desire and develop it over the years. That is a God-given talent. It is the reason that 75 percenters are natural leaders.

It is a lot easier to keep your thumb on the 75 percenter and help him keep his behaviour under control than it is to teach the 25 percenter how to think on his own. It is so much easier just to tell a child what to do than it is to teach him how to think.

However, don't come down too hard on a 75 percenter while working with behaviour control, because you can make him angry too. A 25 percenter becomes angry because of accumulated guilt, while a 75 percenter won't be hurt at the moment, but will develop a 'get even' attitude toward you which will eventually surface.

Too many Indians, not enough chiefs

Most Christians, I think, tend to be 25 percenters. This is a critical fact. The church is more likely to lose the 75 percenters, and these are the people who are our natural leaders. There is nothing wrong with 25 percenters, but we can't do without 75 percenters in the church.

Right now, the church has too many Indians and not enough chiefs. Because there are so few 75 percenters in the church, when one does show up, he automatically becomes a leader. This can hurt the church because we don't have enough 75 percenters to achieve a balance. Any leader who has no competition or feedback listens only to himself and gets more and more caught up in his own ideas.

This helps explain why so many churches teach extremely authoritarian doctrine. Today's leaders are leaning in that direction and teaching it as law to the 25 percenters in the congregation. And they are seldom questioned.

For example, most Christians can question what the Apostle Paul and the Apostle Peter mean in their epistles. They can even question what some of Christ's statements mean. But they don't dare question today's 75-percenter, national Christian leaders about *their* thinking.

The danger of all this is that most of these leaders advocate the same thing about raising children and teenagers. They say that the primary way of relating to a child is by disciplining him, especially by beating him with the rod. Such child-rearing theories are a backlash against the 'do-your-own-thing' parental passivity of the '60s. And child-rearing at this end of the pendulum means rigid, forceful discipline. Verses in Proverbs dealing with authoritarian discipline are used as proof texts for this school of thought, but they are used with no balance. Nor does this school of thought mention that the shepherd's rod referred to in Scripture was used almost exclusively for *guiding* the sheep, not beating them, as Psalm 23:4 ('your rod and your staff, they comfort me') clearly shows.

In my judgement, this misguided teaching is one of the main reasons why so many 75 percenters turn against the church. By the time they are seventeen or eighteen, they are still angry because of their authoritarian upbringing. So, the last place you are going to see them is in church.

The 25 percenter, on the other hand, is more likely to make a commitment to Christ and join the church regardless of how he's treated, because he needs to be under authority.

We are losing the 75 percenter to the temptations of today's 'me first' lifestyle. We are losing him to this lifestyle because it has a built-in anti-authority flavour, and anyone who has enough anger left in him beyond the normal period of adolescence will have an anti-authority attitude and align himself with anti-authority movements.

A minor rebellion!

'I'm not going to church today, thirteen-year-old David stated flatly one Sunday morning a few years ago.

'Oh, come on, David, I replied. 'You know that once you get there, you have a good time.'

David gave in and went with us. He didn't say any more about it for three or four weeks. And then again, out of the blue, he announced, 'I'm not going to church today. I told you before that I didn't want to go, so I'm not going.'

This time I could see that it was useless to talk David into going. He was determined about the matter that forcing him would have created a destructive anti-church, anti-spiritual attitude that could be extremely difficult to reverse. I had to handle this crisis without alienating David, and yet keep him on the long road to maturity.

'Do you like Sunday School?' I asked.

'Yeah, I don't mind Sunday School.'

'OK, I'll tell you what we'll do. You go to Sunday School and your mother and I will take turns taking you home during church and stay at home with you.'

David agreed to the concept. Pat's and my strategy here was to prevent that vicious anger toward spiritual things which can develop when church attendance or spiritual matters are forced. Knowing that David is a 75 percenter, which makes him naturally anti-authority, we chose for the moment not to pressure him and lose him from the church permanently. We didn't feel we were being permissive; we had a plan.

After all, David was almost fourteen. He knew what we thought and how we believed. He probably knew us better than we knew ourselves. This new arrangement went on for about four or five weeks, and then I could see it was getting old for David. He could tell that Pat and I were really suffering because of it.

He knew that we both wanted to be in church together, that we needed to be in church, so finally he said, 'Oh, all right, I'll go to church for your sake.' And that was that.

Now this worked for the Campbells. I can't promise that it will work for the parents of every 75 percenter. It depends a great deal on what kind of an overall relationship you have with your child in other areas of his life, not just the spiritual area. If you really get to know your child and trust your instincts, you'll be able to handle your particular situation. The key is to keep things positive, and try not to become too authoritarian with your 75 percenter.

The same principle applies to your 25 percenter, but even more so. He is so prone to guilt, that a strong, negative, authoritarian attitude can really damage his ability to think and make decisions.

Those anti-everything children

Now let me tell you about a very sophisticated, self-reliant, middle-aged 75 percenter who just this year found Christ.

Jane is definitely a 75 percenter, born to a very definite 75-percenter mother. As a little girl, she constantly exhibited her anti-authority nature, but her mother kept the upper hand, and would almost always see to it that Jane did exactly as she was told. Fortunately, Jane's best friend attended her church, so she enjoyed Sunday School and tolerated church, sitting defiantly, but nonetheless sitting, beside her mother.

When she became a teenager, she openly rebelled against going to church, but again, her mother won and saw to it that Jane not only went to church, but that she earned perfect attendance awards.

Jane was a rebellious teenager. She was anti-academics, anti-church; she was anti-authority in general. She was very antisocial and made only one or two friends. When she moved away from her home town and started college (the college of her mother's choice), she stopped going to church altogether.

She even adopted the belief that Jesus Christ was nothing more than a 'Good Guy'. She vigorously denied the Virgin Birth, claiming it to be simply a myth. She was determined to go in exactly the opposite direction of her mother.

Jane managed to graduate with a degree in nursing, and immediately went to work in a large city hospital where she met and married a doctor. This marriage produced two children, but ended in a bitter divorce.

During these years of working and child-rearing, she rarely visited her parents. When she did, she spent most of her time arguing with her mother.

After her divorce, she met and married quiet, steady Fred. He offered her sons, who now were teenagers, all the love and support he could give them. He was patient with Jane's angry, anti-everything nature.

Fred encouraged Jane to try to develop some kind of a positive relationship with her parents, especially her mother, so again she tried to communicate with her mother.

During one of these visits back to her home town, a visit when she was attempting to heal some of the wounds of the past, Jane shared this realisation with a long-time friend: 'You know, just before we came to Mother's, my oldest son came to me feeling very down. He had applied to two rather prestigious law firms for summer work, and was turned down by both of them.

'In my attempt to console him, to let him know that even when we are at our lowest there is hope, I realised that my words were empty without God. Right then and there, I came to the full understanding that I couldn't encourage him to keep on looking, to feel confident in himself unless I had a strong belief in something that could give me hope, and that something is God. After all these years, I have to admit that Mother was right, at least about God.'

It is so sad that Jane's mother didn't understand her daughter's personality and even her own so that they could have been spared the pain they both suffered all those years. What's more, they had been robbed of many years of what should have been a blossoming relationship, spiritually and otherwise. But that's what happens when 75 percenters are pushed to the point of getting even. In doing so, they often hurt themselves just as badly as they hurt you.

Let's go back to the story of Denise and Bill from chapter 3. Denise, you remember, is a 25 percenter, while her brother Bill is a 75 percenter. In this particular case, we can readily see that unless parents understand different personality types, whole families can be seriously damaged.

Mum and Dad were just as hard on Bill as they were on Denise, but he went on his way regardless.

Bill's parents forced him to go to college, so he went one year and left. His mother had tried to direct his life just as she did Denise's, but his natural 'I-can-do-it-myself' attitude made this extremely difficult. Bill and his mother were constantly at odds.

When Bill and Denise argued and their parents came down hard on them, Bill got angrier and Denise felt guiltier. As soon as he could, Bill got completely away from his family, adopting none of their values. Why should he? His parents were so busy manipulating his life that they rarely let him know how much they loved him.

However, when Denise's problems surfaced and the whole family entered counselling, many issues were brought to light and resolved. This family is so very fortunate. It is healing and the individual members are at last living happy, productive lives.

The stories of Denise, Bill and Jane illustrate the extreme importance of thoroughly understanding each of our children on an individual basis. Unless we know who we are as parents, and unless we become intimately acquainted with our children, we can unintentionally do irreparable damage.

Understanding each personality is the key to understanding how to handle each individual situation. Even though we are not more restrictive or more condoning or more permissive to either the 75 percenter or the 25 percenter, the better we know the personality, the better we are equipped to handle the whole child.

Very few children have equal traits of both personalities, but they do exist. Such youngsters actually tend to lean one direction or the other, but not to the extent of the true 75 percenter and the true 25 percenter. Our daughter, Carey, is one of these middle-of-the-roaders. We were fortunate in having Carey first. If either of our two boys had been born first, then we would really have had problems.

If David had arrived first, I know he would not only be anti-Christian, but he wouldn't even be able to talk about it without going into a rage. Dale would probably be a Christian, but not a happy one who arrived at the decision of his own volition.

Now that you know whether you have a 25 percenter or a 75 percenter, you are armed with a tremendous amount of help to guide that child through life into spiritual adulthood. Spirituality will surely develop in the child whose parents have bothered to learn about his particular idiosyncrasies and have taken the time to show him that they love him unconditionally.

5

A resentful generation

'A gentle answer turns away wrath, but a harsh word
stirs up anger' (Prov. 15:1).

What's for supper, Mum?' fourteen-year-old Tommy
asked as he tossed his books and sports bag onto the
kitchen table.

'I haven't cooked any supper, Tom, but I have things
all set to go for you and Daddy when he gets home,' his
mother answered. 'I have to work at the office this
evening.'

'Oh, brother! I hate getting supper. Can't you do it for
us before you leave?'

'You'll be fine. Don't grumble. What's wrong anyway? You were angry the minute you walked through
the door.' Tommy's mother handed him the hamburgers. 'How was football practice?'

'Fine!' Tommy snapped as he slammed the frying pan
down on the stove. 'You wouldn't care even if it was terrible, he muttered, tossing the hamburgers into the pan.

'Watch your tongue, young man! You don't need to
get upset just because you have to fry two hamburgers.
I don't want to hear any more from you!'

Tommy's dad walked in the back door. 'I'm home! Hey, look who's getting supper!'

'Yeah. Mum has to go to work.'

'Looks as if you have things pretty well under way, son. I'll make a salad. What's new?'

'Nothing,' Tommy replied sullenly.

'Hey, what's the trouble? You sound as if you're in a bad mood.'

'He's cross because he has to help with supper, and he must have had a bad ball game,' Tommy's mother answered for him; then kissed her husband on the cheek. 'I'm going to work.'

'I am not, Mum,' Tommy angrily called to her as she left the room.

'Wait a minute, now; let's settle down. What *is* wrong with you, Tom? Why were you arguing with your mother when I came home?'

'I had a terrible game, Dad. Nothing went right.'

'Hold on, Tom. I don't want to hear you complain about your football. You're a good player and you know it, so just show them what you can do, and stop complaining.'

'That's just it, Dad. At football today I didn't do so . . .'

'I don't want to hear any more about it! Either stop complaining or stop playing. Which will it be?'

'I'll play football,' Tom conceded quietly.

'Now, what kind of dressing do you want on your salad?'

'Doesn't matter.'

'Just leave the kitchen, Tom. This mood of yours is not something I want to put up with all evening. I'd like to know what in the world is wrong with you.'

'But, Dad, I'm trying to tell you. At football today...'

'No more talk about football. Go to your room, and I'll call you when supper is ready.'

Have you ever hit your thumb with a hammer and yelled? Have you ever had a tough day at work and couldn't wait to get home to discuss it? Have you ever felt angry and frustrated after watching the evening news and turned immediately to your spouse and voiced your opinion?

The chances are, you were able to answer yes to all these questions. All of us have felt anger and have felt the need to release that anger by yelling at or talking to someone.

Imagine how you would have felt if you were told you could not yell when you hit your thumb. And what if your spouse refused to listen to your tale of a bad day at work, or ignored you when you wanted to comment on the news? Wouldn't that have been frustrating and made you angrier?

That's how Tommy felt when he tried to talk with his parents about his football practice – more frustrated and more angry. All he wanted to do was to get his anger out, but his parents were too busy to listen. It happens to all of us and we don't realise it. We get so involved in our own lives that we don't take the time to listen, really listen, to our children. Fortunately for Tommy and his parents, they resolved the problem the next morning.

Tommy's dad put his hand on the boy's shoulder and said, 'Son, I'm sorry about last night. I should have listened to you instead of sending you to your room, but I'm not used to coming home and getting supper, so I wasn't in the best of moods either. Let's hear about the football practice. Everyone is entitled to a bad one now and then. I know, I had my share of them.'

'And I was so busy getting ready for work that I didn't really take time to listen either, Tom,' his mother added. 'Don't give up on us, son. The next time something goes wrong for you, we'll behave more like adults and listen to you.' She smiled and gave his arm a squeeze.

The causes of anger

Before further discussion on how to handle anger, let's find out what causes it. Any person will respond in an angry way if his emotional needs are not met as he expects they should be. Take a young child, for instance. When an infant is not fed the moment he wants to be fed, he becomes angry. If his nappy goes unchanged and he becomes uncomfortable, he gets angry.

As he gets a little older, he develops an emotional attachment to someone, usually his mother. It can be someone other than his mother, but regardless of who it is, if that person does not meet his needs, he becomes angry.

A perfect example of this is the time my wife, Pat, attended a weekend conference when our first son, David, was eighteen months old. Pat had never left David for that length of time before.

I anticipated no problems as Assistant Mum and had none. But two days later when Pat got home, David would have nothing to do with her. He was angry with his mother for leaving him – a perfectly normal reaction – and would not let her touch him for about six hours.

Pat was gone for only forty-eight hours, but look at children today. Mothers or other adults leave them for long periods of time, and on a regular basis. And this is one significant reason why children are so angry today – they are not given the loving attention they need to keep that anger from happening. They have a need for an emotional attachment, but nobody is there to fill that need.

The emotional needs of children have to be met in certain behavioural ways by parents. Children react more to *how* their parents behave toward them than what their parents say to them. They need positive eye contact, positive physical contact, focused attention, and loving discipline. I talked about these traits in my book *How to Really Love Your Child*, but I am going to review them briefly here.

All too often, parents use eye contact, that powerful means of communication, in a negative way. Knowing that a child is most attentive when we look him straight in the eye, we reserve eye contact for the times when we need to reprimand him. A young child will obey because of fear, but as he grows older, this fear gives way to anger and resentment. Consciously avoiding eye contact is just as damaging to a child. Indeed, it is more painful than corporal punishment. So let's couple eye contact with a smile and pleasant words, and take care of misbehaviour in other ways.

Unfortunately, parents all too often reserve physical contact only for times when children need assistance, such as getting dressed and undressed or getting in and out of a car. This is sad because physical contact is one of the easiest ways to give children the unconditional love they so desperately need. All of us need positive physical contact with other human beings. Be honest now, don't you feel good when a friend puts an arm around you for an instant and tells you how glad he is to see you?

Focused attention takes work. It may often mean giving up something you had already planned, but it is a vital need in a child's life. Focused attention makes the child feel that he is the only one of his kind; he is special. All parents must take time to spend with each child individually. Recall how good you feel when you can spend time with your spouse, just the two of you, talking over the day, and you will understand the need a child has for that same kind of time.

Discipline is much more than applying the rod. It is training a child in mind and character, to enable him to become a self-controlled, constructive member of society. It involves guidance by example, verbal instruction, teaching, providing learning and fun experiences; in short, it encompasses every type of communication. It also involves punishment. Even though punishment is a negative and primitive factor of discipline, it must be used at times. However, the best form of discipline is guidance toward the correct thought and action, instead of punishment for wrong actions. Discipline is immeasurably easier when the child feels genuinely loved.

By giving our children loving attention in these various ways, we are filling their emotional tanks. Far too many children today are running around with empty emotional tanks, and far too many today are angry.

Lack of emotional nurturing causes depression, and depression causes anger. Many professionals who treat drug and alcohol addiction say that drugs and alcohol cause depression. This is true, but most children who take drugs and alcohol are already depressed, or on the way, because their emotional needs are not being met. Most people who deal with children neglect this fact.

Few people understand that a depressed child is an angry child. And the angrier he is, the more likely he is to become more depressed. It is a vicious cycle, and it can happen to any child regardless of his life experiences. It can happen to a rich child, a poor child, a child with a lot of friends, a child with few friends, a child with many activities, a child with few activities, and so on.

What's the answer? We must, first of all, give our children unconditional love and prevent some of their anger, and then teach them to handle their natural anger. We must allow them to let their anger out, instead of keeping it inside. Suppressed anger is a very dangerous thing.

Passive-aggressive behaviour

Passive-aggressive behaviour is suppressed anger that a child or an adult displays in a negative, albeit unconscious way. Particularly in Western society, it is *normal* in only one time of life, and that is during early adolescence – from thirteen to fifteen. Passive-aggressive behaviour comes from an anti-authority attitude. It is anti-parent, anti-teacher, anti-Christian, anti-employer, anti-anything which represents authority. The purpose of passive-aggressive behaviour is to upset authority – to make authority figures angry.

Some examples of passive-aggressive behaviour are forgetfulness, dawdling, lying, stealing, and chronic lateness. Once you understand what passive-aggressive behaviour is and are looking for it, you will find it everywhere.

Everyone exhibits some passive-aggressive behaviour.

For instance, if I don't watch myself, I tail-gate when I drive. A child displays the same suppressed anger when he soils his pants after he has been toilet trained.

When Daniel was six years old, his mother had a baby boy. Now, Daniel had been the centre of attention in his home for six years, so the arrival of this baby was a drastic change for him.

Every time he asked his mother to do something for him, she would be taking care of the baby. Whenever he wanted to crawl up on his dad's lap and read, the baby would be there. And whenever Daniel made an extra noise at all, his mother would tell him to be quiet because the baby was sleeping.

If Daniel wanted to hold or touch the baby, his parents would tell him that he couldn't. 'You might hurt him,' they would say. He didn't even get to push the buggy.

Poor Daniel. No matter where he turned, that baby was in his way. He wanted to complain, but everyone seemed too busy with the baby to listen.

Then one day, Daniel stood in the middle of the kitchen floor and soiled his pants. 'Mum, come and change me, he called. 'I'm all dirty!'

Daniel was tired of being left out. He was angry and frustrated. He knew he couldn't yell and scream at his parents or the baby, so he chose an indirect way to get back to them. Subconsciously, the purpose of his action was to upset his parents. And it worked.

Passive-aggressive behaviour is hard to see at first because it is so subtle. It almost invariably comes across in fine, upstanding people who initially seem very friendly. The reason they are easy to like in the first place is because they are pleasant. And the reason they appear so pleasant is because they have suppressed all their anger. We see only the pleasant people, but the anger is down there, waiting to come out.

An example of the subtlety of passive-aggressive behaviour is easy to see in children, especially teenagers, and their problems with grades for school work.

At the beginning of the school year, there is no reason for a student to be angry at the teacher or the school. This is especially the case when the student is attending a new school and has new teachers. He starts the school year doing very well. However, as the year progresses, the normal aggravations of life cause anger to build up gradually inside him.

He, like most passive-aggressive people, is very good at suppressing anger, but eventually the anger level gets so great that it starts corning out in passive-aggressive behaviour. The grades start going down. The student unconsciously thinks, 'I am so angry with you that I won't do the work.' He doesn't even realise it's happening. Consciously, he wants to do as well as everyone else; unconsciously, he is releasing suppressed anger in a passive-aggressive way in order to upset authority – parents and/or teachers.

As I stated earlier, younger teens are naturally passive-aggressive to some extent. But if we can handle this phase of their lives correctly, they should be through the passive-aggressive stage by the time they are seventeen or eighteen.

Any thirteen-, fourteen-, or fifteen-year-old is unconsciously and sometimes consciously anti-almost anything – especially those who are 75 percenters. In fact, they are usually angry about something most of the time. What we must do is keep that anger coming out of their mouths instead of allowing them to keep it inside.

This is a very difficult thing for parents to do, because their natural inclination is to quieten their teenagers, suppress the children's anger, and keep peace in the house. But sometimes I have to ask the parents I counsel, 'Would you rather have a son yelling at you, or a son overdosed on drugs? Would you rather have a daughter harping and screaming, or have a pregnant daughter?'

I always tell parents to remove the pressure from their younger teenagers by allowing these children to verbalise their anger. In this way, *they* learn to control their temper in a mature way. In this way, *we* train our children as Proverbs says we should.

Suppressing anger is something like depressing an inflated balloon with a bulge in it; if you push the bulge in, it is going to come out somewhere else. So, if we try to keep our children from expressing their anger, it will only pop out in some other area of their lives – in negative, usually passive-aggressive behaviour.

Bear in mind that you can't totally prevent passive-aggressive behaviour, even though you allow your teenager to express their anger. You need a safety valve for passive-aggressive attitudes to come out in a harmless way. You see, passive-aggressive behaviour is primarily unconscious, and the unconscious mind is amoral. It really doesn't care whether the thought is right or wrong; it just has to get rid of anger.

In passive-aggressive behaviour, a teenager gets rid of anger by making his parents upset. So whatever upsets the parents most is what the teenager is going to go for – the jugular! What would upset Christian parents most? Where is the primary interest in most Christian homes? It is spirituality, of course. So what is the target of their passive-aggressive behaviour? Spirituality, of course.

In non-Christian homes, on the other hand, and in some Christian homes as well, generally the emphasis is on success at school, so most passive-aggressive behaviour starts out anti-academics, anti-learning. Either area can be very destructive in the long run. But what can we do to prevent such a result?

First, we can avoid making big issues out of spiritual things and academics, especially during these years of adolescence. Now, if your teenager comes to you and wants to talk, that's great. You are in a different situation. When a teenager initiates the conversation, that means you are not the one doing the preaching or displaying any negative or authoritarian attitudes. Over-emphasising anything during these years is just handing the teenager ammunition and saying, 'Hey, here's how you can hurt me and yourself. Fire away!'

Now, can you think of a form of harmless passive-aggressive behaviour? (Keep in mind that passive-aggressive behaviour is an unconscious act by a person to do the opposite of what you want him to do.) What about a messy room? That's very normal for almost any teenager, because parents are always demanding, 'Clean up your room!'

If your daughter's room is messy, it's a good place for you as a parent to put emphasis because it's a form of passive-aggressive behaviour which will not hurt anybody. Why?

Because you want to make an issue only out of something that is unimportant and will not hurt the girl. So go ahead and put emphasis on cleaning up that room. She'll eventually outgrow that anti-everything, passive-aggressive attitude and put her room in order again. But how much better for her to exhibit passive-aggressive behaviour by keeping a messy room, instead of going against spirituality or neglecting her school work.

In the child and the young teenager, up to about sixteen or seventeen years old, passive-aggressive behaviour can be changed. That is, we can teach our children to express their anger positively, so that passive-aggressive behaviour will not develop any more than it normally does in that stage of life.

However, once the teenager reaches the age of sixteen or seventeen, passive-aggressive behaviour can solidify. At that point, it can be very difficult, almost impossible, to change. This is why it is so critical to take care of these things as early in child-rearing as possible. Not only should we be careful not to make our children passive-aggressive in spiritual matters, but in all other areas as well, because passive-aggressiveness permeates the whole being.

When passive-aggressive children grow up

Passive-aggressive behaviour is one of the primary forces operating in the world – internationally, nationally, locally, up and down your street. For example, many telling illustrations of adult passive-aggressive behaviour can be found in employer-employee relationships.

An employer does not detect passive-aggressive behaviour when he is conducting an interview with a prospective employee. Indeed, it can take months before a new employee begins exhibiting it. Just like the child starting a new school with a new teacher, the employee starts his new job with a positive attitude. Everything goes well – for a while.

Then things start going wrong. The employee gets a little irritated here, a little angry there, and the anger gradually increases to the point where passive-aggressive behaviour starts exhibiting itself in anti-authority gestures. His job proficiency begins to decrease, and the desirability to have him as an employee diminishes. Finally, the employee causes so much conflict that he has to be fired.

The main difference between passive-aggressive behaviour in children and similar behaviour in adults is that it is largely unconscious in children, and more conscious in adults. It usually only starts unconsciously in adults, and gradually develops into a conscious action.

A short time ago, a businessman friend of mine decided to hire an office manager.

'You know, Ross,' he said to me, 'I thought this would be a perfect arrangement. I could work in the field more, and he could handle questions from clients, some public relations work, collections, etc. In short, Everett seemed like the answer to my problems.

'And he was – for a time. We had agreed on a small

salary until he learned the job, and then he would receive increases based on his productivity.

'All seemed to be going quite well until one of my field men had to stay in the office for a few days to do some work. My secretary was unable to do the typing needed to complete his work, because she was filling in for Everett, who for some unknown reason had taken three days off.'

'Had he asked for the time off?' I asked my friend.

'No, he just took it. I had talked to him a few weeks earlier, and learned that he had had real difficulties getting on with his father, who had just recently passed away. He stated at the time that he might need a few days off to help his mother settle legal matters incurred by his father's death, but he never asked for any particular days.

'At any rate, I considered the circumstances, and let the matter drop. A few weeks later, my secretary told me that Everett was missing work regularly. I talked to him about it, and he said that he had taken a part-time job because I wasn't paying him enough. He had bought a car, and he and his wife were talking about moving to a higher rent area. He said he had understood that I would be giving him a rise, but I hadn't kept my word.

'I reminded him of our original agreement, and he became very angry with me, accusing me of not caring about him or his family.

'Shortly after this confrontation, I had occasion to work in the office for a few days. It afforded me ample opportunity to see my office manager in action. He did very little. He ignored most of the collection matters, turning them over to the secretary. He made no attempts at pursuing possible clients. In short, he was almost non-productive.

'I tried to talk to him, but he became hostile, so I

threatened to cut off his wages if he didn't start to work on some of our accounts.

This threat alarmed him, so for about six months, he made weak attempts at fulfilling his job. I even gave him a rise in pay, hoping this would be an incentive, but still, every time I worked in the field, he found excuses to leave the office. His excuse for being gone so much was that he was interviewing possible new clients, but none ever materialised.

'He was such a burden that I finally fired him. To this day, he blames me for all the problems we had. He contends that he did everything he was supposed to do. He says that he worked like a dog, and I treated him horribly.'

When I learned that Everett had never got on with his father, I was not surprised at the way the interaction between him and my friend developed.

Everett had set up the situation so that he would have an excuse to be angry with his boss. Passive-aggressive behaviour transfers directly from the parent to the spouse and then to the employer. Unconsciously and consciously, Everett was doing all that he could to make my friend angry, all the while rationalising that he was right. The more passive-aggressive a person is, the more he can rationalise. I really could sympathise with my friend. I have worked with passive-aggressive adults, and it is difficult. They rationalise most actions they take.

Another example of working with a passive-aggressive person is when I hired a young woman to work in our clinic. At first, everything went very well. She was a pleasant and kind person and a good secretary.

Then, just like a typical passive-aggressive individual, she became less and less accountable as the months went on. She began to arrive at work late, until finally her tardiness became just plain flagrant. Some days she didn't show up for work at all. And her lunch hour nearly always extended beyond the allotted time.

Since I hate to fire people, I put up with her actions for a long time. Then I began to see her attitude show up in her work. She began to leave work for the other secretaries in the office to complete, which caused them to complain, and rightfully so.

The irony of the situation was that because she was such a pleasant person, those who did not have to work directly with her really liked her. However, those who had to do the work which she left undone resented her. So she created a tremendous amount of turmoil for the entire office.

Anyway, one Friday at noon (Friday is the busiest day of the week for us), she left her job and walked out. There was no reason for her action; nothing unusual had gone wrong in the office; she simply walked out, leaving the other secretaries in a difficult situation.

The next day she phoned me to apologise for her action, then asked for her job back. I just couldn't bring myself to say no, so I told her to come back to work on Monday; she had, as typical passive-aggressive people will do, made promises of doing better.

When I hung up on the phone, I started thinking about the whole situation and realised that things were not going to get better. In fact, I knew that in less than a week, things would be even worse than they were before. So I called her back and told her not to return. I felt terrible doing it, but I knew I had to do it. I can't tell you the difference it has made in our office.

Once more, I want to emphasise that everyone is passive-aggressive to some extent. It shows up in the driving habits of some people; others display it by constantly showing up late for meetings; the list is endless. But it is only when passive-aggressive behaviour totally takes over a person's life that it is a pathological personality disorder.

Passive-aggressive adults will be the end result of today's children if we don't start helping them deal with their anger now.

Helping a child deal with anger

The younger a child is, the more immaturely he will express his anger. As he matures, he should begin to learn to express his anger in a more positive way. This is where we, as parents, must have patience.

I realise that many times parents are so tired that they simply want to tell their children to 'Be quiet!' but that is definitely the worst thing to do. It only succeeds in cramming their anger deep inside them. I would like to discuss ways to help children and teenagers express their anger in a positive way -- a way that will clear the air much better than 'Be quiet!'

In order to help parents deal with the complexities of resolving anger, I have created an Anger Ladder. There are fifteen rungs on the ladder, each step representing a progressively better way of expressing anger:

1. Pleasant behaviour
2. Seeking resolution
3. Focusing anger on source only
4. Holding to the primary complaint
5. Thinking logically and constructively
6. Unpleasant and loud behaviour
7. Cursing
8. Displacing anger to sources other than the original
9. Expressing unrelated complaints

10. Throwing objects
11. Destroying property
12. Verbal abuse
13. Emotionally destructive behaviour
14. Physical abuse
15. Passive-aggressive behaviour

And now we need to put this ladder to good use. As we discussed earlier, passive-aggressive behaviour is the worst way to express anger. Losing control to the point of property destruction or violence toward another person sounds bad, but still is better than passive-aggressive behaviour. Only slightly, but better because it is easier to deal with and prevent than passive-aggressive behaviour.

A still slightly better way of expressing anger is to be in a fit of rage. This may involve screaming, cursing, yelling, name-calling – all directed not only at the source of the anger, but to anyone else who happens to be in the vicinity. As poor as this expression of anger seems to be, it too is better than passive-aggressive behaviour.

Climbing up the ladder, we come to verbal release of anger, aimed at anyone within hearing distance. As poor as this may sound, it also is an improvement over those mentioned thus far.

Getting near the top of the ladder, we find a good way of expressing anger in rung 3, and that is focusing it only on the source. This may involve some yelling and screaming, but at least it is confined to the provoker of the anger.

The top of the ladder is the best of all ways to resolve anger, and that is pleasant and rational expression towards the person with whom you are angry. It is hoped that the person with whom you are having the problem will respond in an equally mature way, so that both parties can rationally and logically examine the issue, discuss it, and agree what to do about it. Few people come to this point of maturity, but if your teenager can occasionally see you handle your anger in this manner, he has a good background for reaching such a point himself.

Expect your teenager to become angry at times, and encourage him to express it verbally. Then, determine where he is on the Anger Ladder, and work with him from there. Find a time after you both have calmed down to praise your teenager in the areas where he expressed his anger correctly; then ask him to correct the aspect you think needs changing.

Let me clarify one point that might possibly be confusing. I am speaking of *verbal* expressions of anger, not behavioural expressions of anger. I am not encouraging permissiveness in behaviour; I am encouraging verbal expressions of anger which can finally be developed into positive methods of resolving anger.

An example of helping a teenager deal with anger happened to a friend of ours whose son came home from school with a very low grade on a maths test.

Jerry, who was bright and outgoing, walked into the house, threw his books on the front hall table, and stomped into the kitchen. Finding nothing in the refrigerator to please him, he slammed the door shut.

'You could keep something around here to eat, Mum,' he growled, and headed towards his room, stumbling over his little brother's blocks. He immediately yelled, 'Bobby, come and pick up these toys! You're more trouble than you're worth! I could've broken my ankle!'

'OK, Jerry, that's about enough,' said his mother. 'I know you're angry about something, but I doubt that it's the lack of food in the refrigerator or Bobby's toys. I do appreciate the fact that you're getting your anger out, but let's try to settle down somewhat and get to the bottom of this.' She remained calm, and placed her hand on Jerry's shoulder. 'Did something go wrong at school today?'

Jerry brought his books from the hall table, and handed his mother the test paper. 'Not unless you call a D on an important maths test something wrong,' he answered her sarcastically.

'Do you want to talk about it now, or wait a little while?'

'I don't understand this low grade, Mum.' Jerry's voice softened. These problems look right to me. I don't know any other way to solve them.'

'What do you think about talking to your teacher about this tomorrow, and maybe he can tell you why he marked them wrong?'

'He won't listen. He's one of those people who know everything.'

'Maybe if you talk to him, Jerry, you'll find that he's not such a bad person. Teachers appreciate the pupil who is interested in learning.'

Jerry finally decided to talk to his teacher. The next evening he was in a good mood. 'Guess what, Mum! You were right. My maths teacher had made an error in grading my paper, and I got a B for the test.'

Jerry's mother was wise in letting him verbalise his frustration, and then in helping him get to the real reason for the anger.

It is so important to understand that whether we are dealing with teenagers, employees, unions, or government, anger is inevitable. It can result from any human interaction. We must also realise that if anger is not dealt with, it will become more and more difficult to control – even explosive. The more it builds up, the more destructive it can become.

Therefore, we must help our teens 'nip it in the bud' if the anger is based on a misunderstanding, or, if the anger is justified, verbally vent it in a slow, positive way so that it can be resolved.

This method of anger resolution does not come naturally to anyone. We, as parents, must patiently train our teens to manage their anger in a mature way. We must guide them towards positive verbalisation of their anger, not allowing behavioural outbursts. We must be careful that our teens' anger does not stay inside, creating passive-aggressive adults.

An angry adult cannot be a productive person. He cannot accept authority of any kind, including spiritual authority. 'For man's anger does not bring about the righteous life that God desires' James 1:20).

6

Handing out discipline

'As a father has compassion on his children, so the Lord has compassion on those who fear him' (Ps. 103:13).

I get very upset when I read child-rearing books written by prominent Christian leaders who advocate hitting, yelling, and pinching as ways to keep children under control. These writers lightly pass over the basic need of the child, which is a need for unconditional love and acceptance.

In this chapter, you are not going to read that beating the child with the rod and pinching him are sound child-rearing practices. You are not going to be told that he is a depraved and evil being who needs his will broken. (I just recently read that description written by an 'expert'.) By the same token, neither are you going to read that total permissiveness is the answer to child-rearing woes.

If you are handling your child in any of these ways, and you firmly believe that you are doing the right thing, then you might be turned off by what you are about to read. But please don't put this book down. Hear me out. If you are turned off because this is not what you are used to hearing, then both you and your child are going to benefit greatly. You are going to learn that you can lovingly discipline your child, and rest in the assurance that he will become an acceptable human being at the same time.

The last thing you want to have to do is use harsh disciplinarian measures on your child. I know that if you follow my suggestions, and take the few extra minutes required to get to the reasons for misbehaviour, much harsh action can be avoided. The misbehaviour itself will often be avoided if you have established a relationship of unconditional love with your child.

It takes time and patience, but who is more important than your child? No talent at all is involved in telling your child to shut up. And anybody can hit a child when he opens his mouth in disagreement. Unfortunately for parents and children alike, too many child-rearing experts are advocating that very thing. This is discouraging, because it results in a child never getting through the normal passive-aggressive stage. He remains passive-aggressive on into adulthood.

Loving, Christlike discipline

I have discussed various ways of conveying love to children, such as eye contact, focused attention, and physical contact. Now I am going to discuss more fully the idea of loving discipline. To administer loving discipline is to train the child in the way he should go. It does not mean forcing the child to go the way you want him to go.

Let's go back a step. Even before you can train your child in the way he should go, he must have and feel from you unconditional love. A child who feels unloved is an angry child, and an angry child will not respond to *any* kind of discipline in a positive way.

Any time you are unjustly harsh to your children, you are violating Ephesians 6:4, which reads: 'Fathers, do not provoke your children to anger; but bring them up in the discipline and instruction of the Lord' (NASB).

Originally, the word *discipline* meant 'an instruction imparted to disciples'. Today, a more negative meaning of the word is favoured. Most Christian child-rearing 'experts' define *discipline* as 'control'. They place minimal emphasis on first loving your child, and then they launch into instructions on how to control your child. This is unfortunate, because too much enforced control only makes children angry.

As I stated earlier, suppressed anger is very damaging to children. It can create all kinds of problems as they enter their teen years. Giving unconditional love and attempting to understand the reason or reasons for children's misbehaviour are the best solutions for solving their problems.

If you can keep the original meaning of *discipline* in mind as you work with your children, it will be of great help to you. The first thing most of us think of when we hear the word *disciple* (discipline being an instruction imparted to disciples) is Christ's disciples. The deepest wish of these twelve men was to be exactly like Christ.

How do you think Christ convinced these men that they should follow Him? Do you think that they believed in Him just because He told them to? Of course not. The disciples followed Christ because of their love for Him and His love for them. 'We love him because he first loved us' (1 John 4:19).

They would never have made such radical changes in their lives if they had not loved Him and felt His love in return. The love of God through Christ was given to the disciples, and they became eager to follow His teachings and spread His Word.

The beautiful example of Christ and His disciples clearly shows us that love and admiration are powerful motives for people to adopt another's values. This example can be followed by parents as they train their children in the way they should go.

Mutual love is the very best way to get children to adopt your values. Once this foundation has been established, not only will your children adopt your general lifestyle, but you will have achieved your primary goal for them – they will want to adopt your spiritual values.

Discipline, then, as I have just defined it, is *training* the child. Physical punishment is only one part of discipline and if the child has had his emotional needs met, a very small part.

The misuse of corporal punishment

Anyone can physically strike a child in a moment of anger, but it takes time and patience to train him. I am not saying that physical punishment should never be used; I am suggesting that loving guidance based on firmly pre-established rules will benefit the entire family structure much more.

A problem that frequently arises is that the punishment far outweighs the crime. I remember talking with a young mother whose four-year-old daughter took two or three board games from the games cupboard and mixed them all together.

'I just had a fit, Dr Campbell, the mother exclaimed. 'I yelled at her, and then demanded that she separate all those pieces and put them back in the proper boxes. It was a task for an adult, but I made her stick at it. It took almost two hours of tears and yelling, but she got it done.'

'How do you think you should have handled the situation?' I asked her.

'I realise now that I should have worked with her. She is too young to have been given such a monumental task and carry it through. What makes me feel so bad is that I spanked her the minute I saw the mess. Parents really can be cruel.'

This mother is so right. Parents can be cruel. They don't set out to be cruel; it just happens. As I read many of the child-rearing books written today, I can readily understand why. Corporal punishment is the main theme.

It makes me sad to see people emphasise the four verses from Proverbs which deal with using the rod (13:24; 23:13–14; 29:15), and then see them virtually ignore Scripture which deals with the child's most basic need – love.

Hundreds of verses in the Bible instruct us to be understanding, compassionate, sensitive, caring, and forgiving. Our children are very deserving, and have every right to these expressions of love.

One crucial point overlooked by so-called child-rearing experts is the fact that corporal punishment can be physically damaging to the child. When the use of the rod is needed, it must be done with extreme caution.

An unfortunate consequence of corporal punishment is that it alleviates guilt. Too much guilt can be damaging to a child, but he must learn to feel some guilt in order to develop a conscience.

A spanking will clear the air; that is certain. The child feels no guilt because he has paid for his wrongdoing by being spanked. The parent has released his anger by spanking the child, so it would appear that everything is under control. However, the lesson learned by the child is not that his misbehaviour was wrong, only that he shouldn't get caught at it the next time.

What you really want for your child is for him to develop a normal, healthy conscience. This will help him control future actions. Feeling guilty once in a while will aid in this development. So, the next time your child misbehaves, try letting him 'sit one out'. Give him time to think about his actions and their consequences. In other words, give him time to feel some good, honest guilt for his wrongdoing.

Another consequence of corporal punishment is aggressor identification. This also is a way of escaping guilt. The child sides with the parent, and begins to agree that aggressive and abusive actions are right. The sad thing about this result is that the child takes this attitude into his adult life, and treats his children and others in the same way.

My strong advice is to stand up against those who are saying that the primary way to discipline a child is to punish him physically. Some of these 'experts' don't even have children of their own. Let us adopt the attitude of Christ which He presented daily to His disciples; let us love our children unconditionally so that they will want to adopt our ways and values.

Dealing with misbehaviour

I don't want to mislead you and let you think that if you love your child unconditionally, he will never misbehave. I'm a parent too, and I know that simply is not true! I have learned though that dealing with misbehaviour is made easier if you have a firm, love-based relationship with your child.

When a child misbehaves, the first thing we should ask ourselves is, 'Why did this child take this action?' or 'Does he have a need that I am not meeting or have not met?' Our first thought should *not* be a negative one, such as, 'What can I do to correct this child's behaviour?'

Remember the story of Daniel in chapter 5? Daniel misbehaved by soiling his pants because he felt unloved. Let's imagine two possible reactions from his parents to this event. If his parents respond to his misbehaviour by spanking him and sending him to his room, they will not solve his problem. They will not fulfil his needs. Therefore, the problem will probably recur.

Daniel's parents need to fill his emotional tank. They need to make him feel loved too. In doing so, they will take away the reason for the misbehaviour, thus eliminating future misbehaviour of this kind.

Teachers sometimes mishandle their students' negative actions. Not long ago, I was counselling Molly, who told me of a very painful experience she had with her teacher.

Molly had been late for school three mornings in one week. On the third morning, her teacher punished her tardiness by making her crawl to her desk. Then he smacked her hands with a ruler. This was an extreme action, and one which proved painfully embarrassing for Molly.

Had the teacher bothered to check, he would have found that the reason she had been late was because the street on her usual route to school had been closed. He would also have discovered that both of her parents worked, and she was left alone each morning to get herself ready for school. If only Molly had been able to give her reasons before such stern punishment was administered, she might not have needed counselling. If only the teacher had taken just a few minutes with her, he could have been her trusted friend instead of just a strict teacher for whom she had no respect.

I am not advocating that you condone misbehaviour. Try instead to arrive at the reason for the misbehaviour. Once that is accomplished, the misbehaviour will be clearly understood and not likely repeated.

Neither am I telling you never to spank your child. I am simply suggesting that you put it on the very bottom of your list of productive and fair ways to deal with misbehaviour – a last resort.

I am reminded of a little girl who lived in my neighbourhood when I was a child. She had a pet kitten which she treated as though it were human. We used to tease her about that cat, and tried to take it away from her, but she guarded it with her life.

One day, she tied a ribbon about its neck and turned it loose. The ribbon got caught in the shrubs, and strangled the kitten.

When her father found out about it, he spanked her and yelled at her in full view of us children. In looking back at that situation, I realise now that she needed some loving forgiveness for her actions. She was not a mean little girl. She would never have harmed that kitten on purpose.

She needed to talk to her father in the privacy of their home, and tell him how sorry she was and how bad she felt. She needed her father's forgiveness. After all, our Father in heaven forgives us when we confess doing wrong; shouldn't we do the same for our children?

Children need to feel forgiven when they are genuinely sorry for their actions. This helps them handle their guilt. I stated earlier that some guilt is necessary in order for the development of a conscience, but too much guilt can be very damaging. Allowing children to feel forgiven will save them untold serious problems of handling guilt in their adult lives.

You are making a grave mistake if you think that punishment in itself will solve anything. Punishment without unconditional love will result in a poor relationship between you and your child. And, if it is allowed to develop, by the time your child is an adult, he will not want to adopt any of your values. He will purposely go in exactly the opposite direction.

Setting an example

Young children have a need to admire their parents. These are the years, up to about age thirteen, that much positive groundwork can be laid for a solid relationship between you and your child. Focused attention during these years is very healthy for the child because it tells him that he is indeed very special. This is the time to teach and train the child in spiritual values, and to emphasise them.

As he matures, he will begin to question much of what his parents stand for. He may even think they are deficient in some areas of their lives. Still, he has the strong need, though it is sometimes unconscious, to be able to love and admire them. So, it is obvious that a good, self-disciplined example set by you as parents will greatly influence the child in a positive way.

The old maxim, 'Do as I say, not as I do' simply will not work with children. A few years ago, a study was conducted on the surge of undisciplined behaviour of teenagers in Sweden. Researchers found that delinquents did not necessarily come from undisciplined, troubled homes. A higher percentage of troubled teens came from homes where the parents did not practise the kind of lifestyles that they demanded of their children. The well-behaved, well-adjusted teenager was found to come from the home of the parents who lived the lifestyle they expected of their children.

Always keep in mind, as you set examples for your children, that you are human and occasionally humans tire. During the child-rearing years, parents can deplete their emotional and physical strength. I especially suggest to parents of teens that they first make sure that their own physical well-being is tended to. By the time children become teenagers, parents are a little quicker to become angry, a little less understanding, and a little more likely to handle their teens' anger with anger. I caution you not to fall into this trap. Keep up your own health so that you will be able to maintain self-control.

Your teenager is going to challenge and/or break some of the rules that you set for him. Since you know this is going to happen, the thing to do in the beginning is to make the rules quite strict and restrictive. Then, as your teenager matures and demonstrates that he can be trusted to behave as the situation demands, his privileges will gradually increase, and parental control will gradually lessen.

In gradually removing restrictions and granting privileges, you are teaching your teenager to become a responsible, trustworthy, independent adult by the age of eighteen. This is not easy. It takes real courage to say no to your teenager when other parents are allowing theirs to do things that you know are detrimental to their well-being.

Let me assure you of one absolute fact. Your teenager, whether he realises it consciously or not, wants your guidance and control. I have heard many young people say that their parents don't love them because their mothers and fathers are not strict or firm with them.

Teenagers must experience consequences for their behaviour. They must experience positive consequences for positive, responsible behaviour, and negative consequences for inappropriate irresponsible behaviour. These consequences must be consistent and fair, not based on how the parent is feeling at the time. Again, parental self-control is of the utmost importance.

It is good to keep in touch with other parents. In doing so, all of you can share valuable information and concerns about your children. You can work together in providing direction and discipline for them.

If you clearly state to your teenager that you are working to help him become a responsible, independent person, he can then feel you are *for* him, not *against* him. Such a positive attitude will greatly improve your relationship.

The four types of discipline

There are basically four types of discipline. The first is an *authoritarian* approach. The child is kept totally under control by his parents. He is offered no love, eye contact, physical contact, or focused attention.

The second type of discipline is the *authoritative* method. This method – based on unconditional love – offers the child a lot of direction, and correction when needed. He also receives emotional nurturing.

Permissiveness is the third disciplining method. It offers the child love, attention, and support, but absolutely no direction. The parent who uses this method just goes along with whatever the child decides, never correcting him or offering him overarching guidance.

The fourth method of dealing with a child is not to deal with him at all – *neglect*.

Recently, a study was conducted on four groups of young adults, each of which had received one of the four types of discipline. The results of the study were compared with the following:

1. Identification with the parents and their value system
2. Following parents' religious beliefs
3. Identification with counter-culture movements (anti-authority attitudes)

The study revealed that the children who were raised under the *authoritative* method (where they not only received guidance, correction, and direction, but unconditional love) turned out the best. They not only *identified* with their parents' value system, but they made it through the anti-authority years and *adopted* the religious beliefs of Dad and Mum.

The children who turned out to be the most unsettled adults were raised in an *authoritarian* manner. Sometimes, this is the way children in Christian homes are raised and, not surprisingly, most reject Christ. The next to the worst way of raising children is pure neglect, and the second best way of raising children is *permissiveness*.

Aren't these findings amazing? Permissiveness, which is what Christian parents are strongly warned against, is superior to authoritarianism, which most Christian parents use. Even more annoying is the fact that the authoritarian method is worse than neglecting the child.

This study affirms my line of thinking: the authoritative way of raising children is the most successful. Children who are lovingly disciplined and guided to adulthood will eventually not only adopt, but *want* to adopt their parents' spiritual values.

A test of our discipline methods

The following situations, which happen to all of us in our daily dealings with our children, can be answered with: (a) Try to find out why, and then deal with the problem accordingly; (b) Verbally punish him, and send him to his room; (c) Immediately administer corporal punishment, and discuss the problem later.

1. When my child lies, I___.
2. When my child does badly in school, I___.
3. When my child refuses to eat his meals, I___.
4. When my child is argumentative with me and I've had a rough day at the office, I___.
5. When my child fights, I___.
6. If my child ever stole anything, I would___.
7. If my teenager puts a dent in the car, I will___.
8. When my teenager comes in after curfew, I___.
9. If my teenager begins to use drugs, I will___.
10. If my teenager cheats on tests at school, I will__.

Honestly check your answers to these random questions in the privacy of your home. If you find that your answers are predominantly 'b' and 'c', then you have probably used the authoritarian approach to discipline.

Re-evaluate your child-rearing methods. Ask yourself if you are giving your child the loving attention and positive direction that he needs. It is critical for the all-around development of your child that he be made aware on a daily basis of your love for him.

7

Children need training

'Train a child in the way he should go, and when he is old he will not turn from it' (Prov. 22:6).

A red sports car pulled up in front of the church and stopped. Two well-dressed little girls, aged about eight and ten, hopped out of the car. 'You wait right here on the church steps after Sunday School. Daddy and I will be back to get you at 11 o'clock.'

'All right, Mummy. See you later.' The children bounced up the steps and into the building while their parents sped away. They didn't want to be late for their tennis game.

'Ah, two whole hours just for us, the husband said, smiling at his wife. 'We can get in about an hour of tennis, and then have a late breakfast before we pick up the girls. Sounds good, eh?'

'Certainly does, Darling. We need this time each week. It's good for both of us.'

Does this scenario sound familiar? Do you see your neighbour here or one of your friends? Or do you possibly see yourself?

Children learn by parental example. What are these girls learning? Sadly, they are learning that just as soon as they are as old as Mummy and Daddy, they too can play tennis on Sunday mornings.

These parents have probably *told* their children that they are Christians, but they are not *living* their spiritual statements. Children are most apt to respond to the value system that their parents *live*, and less likely to respond to what is *told* to them. Parents are very mistaken if they think they can fool their children.

Teaching tots to trust

Children are born ready to learn. In the early months of their lives, they have a built-in survival system. They let out a lusty yell to make their needs known.

A popular current theory on child-rearing advises parents not to pick up a baby every time he cries, because soon he will become spoiled. Actually, just the opposite happens. Babies who have been soothed at their every cry during their early months seem to develop into stronger, more self-confident children than babies who have been left to 'cry it out'.

When their needs are met during these first months, infants are learning that someone loves them. I don't know where the idea of ignoring a crying baby started, but I disagree with it. By meeting his needs, you are establishing a mutual trust between you and your child.

As he develops from infancy into the toddler years, this same trust will be increased as you interact with him. A good method of teaching your toddler that you trust him is allowing him to do simple chores.

As you are putting away the pots and pans, allow him to put one away. I realise that a two-year-old is not going to complete this task properly on his first try, but that's all right. The whole point is to teach him. Even though he places a pan on the wrong shelf in an upside-down position, compliment him. Let him know that you are very pleased about what he did.

'Thank you, Tony. That looks so nice. I like having you help me put things away.' Now Tony is learning two things. He is learning that you trust him, and he is developing self-esteem.

As you go through the toddler stage with your child, and you are trying to develop mutual trust, don't put too many temptations before him. I might suggest that you decorate your home as simply as possible. This serves two purposes. It makes house-keeping chores lighter, and it keeps you from constantly having to stop your child from picking up a favourite vase or knick-knack.

The result of having too many temptations sitting around the house is that you will find yourself yelling constantly because you will not always have your hands free to retrieve that cherished heirloom. Raising your voice to your child has its place, but save it for that place.

On a recent trip to a bookshop, I picked up a book on child-rearing written by a Christian author. As I thumbed through the pages, I couldn't believe what I was reading. The author was telling his readers that it is not only permissible, but actually good, for infants from four or five months to be reprimanded by a loud verbal instruction.

As I said, raising your voice is sometimes necessary, but not in the nursery of a six-month-old infant! An example of the need to raise your voice is if your small child darts away from you into a busy street. Then you would have to yell at him to save his life. However, if you had been raising your voice at him since he was an infant, he quite probably wouldn't have paid any attention to you, and would have continued on his way.

This same author went on to tell parents that incorrect disciplinary actions will do no harm to their children. He explained that children are flexible and tough and forget quickly. Is it any wonder that we have so many troubled children today, with child-rearing books like that on the market?

Swiss scientist Jean Piaget theorised that the development of learning in children is divided into four stages. The age-range of these stages is from birth to two years, from two to seven years, from seven to eleven years, and from eleven years on.

Two- to seven-year-olds believe exactly what their parents tell them. Indeed, until he gradually develops the ability to reason and question, a child takes almost everything his parents say quite literally. Let me give you this amusing, but true example.

Three-year-old Adam sat quietly in the back seat of the car with his eight-year-old sister, Leeann. They were on their way home from the Zoo.

'I'm really tired, Mum,' Leeann announced. 'And I have a headache.'

'I do too,' interrupted Adam. 'Right here on my knuckle,' he continued, pointing to the top of his head.

'Oh, Adam, your knuckle is on your hand, not on your head,' Leeann replied with childish impatience. 'Mum, would you please tell Adam that he can't get a headache in his knuckle?'

'I can, Leeann!' Adam insisted. 'Mummy always pats me on the head, and calls me a little knucklehead!'

You can readily see by the way Adam reacted to being lovingly called 'Mummy's little knucklehead' that it would be very easy to put negative thoughts into the minds of our children because they are so trusting and believing.

I am reminded of an incident that happened to a friend when he was a child. His Sunday School teacher told the class how very pleased she was to be able to teach them about Jesus. 'You know,' she continued, 'Jesus said, "Suffer the little children to come unto me."'

'You know what happened when she read that verse to me, Ross? I began to fear going to Sunday School because I thought I would be nailed to a cross and suffer as Jesus did.'

My friend was like Adam. He believed exactly what was said to him. The point I want to make here is that these trusting young minds are perfect for laying a strong foundation of spiritual values. These are the years when you are in the position to help your child expand emotionally, psychologically, and physically, as well as spiritually. It is absolutely crucial that you begin during these early years to develop your child as a whole person. Only the whole person can develop into a happy, responsible adult who will carry your spiritual values with him.

You can't fool children

Our children are very sensitive to the responses they receive from us. They know when we are telling them something just to keep them quiet; they sense that we're not really interested in them at that moment.

A busy, single mother of three sons told me of an incident which occurred in her home, and it points out just how well our children know us.

She works during the week, so Saturday mornings are reserved especially for the boys. They plan shopping trips or whatever else pleases them for these special hours.

On a particularly busy Saturday when she was helping them dress for a trip to the shops, the oldest asked for assistance in tying his shoes.

'Sit here on this chair and I'll help you,' she rather absentmindedly stated. He quickly complied, and as he hopped down with his shoes neatly tied, the second one asked the same favour, and then the third.

Realising that their mother wasn't really listening to them or paying any attention to them, the oldest boy untied his shoes and got back up on the chair. 'Will you tie my shoes, Mum?' he asked again. The second boy caught on, and untied his shoes, giggling quietly.

'Sure,' the mother said, and began round two of tying shoes. Before the third one could get up on the chair, the mother saw what was going on.

Given the pressures of daily life for this young mother of three, it is understandable that this amusing incident happened, and probably many others which were at times unfair for the boys. But she has developed a stable, good family unit, and so the significance of the negative incidents is minor.

As your child begins to mature to the point of not needing parental help with basic daily tasks, such as dressing or washing, it is very easy for you to fill this time with other jobs. The danger here is that soon you will find yourself spending less and less time with your child. Finding time in today's hectic world is difficult, sometimes seemingly impossible, but you must do it. You must steal away a little time each day for your child, even if it means giving up something that you wanted just for yourself.

The power of family togetherness

Today, more than at any other time in history, children are being influenced by forces outside the family. Many times children would rather spend time with the television than with you. Given what is offered on television, you have all the more reason to make the time to spend with your child.

Children just naturally want to learn. If you don't take the time or think you don't have the time to teach them, they will learn from someone else. They can be easily influenced by negative experiences outside the home. Research shows that even children as young as ten are experimenting with drugs and alcohol.

A good way to teach your child is to share your daily life with him. Make the stories fit his level of maturity, and share with your child events in your life as they happen. In this way, your child can learn through your experiences, and will more readily adopt your value system.

When you turn to God with your problems, let your child know the result of your prayers. Help him understand the comfort you receive by praying. This is an easy way for him to see God working in your daily life.

Another good way to teach a child is by reading to him. This accomplishes several things. You are giving him physical attention, because most children sit on parents' laps when story time comes around; you are giving him focused attention; and he is learning the contents of the book. Bedtime is usually the best time for reading, especially for working parents who must make every minute count.

Include stories other than Christian stories once in a while – especially stories that you make up yourself. My children still remember some of the stories that I made up for them. They almost always asked for one of 'Daddy's stories' before we finally turned out the lights.

Story time is one of the best times of the day for close fellowship with your child. I always advise parents whom I counsel to take a few minutes at bedtime with each child. Share the problems and the joys of the day, read to him, and then pray with him. You are not only enriching your child's emotional being, but you are enriching his intellectual being by choosing informative, educational, and interesting stories.

One parent told me that she wanted to read some of the classics, so she brought a couple of books home from the library. Then she invited her husband and fourteen-year-old son into the family room and offered to read these stories aloud. 'You can imagine a fourteen-year-old allowing his mother to read to him,' she said. 'But I struck a bargain with him. I told him that if he would listen for just thirty minutes, he could leave after that. Since it was a snowy day with nothing much else to do, he agreed. After the thirty minutes were up, I told him he could go, but he stayed.'

'Oh, well, as long as I'm here, I might as well listen to the ending,' he said, twisting in his chair. 'You'd probably be cross if I left anyway.'

This is a very wise mother. She not only enriched her own mind, but was able to bring her family together for a few winter evenings.

'We received many benefits from that experience, she concluded. 'We gained knowledge, and felt a keen sense of love and caring for each other as the reading sessions began to end in discussions of the stories we had read.'

This mother was lucky that her teenager became involved. Her story points out that children always have a need to feel loved by their parents, but as they mature, they also need to know that they can have their own way about some things.

Imagine the consequences of starting a family story time very early in the life of your child. There is no end to the benefits the entire family would receive from it.

It's never too soon to start

It is vital to the quality of your child's life that you spend time with him during his young years, when he is so willing and pliable. It is a time when he is more positive in his attitude towards you. *It is the very best time to teach spirituality.* Children very much enjoy learning spiritual things, and their attendance in Sunday School and church will continue their spiritual learning process. It will enhance what you are teaching them at home.

Early learning experiences remain with children throughout their lifetimes. And if you are consistent and caring, and always give your child unconditional love, he is well on his way to becoming a strong, self-confident teenager and adult.

Recently, an acquaintance of mine took a college course on the Old Testament. It had been forty years since she had attended summer Bible school as a child, but what she had learned forty years earlier had stayed with her.

One requirement on the course's final exam was to list the names of the Old Testament books and list the Ten Commandments. All this information was still with her from her Bible school lessons so long ago. Why? First, because she is a Christian and through the years has had this information before her, and secondly, because her mind was so pliable and receptive when it was first presented to her.

Parental spiritual values imparted to young children will stay with them over the years. I am reminded of the story of a prisoner of war from the Vietnam War who spent seven years in captivity in North Vietnam. As the weeks dragged into months, he began to pull Bible verses and hymns from his memories of Sunday School, just to keep his mind busy. Soon, this daily mental exercise helped him re-establish his relationship with God. This young captain had not been a practising Christian as an adult, but his background of Christian teaching sustained him through seven years of imprisonment.

Now your child may not decide to go back to college when he is fifty years old, and I pray that he will not be a prisoner of war. The object of telling about these two totally different people is to point out why it is imperative to the spiritual life of your child that you instil these values into him at an early age.

An interesting fact about learning is that the atmosphere surrounding the learning experience plays a great part in how well the information is received and retained. Children who are taught in a loving atmosphere not only remember the messages but usually can tell you something about the person or the location involved.

Recently, a young, single, working mother of two came into my office. 'You know, Dr Campbell, I am so afraid that I will not be able to give my daughters the same kind of life that I had. My mother didn't work, and she and I would spend a few minutes at the breakfast table each morning just talking.

'I can still remember that kitchen and my mother's attitude as she cleared the table for our visits. When I was very small, she spent these times teaching me the alphabet and my numbers. She taught me how to draw and use water-colours. As I grew older, she and I discussed everything from dress patterns to boy-friends.

'I think those mornings spent with her were some of the most beneficial learning experiences of my life.'

This young mother had made an appointment with me because she was worried about helping her children develop into productive, self-confident adults. I suggested to her that she take some time from her daily routine and reserve it for some focused attention for her daughters.

I agreed with her that it would be difficult, but once done, the benefits would far outweigh the extra effort spent. Focused attention in a loving atmosphere develops self-esteem, which is extremely important to the overall well-being of your child. You just can't give him too much positive, loving attention. And, of course, a happy, confident child is more than receptive to his parent's spiritual values.

As we close this chapter, and delve into the complexities of teenagers, I want to remind you again that these are the good years to lay a strong foundation. Children are like sponges. They tend to soak up all that surrounds them. So, it stands to reason that if they receive positive emotional, physical, intellectual, and spiritual experiences during these early years, they are more likely to grow up to be healthy adults in every sense of the word.

Unconditional love is crucial. Infants who receive little more than routine physical care are slower in reaching almost every milestone in their development. They are prone to developing emotional problems which inhibit their overall growth and limit their potential. They usually become angry, dissatisfied adults, incapable of accepting their parents' spiritual values.

If your child knows that he is loved, he is sure to want to follow your example throughout his life because of his respect for you. So, you must be very careful to be a good model in every area of his life, not just the spiritual area.

A few years ago, some friends of ours announced the arrival of a son after fifteen years of marriage. Of all the cards and wishes for happiness received, the following poem (which the father keeps on his desk) was the most appreciated. I do not know who wrote it, but I think it is a most appropriate ending to this chapter.

A LITTLE FELLOW FOLLOWS ME

A careful man I want to be –
A little fellow follows me;
I do not dare to go astray,
For fear he'll go the self-same way.

I cannot once escape his eyes;
Whatever he sees me do, he tries;
Like me he says he's going to be –
The little fellow who follows me.

He thinks that I am good and fine –
Believes in every word of mine;
The base in me he must not see –
The little fellow who follows me.

I must remember as I go,
Through summer's sun and winter's snow,
I am building for the years that be,
For that little chap who follows me!

8

Being reasonable with teenagers

'Be completely humble and gentle; be patient, bearing with one another in love' (Eph. 4:2).

When your child becomes a teenager, the day of reckoning is at hand. If you have consistently given him unconditional love and good examples, and taught by life and letter Christian values and principles, your responsibility to your budding adolescent will be much easier; continue being a good example, and keep his emotional tank full. These things, coupled with firm guidelines and patience, will see you and your child through the next four or five difficult years.

Your teenager is no longer the child who believes in every word you say and every move you make. Even though you have surrounded him with unconditional love, he is still going to question you. Yes, even if things have gone relatively well throughout your child's early years, the magic age of thirteen and the adolescent attitude of 'No! I won't do it!' arrive.

This is where firm, loving rules and patience come in. Your teenager is going to question you because the Creator gave him the drive to establish his own identity.

Gradually through these next few years, he will be learning how to leave the nest, and that isn't easy!

The other evening, I opened a newspaper to a picture of a father standing beside a six-foot sign which read, 'For sale, one set of encyclopedias – never used. Teenage son knows everything!' An amusing way to sell encyclopedias, yes, but the irony of the story is that your teenager *does* know everything, that is, practically everything about *you*; that is important.

By the time your child is an adolescent, he knows exactly how you think and what you think. He knows that you want him to adopt your spiritual values; he knows that you want him to do well at school; he knows what makes you angry; he knows what makes you glad.

Reducing school-work skirmishes

Nagging your teenager about anything that you want him to do will only succeed in making him angry. The angrier he becomes, the less likely he will be to do what you want. Your best option is to set firm rules that all in your household can live with, and help him abide by these rules.

For instance, homework must be done before bedtime. Your teenager knows that. It was the rule for his older brother, and he knows it is the rule for him. The worst thing you can do is start reminding him every half hour that he should do his homework. Flared tempers and poor homework are about the only results of this action. Telling him every few minutes that he must do his homework is like telling him that the earth is round – he already knows it, and he's going to get mighty tired of hearing it.

Imagine you and your son on his thirteenth birthday. All his guests are standing around waiting for him to blow out the candles, and you pull him aside. Putting your arm around his shoulder, you say, 'Son, the earth is round. I want you to remember that.'

'Yes, Dad, I already know that.' Then he will blow out the candles and try to continue with his party, but you interrupt him again and say, I know you know that, Son, but I just want you to remember it.'

'OK, Dad, I'll remember.'

The very next day, you approach your son and say to him again, 'Son, the earth is round. You got that?'

'Yes, Dad, you told me that yesterday.'

On the third day you say, 'Son, I want you to know that the earth is round.'

'Good grief, Dad, you've been telling me that for three days now. I know the earth is round. Do you think I'm stupid?'

Imagine how your son would feel if you told him that every day, week in and week out, month in and month out, year in and year out. Pretty soon he wouldn't be able to handle it any more. He would become destructively angry.

I'll tell you how we handle the homework issue at our house. Usually right after our evening meal, I pick a moment when the boys are in good moods, and ask them about their homework, saying something like, 'You fellows have any homework this evening?'

The answer is usually, 'Yes, plenty.'

'OK, just get it done before bedtime,' I reply, keeping the tone upbeat and pleasant. Then I don't say any more about it. If they need any help, I give it to them, but I don't give them the answers. I usually read through the information they've been given to study, and suggest where they might find an answer.

You are accomplishing two goals when you use this attitude with your child towards his homework. You are not making him angry by making an issue of the given situation, and you are teaching him that he must take the responsibility for his homework.

If you have been taking an authoritarian approach to your teenagers' school-work and switch to a more authoritative one, he might not pick up on the responsibility of doing his homework immediately. A 'dead time' will occur when neither your teenager nor you is taking the responsibility. This is usually the time when most parents drop the ball and stand over their child until the work is done. Don't give up.

Your teenager's grades may go down initially – but stand firm and be patient. When your teenager finally realises that his work is his responsibility, he will assume that responsibility.

In this area, the 25 percenters and the 75 percenters are really different. The 75 percenters try to get away with all they can, because they don't have the tendency to please. So if you handle the situation in the right way, the 75 percenter will feel no pressure, but do only what he has to to get by. The 25 percenter, on the other hand, will simply tend to pick up the total responsibility for his homework without an argument.

Take my David, my 75 percenter, for example. He is a bright young man, no learning disabilities, and yet from the age of twelve to fourteen, he got only average grades. But I didn't pressurise him, because I knew that one day he was going to have to take the responsibility for his own grades. I knew that it was impossible for me to *make* him responsible.

I realise that it is very difficult for parents to understand that they cannot make their teenager responsible, but they can't. The *only* way to create a responsible attitude in your teenager is not to take his responsibilities on yourself, but to be an example for your teenager to follow.

Back to David. Like a classic 75 percenter, his schoolwork was only average. Then one day, his sister asked, 'David, have you decided where you are going to college?'

'No, not yet,' he replied with little apparent interest. Shortly after, a friend told David that he was going to Yale the following year.

'Hey, that's great! What kind of grades do you have to have to get in there?'

'High ones,' his friend answered.

David thought about this. After a while a few more of his senior friends began discussing where they were going to college. David began to realise, on his own, that he was going to have to take the responsibility of improving his work if he was going to get to do what he wanted to do in life. Bingo! A gradual improvement started. He now does well and hopefully will for the rest of his life. Incidentally, he was accepted by the college of his choice.

That's how most 75 percenters learn responsibility. And it's the same pattern with spirituality, exactly the same.

If we keep telling our children every day that the earth is round, we are going to make them madder and madder and madder. We must avoid pressurising them; then they will adopt our values. We may not think so at times, but they *will* adopt our values in due time.

We must keep our teenager's emotional tank full, and keep living lives filled with spiritual values. And we must be patient with his outbursts. As we discussed in chapter 5, it is crucial that the adolescent keep his anger coming out of his mouth, and that he learns to exhibit his anger in more positive ways.

Failure is not a dirty word

The danger in teenagers knowing how and what we think is that we can transmit our negative attitudes to them just as easily as they learn our positive values.

For example, how do you accept failure when it happens to you, your spouse, or your child? Far too often, failure is seldom discussed in today's families. A typical reaction to failure is evident in the following story about Ryan's school report. His aunt had called in for a visit, and his mother proudly told her Ryan's grades. 'He has an A and two Bs, she told Aunt Janice. 'We're so proud of those grades.'

'But, Mum, I also had a...' but Ryan couldn't finish his sentence because his mother interrupted him.

'Ryan, would you mind getting your Aunt Janice more coffee? It's in the kitchen.'

What Ryan wanted to say was that his mother hadn't read the full report. He had a C on it too.

In Ryan's home, failure is not discussed. We gleam with pride as we discuss family and individual accomplishments, but little is said about failures. When we as parents discuss our own childhoods with our children, we recount with pride our youthful achievements, somehow never getting around to the mistakes we made.

Keeping in mind that teenagers know exactly what we think and what we expect of them, shouldn't we expect them to encounter failure once in a while? Shouldn't we expect them to learn to accept failure as well as success as a fact of life?

One very athletic, accomplished father brought to me a very unhappy, withdrawn, and depressed fourteen-year-old son. The father had told me over the phone that he was a single parent with custody of his son.

'He won't try anything any more,' the obviously self-confident father told me. The boy stood, head down, beside his father.

'Come on in and sit down. Let's get comfortable. Do you like sports, Don?'

'No, I'm not very good at any kind of sports. I played football for a while, but didn't do so well.'

'He just gave up,' the father broke in. 'I told him that he could never succeed at anything if he kept on being a quitter.'

I looked at the father and said, 'I'd like to talk to Don alone for a while. Would you mind waiting for him?' I opened the door to my office, and directed Don's father to the waiting room.

Tell me, Don,' I inquired as I sat down in a chair next to him, 'how do you and your father get along?'

'Not very well, Dr Campbell. You know, I can't seem to do anything right as far as he is concerned. It's not that he's mean about it; it's just that he doesn't want me to fail. He just throws up his hands and walks away when I do something wrong.'

'What do you enjoy doing? Tell me something that you like, Don – not necessarily something that your father would like you to do, but something that you like.'

Don sat quietly for a while, his gaze fixed on the floor. Finally, he looked up at me with tears in his eyes and said, 'I love playing the piano, but I don't think I'm very good at it. At least my dad never takes the time to listen to me. He wants me to play football, and I hate it. I'm so sick of trying to play football because Dad wants me to, and then listening to him after every game, telling me all that I did wrong.'

Don started sobbing. 'Dad would die if he saw me do this. He says men don't cry, just sissies. Well, Dr

Campbell, it looks like I'm going to be a failure as a man too, because I cry a lot.'

'Don, I know that your father loves you very much. I know that, because he wouldn't have brought you to visit me if he didn't care for your well-being. Tell you what, I'd like to talk with him for a little while, alone. Then the three of us will talk together, and start planning some happiness for you and your dad.'

'I don't know, Dr Campbell. You'd better not tell Dad that he has done anything wrong. He hates to lose at anything – he hates being wrong.'

The sad part about Don's dad is that he was losing in one of the most important jobs of his life – the job of being a father.

It took some time, but eventually this single parent began to realise what he was doing. 'I love that boy so much, Dr Campbell, that I just can't stand to see him fail,' he told me recently. 'I don't want him to have to go through the hurt.'

'But you see, Dave,' I said to him, 'if you accept Don's failures and allow him to do the same, soon he will understand that winning isn't all there is to life, and he'll be able to drop the guilt he feels when he loses. After all, sometimes you win and sometimes you lose. With this attitude, Don can soon begin to feel positive about himself and develop more of an adventurous "I-can't-wait-to-see-what's-out-there" outlook on life.'

After a few weeks of counselling, Don's depression began to lift, and his father, Dave, began to understand his own feelings about failure. Together, they learned to add a touch of humour to some of the losing situations in which they found themselves.

In Dave and Don Wilkins' case, Dave was not developing the whole child. He had been trying to meet Don's physical, intellectual, and spiritual needs, but had only depleted his son's emotional strength. How could Don, who was building up so much hate for his father, ever want to accept his father's spiritual values, or any other adult values for that matter?

Not long ago, I read of a famous sportsman who feels to this day that he is a failure. Can you imagine that – someone who has achieved major success feeling like a failure?

Apparently, when he was nine or ten years old, instead of praising his achievements, his father said, 'If only you had . . .' As the boy grew to manhood, no matter what he did, his father's criticism would come back to him.

Our Father in heaven accepts us with all our faults, never saying, 'Son, if you would just . . .' We must do the same for our children. Our teenagers know that we want them to win, but we must also let them know that we want them to be happy with themselves. They would never enjoy the exhilaration of winning if they could not measure it against a failure or two.

Teens today are tempted by anything and everything.

The only way they can come close to resisting these temptations is by feeling good about themselves. If we have filled their emotional tanks on a daily basis, they have a good start. As in the story of the father telling his son the world is round, we cannot tell our children every day that they can't do this and can't do that. So we must simply set up the ground rules and lovingly guide them to abide by them.

The importance of questions and doubts

Keeping up an honest, open line of communication is one of the best ways to help your teenager abide by your rules. Your teenager many times wants to talk to you about anything and everything – he just doesn't know how to get started. He sometimes wants to talk about moral issues, including sexual morality, faith, and family closeness. He values your input above peer input. He just doesn't know how to go about letting you know this.

Unfortunately, it is difficult for many Christian parents to discuss these things with their teenager. If you are having such a problem, go back to chapter 2 of this book and question your understanding of yourself. When you understand who you are and what makes you feel the way you feel, you will be better able to talk to your teenager.

I have found the very best place for talking is in a car. Every time our family goes on holiday my teenagers and I have some interesting conversations.

I just drive along, saying nothing. If there is anything a teenager gets uneasy about, it's silence – especially when a parent says nothing. Soon, he starts talking. If you are patient enough, and just answer his questions, not taking on a 'preachy' attitude, he will soon get to the real reason he started the conversation. It is during these times that your topics of conversation can run from why babies cry at two in the morning, to girl-friends, and to spirituality. Holidays are wonderful times to get to know your teenager.

Your teenager knows you want him to accept your faith, but he is uncomfortable with a restricting God. He needs to see God as One who liberates. He needs to know God's unconditional love and forgiveness. If you tell him only of the God who controls and disciplines, and you start demanding that he believe exactly the way you do, you will lessen the chance of him following your teaching. Your teenager must feel free to question and doubt, and arrive at some of his own answers about spirituality.

Your teenager is a wonderful human being. He has arrived at a traumatic time in life and needs your unconditional love and support to get him through these next few years.

When he looks in the mirror, he rarely sees a perfect image looking back at him. He sees someone who is too short or too skinny or someone who has a bad complexion or a brace on his teeth. Couple this with the fact that the Lord has given him the desire to start questioning his parents and anyone else who is in authority, and you have a very interesting person. A person who needs his parents' love and attention, but will not ask for it. A person who loves to have his mother tuck him into bed at night, but will defend to the death his right for privacy in his room. A person who refuses his father's offer to help him write his college application form, but finds his way to his parents' room when the lights are out, and timidly asks, 'Dad, do you have a minute? I want to ask you about a couple of things.'

A very wise minister accepted the challenge of giving a speech day address. He stood before the school and said, 'I really like teenagers. They are some of the finest people I know. I'm not going to stand here and tell you the world is out there just for the asking, or it's tough out there but you can do it, or life is what you make it. You already know all of that. I am simply going to say that I have faith in you. I know you will make a few mistakes, but I also know that you'll make a lot of right decisions.

'One of you could be a President or a Prime Minister. Another could own a large business. But more than that, what I want for each of you is to be happy with who and what you are, and I pray to God that this will be your main achievement.'

It takes a lot of time and patience to get your children through the rocky teen years. Pat and I still have one teenager at home, and another away in college, and as this minister said, they are among the finest people I know – and the most questioning, I might add.

We must not treat our teens like little children. They know far more about us and the world than we imagine. They are also still learning and seeking their way. Be open to their questioning. Listen to them, with respect for their opinions. Admit it when you don't know something; then say, 'Let's try to find the answer together.'

Allow your teenager to grow as he questions and seeks to become more independent. In a few more years, he too may be a parent. If you have allowed him to be himself, and to become what God wants him to be, he will be way ahead of the game in his own child-rearing.

9

The harm of negativity

'But you have neglected the more important matters of the law – justice, mercy, and faithfulness. You should have practised the latter, without neglecting the former. You blind guides! You strain out a gnat but swallow a camel' (Matt. 23:23–24).

Negative Christianity. Sounds like a contradiction of terms, doesn't it? After all, isn't Christianity love and peace and joy? Yes, but all too often, Christian parents use such negative *approaches* to teaching spiritual values to their children that they do more harm than good. Christian youth leaders have this same problem. They often, unintentionally, try to force the young people in their charge towards a Christian lifestyle instead of leading them to it. Steve, a youth minister I know, is a perfect example of this.

Steve is a fine young man who came straight from theological college to church youth ministry. Unfortunately, when he first arrived, he didn't know how to reach adolescents.

Steve is a very moralistic 25 percenter. Developing leadership qualities is more difficult for 25 percenters, so you can imagine some of the problems they would have leading a group of teens. Leading teens is difficult enough, even for 75 percenters! One of Steve's first encounters with his church youth group illustrates his dilemma.

Steve had invited the teens over to his home. As he stepped out onto the patio, he overheard several young people gossiping about a new member in the group.

'Ross, they were saying some pretty unkind things about that new girl,' Steve told me later. 'I immediately got angry, went back into the house to get my Bible, and proceeded to give them a long lecture. I was determined to get the upper hand, and teach these youngsters a thing or two about love and respect for other people.'

'How did they react to that, Steve?' I asked. 'Did they decide that they would never gossip again, and thank you for the advice?' I knew what Steve's answer was going to be. Of course, they didn't. These youngsters are naturally somewhat anti-authority, because they are teenagers. The party ground to a screeching halt. They all kept quiet for the rest of the evening – a classic adolescent reaction.

Why did the 25 percenters quieten down? Do you think they were angry? Yes, to some extent, but they were primarily hurt, and felt guilty that they had disappointed their leader.

How about the 75 percenters? They had the same reaction as the 25 percenters, but do you think they felt guilty? No way. The 75 percenters were so mad with Steve they couldn't see straight. The nerve of him trying to tell them what to do in that ultra-moralistic, authoritarian way.

Steve would have been much further ahead if he had known some basics about the personalities of youth. He needed to know why all the youngsters reacted essentially the same way, why they instinctively felt hurt albeit for different reasons.

To be harsh and negative with a youngster that age, or any child for that matter, will accomplish little. We must learn to be firm but pleasant, consistent but positive. These rules apply to every age group, but are magnified a thousand fold with thirteen-to-fifteen-year-olds. That's why we need to start learning as young parents how to handle our children, so that we will know what to do when they reach thirteen.

Steve, the youth minister, made a big mistake by coming down too hard on his young people. The success of the youth meeting was totally destroyed. However, Steve is a sensitive person. He knew immediately that he had done something terribly wrong.

'What should I have done, Ross?'

'Well, you shouldn't have been so negative and harsh. They already knew that they shouldn't gossip. How many times have they heard that before? Telling them not to gossip is like telling them the earth is round. Every teenager knows that the earth is round, but if you ignore that fact and continually tell them that the earth is round, you'll only succeed in making them angry.

The same thing holds true about telling them not to gossip. It just made your youth group angry, or left some of them with feelings of guilt.

They knew you were there. You caught them in the act. They were trapped, so they just had to sit there, waiting to see what was going to come out of your mouth. And if anything negative came out of your mouth, that was going to be it. So, you made a negative statement, and that was it. You lost them.

'What you should have said was, "Anybody want mustard on his hot dog?" In other words, you should have ignored their statements.'

The young people in that group knew their leader was upset. They could see it on his face. What he needed to do was to handle the situation meekly. *Meekness* doesn't mean 'weak'. *Meekness* means 'withholding your power', or 'holding your power in reserve'. Christ was all-powerful, but He always held it in reserve.

That is the way we want to interact with teenagers. We have the power (and they know it), but we don't have to use it. You see, once we have used our power, then we have nothing. There is no longer any reason for them to respect us.

Steve used his power, and the young people lost respect for him. If he had just held his power in reserve, and been pleasant, things would have been different. He could have played the game, 'I know what you are doing, and I know that you know that I know. And I know that you know better, so I am trusting you to take care of it yourself.'

Force is not the answer

You see, the opposite of passive-aggressive behaviour is learning to take care of things for yourself – to take personal responsibility. You cannot expect youngsters to grow out of the passive-aggressive stage and take responsibility for themselves unless you give them the opportunity. Any time you start yelling and screaming, or start lecturing, or become negative with your child or teenager, in his eyes you are telling him that what he has done wrong is *your* responsibility – not his. You are preventing him from taking responsibility for his own behaviour.

That is what Steve was doing. He was 'preaching' Christianity to his youth group in a negative way by chastising them for gossiping. He was trying to force them to think as he was thinking, and to make amends for their actions.

As a parent, you cannot force your values on your child, especially when he becomes an adolescent. Unconditional love and development of the whole child is the only way to keep him free from inappropriate anger, so that when he reaches adulthood, he will want to adopt your values. The responsibility will be his as to whether or not to follow your spiritual beliefs. He cannot be forced to make that decision.

The main theme of Christian child-rearing 'experts' of today is *parental power.* I am not saying that parents should not be in control, and should not set rules. I *am* saying that parental control should be based on love and understanding.

Fill your child's emotional tank. See to his intellectual needs. Help him take care of his physical needs. If you do these things, his spiritual needs will be fulfilled by your daily example and guidance. Displays of force and power will not be necessary.

Not too long ago, I heard a prominent Christian 'personality' speak on the subject of getting children back into our churches.

'When my daughter was five years old,' he began, 'she didn't want to wear a certain dress to Sunday School. So what do you think I did? I stuffed her into the dress, and made her wear it to Sunday School.'

Then,' he continued, 'when she was fourteen, and decided that she didn't even want to go to Sunday School or church, how do you think I handled that? Well, I used basically the same principle. I stuffed her into the car, and made her go to church!'

I couldn't believe my ears. Just imagine the anger that girl was feeling. Her feelings and needs obviously were not being considered; only her father's need to have her in church and Sunday School was being met.

Don't do this to your child. Don't 'stuff him into Christianity. It simply won't work. No one can be dragged, kicking and screaming, into the kingdom of God. If you have met your child's needs, and you really have a daily Christian lifestyle, your child will probably follow.

Recently, I had the opportunity to talk to Terri, an eighteen-year-old who was fifteen when her parents became Christians.

'I didn't think it was too bad,' Dr Campbell, she told me. 'I had always enjoyed going to church and Sunday School, so the change in my life concerning church attendance wasn't drastic. But there *were* drastic changes in our family life. We could no longer watch television, go to the cinema, or listen to rock music. My sister Lynn and I even had to stop wearing blue jeans or trousers.

'I went along with it. It was easier to do that than argue with Mum and Dad. But Lynn was a different story. She didn't want any part of it. She hated giving up her tapes and her favourite jeans. It must have been awful for her when Mum and Dad first started going to church. She really rebelled. I remember one time when my cousin invited us to go shopping. When we got far enough away from our house that my folks could no longer see us, Lynn pulled off her skirt and blouse in the car, and there she was in her favourite jeans and T-shirt. I nearly fainted.

'But gradually, Mum and Dad cooled off on some of their restrictions, and our lives got back to normal. I'm so glad things turned out the way they did. I don't think Lynn would have lasted. Now that I look back at it, we were held down so tightly that it was like wearing blinkers – you know, those things they put on horses to keep them from seeing anything except the centre of the road?

'When I went to college and got out into the world, I realised how very limited my view of life had been. I wondered how Lynn would handle getting away from home. I was afraid that she might be pretty wild and reckless for a while. And so, during my Christmas vacation, I was very glad to see that Mum and Dad had let up somewhat. I think it's the best thing they could have done for Lynn.'

Terri is an intelligent young woman. She realised what was happening to her sister and that her parents' demands were causing Lynn to go in the opposite direction.

Terri and Lynn's parents had become Christians when their daughters were at crucial ages. Parental stability is a must in the life of an adolescent. And here were Terri and Lynn's parents going through some tremendous changes. However, they soon saw what negativism was doing to their daughters, and backed off on some of their inappropriately harsh demands.

The film *Footloose* came to mind when Terri was telling me about her parents. I don't know if you have ever seen that film, but it is a perfect example of forcing teenagers into a specific lifestyle. The film has some rough language in it, but it serves only to portray exactly what teenagers will do if they are held down tight enough. They will rebel as the teenagers in *Footloose* rebelled.

The youngsters in the film were not allowed to listen to anything but classical music. They were not allowed to dance. They were not even allowed to read anything unless it was sanctioned by a church committee. It is not a true story, but it is a clear example of passive-aggressive behaviour and anger.

Teenagers are naturally going to question you and your actions. If you constantly restrict them, and force them to do exactly as you say, you will lose them. The teen years are very trying for parents, but if you have established a strong foundation of love and spiritual basics, you can get them through these years with a minimum of pain.

The gentle nudge of love

When my wife, Pat, and I lived in California, I met a man who said he and his wife were agnostics. They didn't believe that anyone could know God or His great love. They didn't even believe in love. He explained to me that love between a man and a woman was nothing more than physical attraction. He defined parental love simply as nature's way of assuring continuation of the species.

When their first child was born, this couple decided that if the child wanted to become a Christian, or wanted to form any kind of spiritual beliefs, he would be allowed to make that choice on his own. They vowed they would not interfere. Talk about a negative approach to Christianity! I felt so sorry for them and their son.

One afternoon, when their child was still an infant, Charles and I were talking. 'You know, Ross,' he said, 'Meg and I believe there is no such thing as love, but when we hold that baby, we get the strangest feelings. They are quite difficult to describe.'

I couldn't believe what I was hearing. I talked to him of God's love for human beings, and of human love for one another, but he just didn't want to hear about it. These were the most unusual people I had ever met.

A few months later, we happened to see each other again, and Charles had quite a revelation to share with me. 'Ross, do you remember when I told you about the feelings Meg and I didn't understand when we held our baby? Well, we know what they are – they are love!'

He went on to explain how he and Meg began to feel an emptiness in their lives. They joined a group that was starting a Christian church in their neighbourhood. 'We have been foolish a lot of years,' Charles admitted to me. 'We were both raised by parents who did not attend church regularly, but at least they did not deny God.'

'How about your son's spiritual life, Charles?' I asked. 'Are you still going to let him make that decision on his own?'

'Well, we won't force him into anything. We hope he will see how Meg and I feel about our faith and follow our example. We certainly do not want him to experience the void which was present in our lives during the past few years.'

Parents with a mistaken liberal attitude of non-influence can do as much damage to children as parents who try to force their spiritual beliefs on their children. It is dangerous to leave young people totally void of spiritual values. Luke 6:49 tells us what will happen if we do not give our children a foundation of unconditional love, and if we do not allow them to see us live our faith daily: 'But the one who hears my words and does not put them into practice is like a man who built a house on the ground without a foundation. The moment the torrent struck that house, it collapsed and its destruction was complete.'

When children are very young, it is easy to teach them about God. They are trusting and eager to learn. But as they enter the teen years, when they naturally become anti-authority about everything, spirituality is one more thing they question. Adolescents want to hear of a loving, forgiving God.

Just think about it. God placed in these wonderful young people the desire to question authority. So how can this desire be wrong? If you stamp out this natural need in 75 percenters, and only give them the doctrine of an angry God who will strike them down at any given moment, you will lose them for sure. This same doctrine taught to 25 percenters will frighten them, make them feel guilty, and in many cases, if it is strong enough, will do serious psychological damage. Children and teens need to know the loving, forgiving God as well as the God of justice and righteousness.

The error of doomsday teaching

We also must guard ourselves against the Pharisaical attitude with our children, especially our teenagers. The Pharisees were good men. They were educated and sincere, but they were so convinced of the absolute rightness of their point of view and their personal experiences that they could not accept even the Saviour Himself.

Parents are so used to being the major authority figures in their children's lives that they all too often overreact in negative ways to the questioning attitudes of their adolescents. They hand out guilt: 'How could you embarrass your mother like that?' (Imagine what that statement does to the 25 percenter.) They hand out 'hellfire and damnation' theology: That music is straight from the devil, and if you listen to it . . .' And they hand out doomsday teaching: 'If you don't do as I say, God will punish you!'

Some of the most serious cases I see are adolescents who have been 'threatened with God'. Parents who sincerely care about the spiritual life of their children but mistakenly take the negative approach actually can and do cause serious emotional problems.

'You'll-do-God's-bidding-or-die-and-go-to-hell' child-rearing will affect 75 percenters and 25 percenters differently. Seventy-five percenters will build up a sweltering anger, and go just as far in the opposite direction as they can just as soon as they can.

Twenty-five percenters, on the other hand, will be scared to death and develop strong guilt feelings. When constantly subjected to Christian negativism, they will become obsessive and injured psychologically. Instead of experiencing the comfort and love of God, they are likely to live in anxiety and fear. Their tendency to low self-esteem will dip even lower.

Sixteen-year-old Brian Starks was brought to me by his parents. I noticed immediately that he stayed very close to his mother. He also appeared to be extremely anxious. Brian's parents were unusually strict. They demanded that Brian and his fourteen-year-old brother, Brady, attend every church function with them.

As I began to counsel this family, I learned that Brady was an extreme 75 percenter. I could see that he was doing what his parents asked of him concerning church attendance, but I couldn't help but wonder if the Starks knew what was in store for them when Brady got a little older.

Gradually, Brian poured out his story. 'You see, Dr Campbell, I've always been jealous of Brady. He seems to be able to do anything. He's clever. He can really play a trumpet, and he's quite a runner. I guess that's where the trouble started.

'A couple of weeks before the big spring track event, Brady began to tease me. I hate it when he brags about everything he can do. He knows I'm not an athlete. Anyway, he just kept on teasing me. Finally, I told him to shut up and I put my fingers in my ears so I wouldn't have to listen. Then I prayed that Brady would get hurt somehow, just enough to keep him out of the event.

Two days later, he went out with some rough friends, and was in a car accident, and broke his leg. I felt awful. I knew that God was going to punish me for causing Brady to break his leg. It was right after that that I began to see the Grim Reaper at my bedroom door. Honestly, every night he was there. I thought that God had sent him to take me because of how I felt about Brady. It was awful.'

Brian suffered severe emotional damage because of the 'God-will-punish-you-if-you-don't...' attitude at home. It will take some time to help him through this, but I have hopes. I am always sad when I have a patient like Brian. He's an intelligent boy; he is just as musically talented as his brother, but his 25-percenter personality coupled with low self-esteem and a negative approach to Christianity has cost him a great deal.

Finding a middle ground

It is all too easy to veer into over-strict or over-permissive methods of dealing with your children. I know. Sometimes I think if I could just say no to everything my children want to do, then I wouldn't have anything to worry about. I would know where they were all the time.

I, and all other parents of teenagers, know that is impossible. We wouldn't really want it for our children. The middle road is where we must walk with our teens. After we have filled their emotional tanks, after we have become acquainted with each of them individually, then we can interact with them in significant and fruitful ways.

As I suggested to Steve, the youth minister, when you're tempted to 'lower the boom', just cool it and change the subject. Don't get all bent out of shape at their negative actions. The more negative reaction they get from you, the more negative action they will give you. Relax, fellow parents – enjoy your precious teenager – the negative and the positive. It won't be long until you will have a young adult in your house who'll say, 'Hey, how about me driving to church today, and cooking the lunch afterwards!'

10

Helping with 'special needs' children

'The King will reply, "I tell you the truth, whatever you did for one of the least of these brothers of mine, you did for me"' (Matt. 25:40)

James was a happy little child. From the time he was born until his seventh year, he didn't appear to have any unusual problems. He walked when he was supposed to. He talked at the right time. He was easy to potty train. To the casual observer and even to his school-teachers, he was an average, everyday child.

No one realised that he was memorising everything in order to get through each school day. But James' mother is a very sensitive person. She knew that some-one was wrong with her child; she just couldn't find anyone who would agree with her and tell her what it was.

Everyone said, 'Oh, boys will be boys.'

Still, she felt that something was wrong. When he was about eight, James began to be hard to manage. He often accused his mother of not really loving him. He argued with her constantly. She never felt that she was really communicating with him in a comfortable, maternal, child-bonding way.

Soon he started having academic problems. He just couldn't keep up with the other children, because learning was going from general concepts into an abstract level. James just couldn't seem to understand. He was still trying to memorise everything. And as a consequence, he was getting poor marks for his work.

Out of utter desperation, he put more and more energy into his school-work because he was basically a good child and wanted to do well. And for about a month or two, he did do very well. Then his total energy output completely exhausted him and his marks started to go down again. He panicked and became depressed.

James' concentration power waned. He couldn't remember simple tasks. He had a behaviour problem at school and at home. He even began having little quirky movements of his body, which were so well hidden that no one really recognised what they were. For instance, he let his hair grow long to make it seem he was flipping it from his eyes when actually he was nervously jerking his head. He shuffled his feet when he walked, making clicking sounds with his heels.

When he was about nine, he just couldn't keep up. His behaviour worsened; he became more defiant and harder to manage. He began to have temper tantrums. At this point, his parents brought him to me for counselling.

After we evaluated him, we found a very depressed child with extremely low self-esteem. He was self-critical, and felt unconsciously that nobody cared about him – that nobody really loved him.

He was filled with pent-up anger, especially towards authority. That passive-aggressiveness was exhibiting itself in misbehaviour toward the number one authority

in his life – his parents, and toward lower authorities –
his schoolteachers.

There were several reasons why James' marks were
going down. Number one, he had perceptual problems.
In other words, the information coming into his mind, as
it was processed, became somewhat distorted. Therefore, his studies were confusing to him. Secondly, he was
depressed, and depression can either create or intensify
a learning problem, because concentration is so difficult
for a depressed person. Thirdly, he was handicapped
due to his passive-aggressive behaviour. He was getting
back at authority by purposely, but unconsciously (that
is to say it was out of his awareness) doing badly. He
was getting back at the chief authority figures in his life
– his teachers and his parents.

This good-looking lad was doing poorly in every area
of his life. His learning difficulties had developed into a
total life problem.

His anti-authority was out of hand. Even at his age, he
was against everything his parents stood for, including
spirituality. He hated church. He hated his Sunday
School teacher. He was a constant disruption in his
Sunday School class.

We began treating James for depression. We counselled his parents to deal with his anger by encouraging
him to get it out from inside where it was destroying
him. And after taking these steps, we got him the academic help he needed.

After about four or five months therapy, he was doing
well. His behaviour had improved, and for the first time
in his life, he was able to be an affectionate child. For the
first time, his parents could really manifest their love
towards him, and he could accept it.

It was the first time he would let them love him,
because now affection was pleasant to him. He could

really believe that they meant it, because at last he was experiencing positive self-worth. He was beginning to develop a positive self-image.

We involved an educational therapist in James' treatment to take away the passive-aggressive, anti-learning attitude that had grown within him. This took the responsibility for his education out of his parents' hands. They were no longer involved in tutoring him.

First, the educational therapist created a positive personal relationship with James. Then she built on that relationship, and turned it into a positive attitude towards learning. She worked with his teachers at school, and got him the special education that he needed. She helped his teachers understand how to help him feel good about himself and continue his positive attitude towards his education.

With his anger subsiding and his depression lifting with therapy, James became less passive-aggressive and less anti-authority. Now, for the first time, he became pliable and receptive to spiritual values and teaching.

James is fortunate. His mother is a perceptive Christian who wouldn't take a 'boys will be boys' answer to her son's problem. And when the problem was finally diagnosed, both she and her husband made a concentrated and sincere effort to solve it. Now, with patience and time, and by Christian example in their daily living, James' parents will be able to help him develop into a well-rounded adult who will want to follow their spiritual values.

Insights on the handicapped

Children with perceptual handicaps or chronic medical problems have the same problems as average children.

The sad thing about these children is that along with the normal everyday problems, they must deal with their own particular handicap.

These special children tend to be anti-authority in every way, including anti-spirituality. They are prone to wrongdoing, even criminal acts. A recent study of perceptually handicapped males shows that adolescents with diagnosed perceptual handicaps are more likely to become involved in juvenile delinquency. The odds of being judged delinquent are 220 per cent greater for these young people than for their non-handicapped peers.

These children are usually quite depressed. Depression is the one thing that we desperately want to avoid in all children and teenagers. The more depressed a child is, the more angry he becomes. Depression produces anger. And angry children are much more likely to be passive-aggressive.

When we take this already depressed and passive-aggressive child, and superimpose the normal depression and normal passive-aggressive behaviour of adolescence, we have a child who is profoundly depressed and profoundly passive-aggressive.

Long before we can teach spirituality to this child, we have to help him through his anger and depression. We have to try to understand his particular problem, and let him know that we love him unconditionally. Then, and only then, are we on the road to helping him understand his need for a personal relationship with Jesus Christ.

Our educational system has become more adept at identifying the child with perceptual problems. We are now in a better position to understand and help this child, but there are many other people who are still unaware of his dilemma. Unfortunately, they think the perceptually handicapped child is lazy or stubborn or just plain stupid. They do not understand that the child does not perceive or take information from his environment through his senses to his mind in the same way that an average child does. This child's understanding of the world around him is distorted due to a neurological problem usually present from birth.

Imagine the child's dilemma. He has trouble academically which creates anger in him. This anger is created from two sources – the child himself because he cannot understand the work, and the parent who nags because he is not doing the work. Therefore, he doesn't feel understood or loved by his parents, causing more anger and depression. He doesn't get along with his peers, so the end result is an extremely depressed child. By the time he reaches adolescence, this depression will probably result in severe behavioural and emotional disorders.

It is critical that the parents of special children fill their children's emotional tanks daily. All too often, a perceptually handicapped child has great difficulty understanding our positive feelings for him. For this reason, he needs extra helpings of love, physical contact, and focused attention from the important people in his life.

To convey love, we use eye contact (visual perception is needed), physical contact (an overwhelmingly complex sense), and focused attention (requires seeing, hearing, and the possession of a certain amount of logic). If a perceptual problem exists in any of these areas, the child's understanding is distorted, thus creating overwhelming frustration for both the child and us, not to mention lack of communication.

A shared suffering

Not only does the handicapped child experience pain and frustration, but so do his parents. They usually run through a whole gamut of emotions before they can come to grips with the fact that their child is suffering from learning disabilities.

They begin by denying that the problem exists, which, in itself, heightens the child's frustration. They take the child to therapists for second and third opinions; they isolate themselves, thinking no one understands their pain.

Then they start feeling guilty. They feel that they caused their child's problem. They question their child-rearing methods: 'Were we too strict?' 'Were we too easy-going?' Anger is usually next. 'We're surely not the guilty ones in this situation. We've done everything we can. It must be that the doctor doesn't know what he's talking about. And this neighbourhood and this school – nobody knows what's going on!'

Parents finally start blaming each other. When the child sees this, he experiences fear and more depression.

At this point, the parents who really want to help their child will commit themselves to counselling. Here they will learn that there is still hope. They will find how to deal with their child's specific problem, and how and where to reach for educational assistance. Soon they will be removing some of the reasons for depression and anger from the child.

Rick, a handsome, dark-eyed ten-year-old, walked into my office, keeping well ahead of his mother, Joyce.

'I do hope you can find out what is wrong, Dr Campbell,' he said, 'because my mother worries a lot about me. Sometimes she even cries. I hate to see her do that. Maybe you can tell her something today that will make her feel better.'

Joyce was a single parent. Her husband left her just a year ago – the same time that Rick's problem began to surface at school. She was a sincere mother who tried to do everything she could for Rick. The teacher at Rick's school had told her that there really wasn't anything wrong with him. Rick's only problem, she said, was too much maternal attention.

'You're trying too hard to compensate for the absence of his father, Joyce, and you're spoiling him. He can read. He's just being stubborn to get all the attention he can,' the teacher stated firmly.

And so, armed with this information, Joyce gave Rick less attention, and tutored him every night after school. Nothing worked. His behaviour problem increased and he failed his exams at school. It was at this point that Joyce brought him to me.

After we had evaluated him, I called Rick and his mother into my office.

'Well, Rick, we'll just see what we can do to make your mother and you feel better.'

I went over the tests with them, and showed them that Rick had a visual perceptual problem and found it slightly difficult to pay attention. 'But don't worry, you're a bright boy, Rick. And I doubt if you are too stubborn to try to read. I think you're all right, and I'm going to try to help you.'

Rick's eyes lit up. 'Listen to that, Mum. I'm not stupid after all. You don't have to worry so much about me now.'

In Rick's case, he was feeling responsible for his mother's unhappiness. Joyce was wise to seek counselling. In doing so, she became aware of his true problem, and he was able to get rid of some of the guilt which also caused some of his depression.

Joyce had gone through all of the frustration that other parents encounter when dealing with a perceptually handicapped child. All of these feelings are normal. The problem with them lies in the possibility that some parents will stay in one of these phases too long, increasing the child's negative feelings of self-worth.

The problems of most perceptually handicapped children can be minimised if they are caught soon enough. James and Rick are fortunate because their parents caught their problems in time. Catching the problem 'in time' means catching it before the child becomes an adolescent. When the problem remains untreated by the age of thirteen, fourteen, or fifteen, the child usually experiences much more than academic difficulties. His problems almost always include drugs, sex, lying, stealing, running away, or even suicide attempts.

In telling the stories of James and Rick, I have tried to help you understand the dilemmas of perceptually handicapped children. It is obvious that their problems, coupled with the normal rough spots of life, can pose a real threat to their overall well-being, including their spirituality. Developing these learning-disabled children into whole children takes more time, patience, and understanding, but it *can* be done.

Children with chronic illnesses

Perceptual difficulties are not the only problems that affect the behaviour of children. Chronic medical problems can also create emotional and behavioural controversies. We can become so involved in the daily physical needs of a chronically ill child (daily correct doses of insulin, for example), that we overlook his emotional needs.

As physically impaired children grow older, they can become increasingly bitter about their disease or handicap. They become angry with caring parents, because the parents have inadvertently replaced the natural giving of love with daily medical attention. These children can become defiant, not only towards their parents, but towards all authority.

Take Linda Walker, who was described to me by her mother as 'a fussy baby from the beginning'.

'We tried everything we could think of, but we just couldn't seem to make her happy. Then, when she was three, the paediatrician discovered that she had a chronic heart defect. From then until now, our life with her has been one trip after another to specialists.'

'How is her physical health at the present?' I asked the Walkers.

'It's stabilised right now,' Paul Walker answered, 'but her pregnancy certainly won't help her.'

'I see you have one other child, a son,' I noted as I scanned their file. 'How is his health?'

'Oh, it's just perfect,' Mrs Walker answered. 'We're so proud of Jeff. He's a fine athlete, and quite an accomplished pianist.'

'Has Linda ever developed any hobbies?'

'No,' her father answered. 'We've been so busy attending to her health problems that we never had the time to do much else with her. Don't get me wrong, it's not that we didn't want to. She has always been such a sickly child that we never could talk her into doing anything other than going to school. And now, here she is pregnant. I guess it's too late.'

'At least she is going to marry the father of the baby next week,' Mrs Walker added. 'Maybe that'll make her happy. We've done all we know to do, Dr Campbell, but we certainly went wrong somewhere. She's been very depressed lately. I'm relieved that we talked her into coming to see you. I do hope you can get through to her. She's in a sorry frame of mind to start a marriage.'

'Why don't both of you wait outside, and let me talk to Linda,' I suggested as I ushered the Walkers toward the door.

Curled up in a chair in the corner of the waiting room was Linda – seventeen years old and pregnant.

'Would you like to come in, Linda?' I asked as I walked over to her.

'Why not? That's what they brought me here for.' As she sat down in a chair in my office, she said with a frown, 'I don't know what good my being here is going to do. You can't change things.'

'You're right, Linda; I can't change things, but maybe in time I can help you to change the way you feel about some things.'

When Linda began to open up, my suspicions were confirmed. She was a classic example of the chronically ill child whose parents spent so much time caring for her physical needs that they forgot about her emotional needs.

'Jeff can do this – Jeff can do that! That's all I ever heard. "Let's go to Jeff's match, Linda. It'll do you good to get out of the house. Let's go to Jeff's piano recital, Linda. Maybe you'll decide to start taking piano lessons." And you should see the grades Jeff gets – all are A's. I got C's and I think that's quite good enough.'

I've just started counselling with Linda, but I feel she can be helped with her depression. I know that her parents love her. They didn't realise that they had been substituting emotional attention with medical attention. Linda's poor schoolwork and her pregnancy both were subconscious acts of defiance against this seeming indifference.

There are other reasons why chronically ill children become depressed and bitter, but in my years of treating these children, I have found two principal pitfalls for parents. They are the ones we discussed: a substitution of medical attention for emotional fulfilment, and lack of control and firmness.

Parents of chronically ill children feel such pity and sometimes even blame and guilt that they do not try to control the child's behaviour normally. This results in a manipulative child who will use his illness to control his parents.

As we saw in the story of James, success can come. If the problem is detective and help is obtained in time, both the parent and the child will benefit beyond measure. The child will not only be able to handle his education, but will be able to feel worthy of the love of his parents and friends.

Once he has gone through the normal anti-authority years of adolescence, he will follow his parents' spiritual values, not only because they want him to, but because he wants to.

11

The disintegrating family

'Better a meal of vegetables where there is love than a
fattened calf with hatred' (Prov. 15:17).

Mark Johnson sat across from me, impatiently tapping his
well-manicured fingers on the arm of his chair. He was
obviously a person of financial means. His overall appearance and his mannerisms were flawless. His lovely wife,
Brenda, whose attire and behaviour appeared equally perfect, seemed just as impatient.

'Sorry to keep you waiting,' I began as I finished scan-
ning their file. 'I see you are a lawyer, Mark. My son-in-
law is also a lawyer. I really admire you fellows. There
appears to be no end to the details you have to pursue
before finally presenting your case.

'And how are you, Brenda? Is the world of children's
clothing keeping you busy?' Brenda is the owner and
manager of a fashionable children's clothing shop.

Both Mark and Brenda are Sunday School teachers
and are active in a large church. All outward indications
give them the mark of a very successful couple. They
have two children, a daughter Amy, aged six, and a son
Todd, aged eleven.

So why are they sitting in my office?

'Dr Campbell, we need to talk to you about Todd. Six months ago, he seemed to change from a normal boy into a quiet stranger who was angry all the time. He constantly found excuses to stay away from us. Goodness knows, we have very little time to spend with each other as it is. Mark's work load seems to be increasing daily, and my shop keeps me past 10 o'clock many evenings,' Brenda began.

'Yes, Dr Campbell,' Mark agreed, 'and you'd think that the children would appreciate all that we can give them because we work all those long hours. Amy hasn't given us any trouble, but Todd is a different story.

'A few nights ago, some of his older friends brought him home drunk. What in the world would make an eleven-year-old who has everything do such a thing?'

'We're shocked beyond words.' added Brenda. 'And to make matters worse, he's disrupted the entire household with this silly trick. Mark had to reschedule his clients, and I'm taking time away from the shop to keep this appointment with you. Don't get me wrong, we want to help Todd, but we can't understand why this happened. As Mark said, we've given him everything, and this is the way he thanks us.'

'What in the world is wrong with our boy, Dr Campbell?' Mark said as he began to pace the floor. 'Or could it be us? I can settle legal matters of the most important people in this city, but I can't make my own son happy.'

Yes, what is wrong? Why would an eleven-year-old drink alcohol on a regular basis? I found, as I counselled the Johnsons, that Todd had drunk alcohol many times, but was able to conceal it from his parents before now.

Why is there an increase in the number of ten- and eleven-year-olds who are trying drugs and alcohol?

Why did 57 per cent of a group of fourteen-year-olds in a recent survey state that they had drunk alcohol more than once in the past twelve months?

My answer is because family life is deteriorating. Parents are too busy to make special time for their children. Young people are receiving little or no love and attention.

Their emotional tanks are empty. They do not feel loved. As a consequence, they are succumbing to negative peer pressure for attention and acceptance.

Stresses and strains in the home

It takes a lot out of parents to keep both career and family intact when both of them are working. And far too many parents just don't have the desire or the perseverance. Therefore, something slips, and it is almost always the quality of family life.

Divorce is usually quoted as the big offender. But that isn't always true. A single parent can be supportive and give the child loving discipline and training just as two parents can, sometimes even better. (I don't advocate divorce, but sometimes it is necessary for the health and safety of all involved.)

Mark and Brenda Johnson are prime examples. They are so busy with their careers that they don't even know where their son is. They put up a front of the perfect parents. They are successful financially; they are active in their church; and they have two lovely, but very unhappy children. Yes, we discovered six-year-old Amy is an angry child.

The key to a successful family is not whether or not it has two parents; it is whether or not the parental focus is on the right things for the child. A single parent can raise a child and guide him through the 'terrible teens' into responsible Christian adulthood just as two parents can. I have seen it occur countless times.

We don't have to look too closely to see giant cracks in the framework of the family unit as we know it. Even Christian parents like Mark and Brenda Johnson are not immune. The overwhelming desire for material possessions fails to leave time for the basic needs of children.

Christian parents sometimes rationalise their absence from their children by taking them to church and Sunday School every Sunday. In so doing they think they are filling the spiritual needs of their children, but they are not. As we learned in chapter 5, young people like Amy and Todd Johnson are too angry to accept any kind of spiritual teaching. Their emotional tanks are so empty that they feel unloved and try to 'get back' at their parents in any way they can. Todd Johnson chose to experiment with alcohol.

Quality time, quantity time – those expressions are often heard. The basic term is neither quality nor quantity, but just *time*.

'Hey, Mike, I don't have to be at my meeting until 7. Want a game of table tennis?'

'OK, Dad.'

'Lisa, you need a new pair of shoes. Shall we go to the shops and have a pizza afterwards?'

Spending time with your family – getting to know your children, telling them you love them, and letting them know they are important to you – these are the important issues.

Some of the real worries about the breakdown of families are solved by the time we invest in each other. Commitment to Christian family structure is based on the idea that we love each other. It hinges on the fact that we care about the emotional, physical, psychological, and spiritual needs of all family members.

It doesn't really matter what we do, or exactly how we measure the time we spend with our children. We can play table tennis or go shopping or just go for a drive, as long as we let our children know that they are loved. It is worth conquering the outside and inside influences that tend to separate parents and children.

Loving times shared by a family, regardless of how large or small or how many parents it has, add to the strength of the individuals and the family as a unit. If I asked you to recall a happy personal family experience, what would it be? Do you look back with fond memories on the *things* your parents gave you, or do you more vividly remember shared personal moments?

I have a friend who tries to make breakfast the highlight of the day for her family, because she had such a happy time at the breakfast table when she was a child. She says that everyone around the table talked and shared plans for the day ahead, including her parents. Above all, she remembers a feeling of closeness, a feeling of belonging and being loved.

Maybe you remember a time when your mother made dolls clothes for you, or a long walk you took with your dad. Perhaps an eleventh birthday party or a special family joke comes to mind. All of these memories add to your sense of security and acceptance. And most are of simple times made special by the love and togetherness of the people involved.

Keys to keeping together

What can you do as a Christian parent to prevent your family from falling apart? There are no simple, pat answers to this question, but that doesn't mean the goal is not achievable.

As I counselled Mark and Brenda Johnson and Todd, they began to find ways to change some of their habits.

Mark discovered that if he could take time to attend counselling sessions for his son, he could surely make time to enjoy his son, and possibly prevent the need for future counselling. Both Mark and Brenda realised that their present pace was damaging not only Todd, but their daughter Amy.

They began to allow the teaching of their faith to show in their daily lives. Before Todd's problem surfaced, Mark and Brenda were only Sunday Christians. This is a very dangerous message to give to children. It almost always ensures that the children will not understand their parents' spiritual beliefs because of the double message.

It takes time to correct the old, established patterns, but the Johnsons are determined to make a better life for themselves and their children. They were faithful in attending the counselling sessions, and soon brought their family together again. They learned how to give the love that they felt deep inside for Todd and Amy, but didn't take the time to show.

Look at your children as individual whole beings. Don't merely satisfy their desires for material things, and then expect them to grow properly. Don't take them to church on Sunday, and then leave spiritual values out of their lives the rest of the week.

Be mindful too of your child's emotional needs. If he is not loved, he cannot feel worthy of anything else you give him or try to teach him. The plight of an angry child is sad indeed.

I cannot stress enough the importance of getting to know your child on an individual basis. Not long ago, I talked to a young father who is concerned that his son is going to be 'too soft'.

'I'm going to take that boy to some karate classes,' this man said to me. 'He has to learn that he can't go through life being nice all the time. He has to learn to stand up for himself.'

'Is he pretty excited about it?' I inquired.

'I haven't told him yet nor have I told his mother about it. If she had her way, this kid would be a big sissy. She thinks every disagreement can be settled by talking. I know better. A child, especially a boy, has to learn how to fight and defend himself if he is going to make it in this life.'

The child who is going to be the recipient of karate instruction is a quiet 25 percenter who loves tennis, and music. He may suffer as he tries to live up to his father's macho expectations. He will definitely suffer as he listens to his parents argue over how he should be raised. If this father will just take the time to know his son, and love him unconditionally, not only their relationship but the whole family will benefit.

Entire families pay the price when there is no communication. This father should honestly examine himself and his attitude toward his wife, then work to reopen the lines of communication. The two need to agree about child-rearing in order to make the way smoother for their son. The boy will benefit from this atmosphere of love and affection between his parents, and the entire family structure will improve. Unconditional love allows for free and honest expression.

Above all, take time to show your children love. They never outgrow the need for affection from you. One of the most poignant stories I've ever read along this line was in a recent edition of *Reader's Digest*.

Carmen, a wealthy friend of Rhea Zakich, author of the communication-building Ungame, recalled that when she became six, her mother told her she was now too old to be kissed. The little girl felt so bad that every morning she went into the bathroom and looked for the tissue on which her mother had blotted her lipstick. She carried it with her all day. Whenever she wanted a kiss, she rubbed the smear of lipstick up against her cheek.

Not until she was forty-three years old did Carmen admit that her mother's denial of a real kiss had been one of the most hurtful moments in her life.

Now is the time to avoid those hurtful moments. If you have some weak areas in your family, whether it be a single-parent or a two-parent family, look at them as objectively as possible, and begin to repair them. Be willing to make sacrifices for each other; exhibit unconditional love; become genuinely involved in interests of family members – all these things help unify family life.

Special times for special people

Not long ago, I read with great interest the story of a devout Christian family. A young student, who recognised how much his mother had influenced all the family in a very positive way, wrote to her, asking about her methods of educating and training her children. He wanted to impart this information to the young parents to whom he was ministering.

This woman, who raised ten children to adulthood, wrote back that her main goal was to teach her children to respect God and each other. Some of her specific rules were:

1. No child spanked twice for the same offence was ever upbraided for it afterwards.
2. Each child was to respect the property of the others, even in the smallest matter.
3. Every act of obedience was commended and frequently rewarded.
4. Promises were strictly kept.

But the most important thing that this mother did for her children was to set aside a special hour for each of them on an individual basis. She recognised the child's need to spend time alone with her.

Her husband was gone a great deal, so it was up to her to see to the spiritual and emotional needs of her children. She also taught in Sunday School and led devotions, besides caring for her large family on a daily basis.

Is it any wonder that the student son was proud of his mother and wanted to share her methods with his parishioners? And this mother was truly rewarded by the Christian lifestyle of her son, for his name was John Wesley and she was Susannah Wesley. Their correspondence took place in 1732. Susannah Wesley knew instinctively then what I am suggesting to you today: develop the child's whole personality, and give him focused attention.

Mrs Wesley's daughters, as well as her sons, were taught to read and were educated under her expert instruction. She not only encouraged Christian values, she lived them daily. Love and understanding were ingrained to such a degree that Susannah Wesley was always a close friend to all of her children, especially John.

Susannah Wesley's family was for all intents and purposes a single-parent family, and yet she did not allow it to deteriorate. She took the time to give her children focused attention; she let them know that she loved them; her spiritual values were evident in her daily life.

I know it is difficult. I know parents tire. I am a parent too. There have been many times when I would have found it much easier to fall asleep on the sofa than attend a football match, but I was always glad I went to the game.

If you don't work to keep your family together, your children will not have a good example to follow when they try to establish their own families. The love and respect you give to your children will be returned a hundredfold. By the same token, the damage received in an unloving family will manifest itself over and over in families to come.

I counselled a couple who were about thirty and thirty-five years of age, and were contemplating a divorce.

'I just can't take it any more,' Nancy White said. 'Randy is too distant. I have lost all feeling for him, because he is so cold. He never was one to do much touching, but now it's awful. I don't think he loves any of us.'

Randy White sat silently listening to his wife's words. 'He doesn't even hug the children any more,' she continued. 'Because he is a pilot, he has very little time to spend with us, but when he's home, he shows us no affection.'

'I can't help it, Nancy,' Randy blurted out. 'Nobody ever touched me or said "I love you" or displayed any signs of affection in my family. I can't do it. I don't know how.'

Unfortunately, this couple divorced, but Randy later returned for more counselling. As I got to know him, I learned that he felt totally unworthy of giving or receiving love because of the way his parents treated him.

Raising a child is like throwing a small stone into a still pond. The results of how you treat or mistreat your child will echo for years and years into countless families, just as the rings from that stone ripple across the water.

Whether it be play or work, the time you spend with your child is priceless. Then, and only then, can you get to know him and offer him your love and understanding. You cannot give this love to him over the telephone or on a note magnetically attached to the refrigerator door. These things are fine in their place, but one-to-one attention is imperative.

12

Bringing up children – and common sense

'Finally, brothers; whatever is true, whatever is noble, whatever is right, whatever is pure, whatever is lovely, whatever is admirable – if anything is excellent or praiseworthy – think about such things. Whatever you have learned or received or heard from me, or seen in me – put it into practice. And the God of peace will be with you' (Phil. 4:8–9).

Al and Brad Stockman eased their dad's car around the corner onto Pinewood Drive.

'Al! Turn out the lights now,' Brad said to his brother. 'If Dad sees us coming home this late, we're dead. The first time we're allowed to take the car out, and we're two hours late getting back.'

Al Stockman pulled the car slowly into the drive. 'Open the garage door, Brad,' he whispered to his younger brother.

Brad slipped quietly from the car and lifted the door. He guided the car into the garage, and then cautiously dropped the door back down.

'Do you suppose Mum and Dad could still be up?' he whispered to his brother.

'I hope not, Al answered. 'It's 1 o'clock in the morning, and we were supposed to be home by 11. If we can just get past the kitchen without bumping into the table, we'll be all right.'

The boys crept up the back steps, carefully opened the door, and tiptoed halfway across the kitchen. Suddenly the room was flooded with light.

Sitting at the kitchen table was their mother, sipping a cup of coffee. Dorothy and Jack Stockman had been waiting up for the boys. Jack sat back down beside Dorothy.

'Now we're in for it!' Al murmured, as he jabbed Brad in the ribs. 'Don't say a word, just take my lead.'

'Well, boys,' their father began, 'it seems you're a little past your curfew.'

Dorothy Stockman wrapped her blue housecoat more closely around her shoulders. 'Are you two OK? Where in the world have you been? We've been worried about you.'

'That's daft, Mum,' Al growled. 'Gosh, I'm old enough to drive, and you're treating me like a baby.'

'We really couldn't help it,' Brad interrupted, seating himself at the table with his parents. 'We came out of the theatre in time to be home at 11, but the right rear tyre on the car was completely flat.'

'I'll handle this, Brad,' Al snapped at his younger brother. Turning to his father, he said, 'Yeah, and when we opened the boot to get the spare, it was flat too! Then we had to call a garage for a tow so that we could get the car to the garage and put air into the tyre. I thought he'd never get there, and then the man at the garage was as slow as molasses in January. It wasn't our fault that he took so long.'

'You're right, Al, it wasn't your fault,' Jack Stockman agreed, 'but surely you knew that your mother and I would be concerned when you didn't arrive home on time. Didn't you think of that? Why didn't you phone us and let us know what was going on?'

'Dad's right, Al. We should have called.'

'I don't think it's any big thing, Al retorted. 'We're home, and everything is OK. Why all the fuss?'

'Yes, boys, you're home and everything is fine, but your mother and I didn't know everything was fine an hour ago. I think two weeks without the privilege of driving that car will help you to remember how to use a telephone, and let us know when things like this happen. Let's get to bed now.'

Jack and Dorothy Stockman are fine Christian parents. Their spiritual values have been evident to their sons from the beginning. They know their boys. They have taken the time to get to know each one as an individual.

They knew they should allow Al to vent his anger about the flat tyre. They also knew Brad would probably need to be encouraged to discuss the situation further. So they handled things accordingly.

In another family, the same happening might be handled differently, depending on the personalities involved. In yet another family, the late arrival of two teenagers might create such an upheaval that one or both of the parents might feel it necessary to go outside their home for help in dealing with the angry words which almost always result when teens misbehave.

The point I want to make here is that there is no clear-cut answer to any given problem. When you are working with children, the accent lies not on the magnitude of the problem, but rather on the reaction of the parents to the problem. If you react to problems in your household by seeking outside help, more power to you. A wise parent seeks help.

Parents can't do it alone

As a Christian parent, you must realise that despite your wishes to the contrary you can't do it all by yourself. Many times you will need help. Don't feel guilty and consider yourself a failure as a parent when this happens.

Outside help is almost always needed when dealing with the spiritual lives of your children, especially your 75 percenters. If you try to guide them toward spirituality by yourself, you stand little chance of success because of their natural tendency to rebel against parental guidance.

I go outside our home for help. I have been a Christian for over thirty years, and a physician for almost twenty, yet I realise that I cannot lead my children to Christianity all by myself.

First, I look to the church. I would change churches if I had to for the sake of my children. A church with a good youth leader is an absolute must for teenagers.

David, our oldest son, was one of the more difficult children to bring to Christ. He is a muscular, macho athlete who, like others of his breed, saw Christianity as kids stuff. So, when David became an adolescent and developed an anti-church attitude, we were grateful that our youth leader was a former football player, six-foot-four, weighing well over 14 stones. He and David became good friends. We couldn't have been more fortunate. Who is better qualified to teach a macho kid about Christ than a macho adult?

If you need it, please don't be too proud to ask for help. It could make the difference between Christianity and a life void of any spiritual values for your child.

I read a research questionnaire which asked Christian families about this very thing. The families were given a list of situations, and asked where they would be most likely to turn for help. The situations given were:

1. If my child got involved with drugs or alcohol.
2. If my child became sad and depressed for a long period of time.
3. If my child had a lot of questions about sex.
4. If my child got into trouble a lot.
5. If my child hung around too much with friends I did not like, I would go to _____ for help.

Most of the families agreed that they would ask for help, and the following sources were given in this order:

1. Relatives
2. Friends or neighbours
3. A priest or minister
4. A medical doctor
5. A teacher or school counsellor
6. A community agency or social service

All of these sources are good and should be sought when the need arises. You cannot be a superparent and solve every problem you encounter with your child in exactly the right way.

The unique pressures of Christian parents

All caring parents love their children, but Christian parents often feel the pressures of child-rearing more than others. They try very hard to do a perfect job. They want the very best for their children; they want them to be accepted in society; and most of all they want them to mature into fine Christian adults.

Many Christian parents feel that their children should be perfectly behaved at all times, and take on a great deal of blame and guilt when anything negative mars this unrealistic expectation. They take their responsibility as parents so seriously that in the long run they damage instead of enhance the lives of their children.

You are *not* perfect. One of the pillars of the Christian faith is that no one is perfect but the Lord Himself. That believers have the freedom to fail, and to be forgiven, is a gift from God. Use it wisely. Where you spot weaknesses in your interactions with your children, seek help.

An obvious example of parents who think they should raise perfect children is church leaders, especially clergy. We have all heard of the 'preacher's kid' syndrome. These poor people think they must do everything perfectly and allow no one to see a flaw in their family structure – after all, they are teachers of the Word of God.

Children living in this kind of atmosphere really suffer. They are pressurised by their parents to lead strict spiritual lives, and their peers and the community exert more pressure on them. Twenty-five percenters in the homes of Christian leaders can be damaged by feelings of guilt and suppressed anger, while the open rebellion of the 75 percenters can be spectacular indeed.

One Christian mother, the wife of a Protestant minister, gave me some insight into the life of the 'preacher's kid'.

'I'm telling you, Dr Campbell, you wouldn't believe how I used to expect my poor children to be the 'perfect kids' every day of their lives. When they were young I thought it was my moral obligation to have all three of them starched and dressed and seated on the front pew every time the church doors were opened. *My* children couldn't make a noise or be disruptive. And heaven forbid that the boys' shirt-tails were out or that they would want to run around outside before services.

'I realise now that the boys are both 25 percenters, and Janet is a 75 percenter. Peter and Kevin were always well-behaved children, but Janet was altogether different. I'm sure the boys often resented the demands I made of them, but they never complained.

'Janet resented authority from the day she was born. You can just imagine her reactions to strict parental control. I had quite a time keeping her in line when she was a child, and her entrance into adolescence made me realise that I would have to make some changes in my thinking, because Janet wasn't going to change.'

'What sort of changes did you make, Carol?'

'Well, first of all, seeing the way Janet was reacting to this strict lifestyle I was demanding of my family, I wondered if the boys had the same feelings, but wouldn't tell me. My husband Phil and I discussed it. We soon realised that we were strangling our children to please everyone in the congregation. We were trying to be the world's ultimate parents.

'As we talked about what we were doing, we began to develop an understanding of our children on an individual basis. If we really loved our children, we knew that we were going to have to let them be just who they were, and gently guide them with love and daily examples toward Christianity. Then, instead of doing a complete about-face overnight, we gradually implemented our new lifestyle.

'If the boys stayed overnight with friends and didn't make it to church on Sunday morning, we didn't panic as we had before. I could see them start to relax as we became less rigid and demanding with them. As small children, the three of them had formed a singing group.

As a consequence, they were constantly asked to perform at one church function or another. In the past, we always made them accept. Janet always rebelled. Now that we have let up on this and allowed them to accept or turn down those offers on their own, they are beginning to enjoy their music more. Even Janet doesn't complain quite as much about singing.

'The boys are seventeen now, and I think we have got through this with relatively few scars. I still have to be careful not to take advantage of their easy-going personalities, but Phil and I have learned a lot.

'Janet is fourteen. Helping her through these next few years will be a different story, I'm sure. Only last Sunday as I was putting the roast in the oven just before church, Janet strolled into the kitchen still clad in her pyjamas. Shocked at seeing her totally unprepared to leave for church, I blurted out, "Why aren't you ready for church?"

'You can imagine my surprise when she placed her hands on her hips and told me in no uncertain terms that she wasn't going to Sunday School or church.

'"Why, Janet? What in the world has got into you?" I asked.

"The whole thing is boring, Mother, and I'm just plain tired of it."

'My old attitude of "you'll go or else" surfaced briefly, but before I blew the whole situation, I calmly closed the oven door and turned to her.

'"Janet," I said, inviting her to sit for a minute at the kitchen table, "I'm sorry you feel this way, but I'm glad you told me. My concern is, how will your Sunday School classmates feel when you're not there? You are the leader of that class. Couldn't your absence possibly be letting them down?"'

"What do you mean?" she asked.

' "Well, for instance, your teacher relies on your knowledge of the Bible. That class is going to be rather quiet without you."

'Janet started to reply, but didn't. "I understand that everything gets tiresome once in a while, Janet," I continued, "but instead of making a decision this very minute, why don't you think about what I just said?"

'I really wanted her to go to church with us, Dr Campbell, but this time I wasn't going to force the issue.'

'How did it work out?'

'She pondered the problem for just a minute, then jumped up and hurried out of the kitchen. "I'd better hurry, if I'm going to be ready in time to get a lift with you," she said.'

This Christian mother is a perfect example of a parent using common sense. She instinctively knew that an argument with her daughter would result if she had demanded that she went to church. So, she played it cool. She had at last learned that she was not going to be able to force her children into her lifestyle. She knew that understanding and gentle, loving guidance were the only answers. She and Phil had tried 'superparenting' and it had just about destroyed all of them.

When Carol and Phil finally set aside their worries of 'what will everyone think?' they could really help their children grow as individuals and develop as whole human beings. In turn, their sons and daughter could really have their emotional, physical, psychological, as well as spiritual needs met.

Carol's solution to the 'I'm-not-going-to-church' dilemma was different from the Campbells', but worked equally as well. This enforces the fact that there is no pat answer to every problem. Individual personalities and situations must be considered.

Learning to read emotional signals

A parent's instinctive reaction cannot be overlooked. Carol knew, without consciously developing the thought, that she would not be able to come down hard on Janet, and it worked. Never underestimate your instinctive ability to perceive any given situation. If your family really has been getting to know one another in an environment of unconditional love, then instinctively you will be pretty good at reading basic signals of anger, fear, anxiety, and other emotions.

If this is not the case, perhaps the following incident will help you know where to start:

Ruth Dawson hurried from her kitchen onto the patio with a plate of sliced tomatoes. 'There,' she said to no one in particular, 'everything is ready for tonight.'

Her daughter, Michelle, came outside to join her. 'Anything else I can do, Mum?' she asked.

'No, we're ready now. Go and get ready. You must be excited. You haven't seen Susie for four years. I'll bet she's changed a lot too. Just think, you're both sixteen now.'

'It won't take me long to get ready, Mum. Why don't we just sit here and drink a glass of lemonade before they get here?'

'I don't have time, Michelle. I still have to wash my hair. I can sit down and rest after our guests arrive.'

Michelle reluctantly went into the house and dressed for the evening. Just as Ruth was putting on her earrings, Michelle called to her. 'They're here, Mum. Come downstairs.' In no time, the old friends re-established their friendship, and Michelle and Susie found they still had much in common.

'I'd better go in and see if I can help Mum,' Michelle said after a while. 'How's it going, Mum? What can I do?' she asked as she came into the kitchen.

'Michelle, what are you doing in here? Go back and talk to Susie,' Ruth told her.

'OK.' Michelle went out for a few minutes, but soon found another excuse to be with her mother.

'I can't work out what's wrong with Michelle,' Ruth said to her husband after everyone had gone. 'She hadn't seen Susie for years, and yet she wanted to hang around me all evening.'

'Did you ask her?' her husband inquired. 'Maybe she wanted to talk to you about something.'

As they left the Dawson house, Susie said to her mother, 'Boy, I felt really sorry for Michelle tonight. Her boy-friend called her today and said he was seeing someone else. She's miserable.'

Ruth Dawson was missing the distress signals that Michelle was giving her. Her common sense and instinct should have told her something was wrong, but she was so involved in having a perfect party that she didn't pay much attention to Michelle.

I'm not suggesting that you can be 100 per cent in tune with every thought and action of your child. That is totally unrealistic. But just a little common sense will many times correct a problem before it becomes a major event.

Keep communication flowing within your family. Don't assume that just because you and your spouse are not divorced, that yours is a totally healthy family. A healthy family takes work. Seek God's help daily, depend on your common sense, and love your child as God loves us – unconditionally.

Our challenge for the future

Fellow parents, our inherited and precious faith must be passed on from generation to generation. It is, of course, impossible for Christianity to skip even one generation entirely. But still, many are concerned why we are having severe difficulty in passing it on from our generation to the generation of our children and teenagers. As stated in chapter 1, recent findings show that only a small percentage of people brought up in Christian homes become followers of Christ.

We must not allow the events described in Judges 2 to take place in our country. That passage records the fact that the Israelites remained faithful to God during Joshua's generation, but failed to pass on the faith to their children. 'After that whole generation had been gathered to their fathers [died], another generation grew up, who knew neither the Lord nor what he had done for Israel. Then the Israelites did evil in the eyes of the Lord and served the Baals. They forsook the Lord, the God of their fathers' (Judg. 2:10–12).

Parents, I fear this is what's happening in our times. Yes, there are fine Christian young people developing today, but their numbers and influence are small. Their generation is rejecting what we and our forefathers have held dear. The spiritual battle is being lost. Where is it being lost? In our homes. I am thrilled with the work and success of youth groups and organisations devoted to our youth. But even their findings, statistics, and experience confirm what we are saying. Successes in their ministries can never overcome the multitudes of children lost spiritually from Christian homes. The hour is late, but not too late. We, with God's help, can reverse this trend by raising children and teenagers in the right way. We need to learn to know and understand them, to keep their hearts soft and open to a personal relationship with Christ, and to allow God to mould their characters and lives.

I have tried to show how this can be done in each Christian home. I realise that many principles I have stated are in opposition to what other voices have been saying over the last two decades, and will be rejected by Christians who adhere to these harsh, authoritarian approaches to child-rearing. The consequences of such authoritarianism, as we have seen, have been tragic. What bewilders me is that as the situation and our young people become more and more desperate, these 'experts' fail to see the light and change their message.

However, I pray that you, dear parents, have read (and I hope will reread) this book with an open mind, and compare its content with the whole of Scripture. I feel the insights you gain in the process will help you understand the changes which must be made in most Christian homes in order to pass the faith on to the next generation. At present we are losing the battle. Let's win the war!

> 'Give, and it will be given to you. A good measure, pressed down, shaken together and running over, will be poured into your lap. For with the measure you use, it will be measured to you' (Lk. 6:38).

Teenagers: Why Do They Do That?

Nick Pollard

Concerned about teen drug-taking, pregnancies and eating disorders? Baffled about what drives many teenagers to such behaviour? Worried that 'it must be my fault'?

This brilliantly enlightening book argues that understanding the culture in which teenagers are growing up is the key to understanding why some inflict tragedy upon themselves or others.

Nick Pollard, a specialist in teenage spiritual and moral education, provides adults with invaluable insights to enable them to open doors of communication with teenagers and begin to influence them for good.

978-1-90475-313-1